CW00677290

FOR BAKA'S HOMELAND

Eyewitness to the Birth of a State

FOR BAKA'S HOMELAND

Eyewitness to the Birth of a State

Michael Palaich

Copyright © 2019 by Michael Palaich

All rights reserved, including the right of reproduction in whole or in part in any form without the permission of the publisher, or author.

author@forbakashomeland.com
crolibertaspublishers.com

Library of Congress Cataloging-in-Publication Data
https://lccn.loc.gov/2019913845
For Baka's Homeland: Eyewitness to the Birth of a State
/Michael Palaich.Chicago: CroLibertas Publishers, 2019.
    pages cm
    ISBN: 9780999822753 (paperback)

Cover design by Ante Mihaljević

10987654321

CroLibertas Publishers
Chicago, Illinois
2019

To the thousands of Croatian men and women who sacrificed their lives defending their homeland, families, cities, towns, villages and brothers-in-arms.

To all disabled veterans of Croatia's War of Independence who were willing to sacrifice their lives so their people could live in freedom.

To the mothers, fathers, sons, daughters, brothers and sisters who suffered the loss of loved ones killed during Croatia's War of Independence.

To the Croats in diaspora who lived a life in exile from their family and homeland rather than perpetuate the lie called Yugoslavia.

TABLE OF CONTENTS

List of Acronyms

BiH	Bosnia-Herzegovina
EU	European Union
HDZ	Croatian Democratic Union
HIS	Croatian Intelligence Service
HOP	Croatian Liberation Movement
HOS	Croatian Defense Forces
HRS	Croatian Republican Party
HRZ	Croatian Republican Union
HV	Croatian Army
HVO	Croatian Defense Council (Herzegovina)
JNA	Yugoslav People's Army
KOS	Army Counterintelligence
NATO	North Atlantic Treaty Organization
NDH	Independent State of Croatia 1941-1945
OTPOR	Croatian National Resistance
SIS	Croatian Security Intelligence Service
SFRJ	Socialist Federal Republic of Yugoslavia

UDBA	Yugoslav Secret Police
UN	United Nations
UNPROFOR	United Nations Protective Forces
UNS	Croatian National Security Office
ZNG	Croatian National Guard

Pronunciation of Croatian Letters

c is "ts" as in bats

č is "ch" as in chopper

ć is "ch" as in chips

đ or dj is "dg" as in wedge

dž is "g" as in generous

j is "y" as in yes

lj is "lli" as in William

nj is "gn" as in gnocchi

š is "sh" as in shook

ž is "su" as in pleasure

u is "oo" as in loop

Prologue

"FEDERAL AGENTS, open up!" The shouting was followed by loud banging on the door to my apartment. It was 6:00 in the morning and from that moment on for the next five years I would live my life in a kind of limbo.

The U.S. Government's case against Michael Palaich (case number 96-80844) began on the day I was arrested in Frankfurt, Germany, on October 22, 1991. That arrest resulted in a search warrant being executed by the U.S. Federal Agents in Detroit, Michigan, a few months later, on May 1, 1992. Charges had not yet been brought against me, but I wasn't completely free either. During the five-year period leading to my indictment, my garbage was collected by federal agents, phone records were subpoenaed, I was personally followed by undercover agents, and my family, friends and employers were questioned by federal agents in an attempt to make a case against me.

It took almost five years and two Grand Juries, but on October 11, 1996 it finally happened. The U.S. District Attorney for the Eastern District of Michigan, Saul Greene, charged me with illegally exporting arms and ammunition to Germany. The indictment triggered another series of events: arraignments, mug shots, finger printing, meetings with pre-trial service officers and surrendering of passports. What followed next was a series of legal filings by my attorney: motions to dismiss for various reasons and motions to suppress evidence, all part of the endless stream of legal maneuverings. The court case against me would last an additional 2 ½ years. I was pursued by the U.S. Justice Department for a total of 7 ½ years.

While trying to endure the legal pressures facing me at home in America, a war was raging in Croatia and I was involved in it. Ironically, it was this period that was, perhaps, the most productive of all the years I spent in the movement for Croatia's liberation. That involvement meant frequent trips to Croatia and eventually becoming a Registered Foreign Agent for the Ministry of Defense. It also meant creating a fake press agency, called Pan National News Agency. This agency enabled me to gain access to United Nations facilities throughout Croatia and Bosnia-Herzegovina, and to secure U.N. transportation into the city of Sarajevo during the siege by Serb/Yugoslav forces. Developing relationships with the ambassadors for Bosnia-Herzegovina also allowed me access to Bosnian military and press during my activities there.

While America's Department of Justice was doing its job, trying to prosecute me in federal court, I continued to do my job: working to help realize a free Croatia.

Why?

People often ask me the same question when they begin to learn my story: "Why?" Why did you feel the need to get so actively involved in the Croatian cause for freedom, even to the point of going to war, or risking a long prison sentence? "You were born in America," they would say.

Indeed: why do young men of any ethnic group who are born in one country volunteer to fight in their parents' homeland? We are all aware of this recent phenomenon among young Middle Eastern men who were born in Western countries and who go to fight in foreign lands that they have never seen. To my surprise, I learned that this phenomenon was also true of the Polish people during WWII. Inside the vestibule of St. Josephat Church in Detroit is a large plaque with names honoring many young Poles from Detroit who joined the Polish Home Guard, first to fight the Nazis during WWII and then the Soviets after Poland was occupied by them.

Sometimes ideology is the only driving force for young men and women who volunteer to fight for a foreign cause – independent of their ethnicity or citizenship. In 1937 three thousand left-leaning American idealists joined the Lincoln Battalion as volunteers for Republican forces during the Spanish Civil War. Thousands more from countries around the world joined Spain's International Brigade to also fight on the Republican side against Franco. One active Soviet Cominform member and future Communist dictator named Josip Broz (Tito) was among the International Brigade's volunteers.

It was Tito's Socialist miscreation called Yugoslavia that installed him as the country's dictator in 1945. It was that same repressive Communist Yugoslav regime that anti-Communist Croatian patriots living in the Croatian diaspora battled with for decades. Most of the clashes took the form of words, with each side attempting to persuade public opinion in the West. In a few cases Croats resorted to highjacking airplanes, killing diplomats and bombing buildings associated with Yugoslavia. The Yugoslavs, in turn, resorted to planting agent provocateurs among Croatian émigré groups, inciting them to commit illegal acts and then working with Western Intelligence Agencies to have them arrested. Many of those impressionable young men spent decades in prison for their actions. According to Amnesty International, the Yugoslav Secret Police was also responsible for sending out hit teams to assassinate Croatian dissidents. In *Yugoslavia: Prisoners of Conscience* published by Amnesty International in 1985, they charged that Yugoslav assassins murdered more than seventy outspoken political opponents of Yugoslavia in this way.

Prologue

Croats were finally able to liberate their people from that insidious regime after four years of war, with help from Croatia's émigrés. That help from the diaspora came in the form of money, lobbying, humanitarian aid, arms and – sometimes – men who volunteered to join the newly created defense forces of the fledgling Croatian state.

Like all liberation movements, however, Croatia's long march toward freedom started decades before the first bullet in the Homeland War was ever fired. This book is not meant to be an all-encompassing history of Croatia's liberation movement leading up to Yugoslavia's dissolution. It is only a story of one person's personal involvement in Croatia's Homeland War, the years of political involvement that preceded it and the people I met on the journey.

1

Baka's Boy

WHY DO WE DO any of the things we do? It's an age-old question: are we just organisms that react and respond to stimuli in our environment? Are our actions and attitudes predetermined by the culture in which we are born? Are they determined by our birthing order amongst our siblings? Does nature or nurture best explain why we act and react as we do to life's events?

My wife and I have a friend living in Croatia who has the irritating habit of dismissing my observations of life in Croatia by saying, "You think that way because you're American." On the other hand, Anglo-Saxons have told me on many occasions that I view Croatian historical events the way I do because I am a Croat. Paradoxically, both opinions may be right and wrong at the same time.

I have come to accept the reality that I will never be fully accepted as a Croatian in Croatia. I am always referred to as "The American" when in Croatia. That will always be the case. Furthermore, at sixty-five years old (my age at this writing) I have also accepted the reality that I will never be fully assimilated into American Anglo-Saxon culture either. My father was born in America and served in the U.S. Army Air corps during WWII. I am a veteran of the U.S. Navy. I have lived and worked in America my entire life. Still, there is much of the Anglo-Saxon culture in America that I just don't understand. In my youth I believed that I was unique in this way. But after making friends with many first- and second-generation Croats living in Canada, Australia, America, Germany and Argentina, I find that many of us born outside of Croatia share this sense of straddling two cultures.

Of course, this phenomenon is not unique to Croats living outside of Croatia: it can be observed in the lives of many who straddle two cultures. They live with one foot in the culture of the family's "old country" and one foot in their family's adopted country. The inability to fully assimilate can also be seen to some degree in Greeks, Italians, Albanians, Middle Eastern people and many other nationalities. The hit movie *My Big Fat Greek Wedding* captured this reality humorously in 2002. Yes, we may be Americans, Australians, Canadians, Germans, Argentines, etc... but we can't help but view our daily lives through the lenses of the sub-cultures in which we live.

To illustrate this, I often tell the story of a Croatian friend of mine. Božo Čačić couldn't understand why he created such a commotion in his neighborhood when he decided to slaughter a lamb in his garage and hang it from one of the rafters to drain its blood before roasting it on a spit. To his surprise the police appeared at his door demanding to look in his garage. Apparently, the neighbors, thinking they were living next door to an ax murderer, became alarmed and called the police when they noticed a bloody stream running down my friend's driveway and into the street. Everyone – including the police – was relieved to discover that the lamb hanging upside down by its legs was the source of the blood pooling at the end of his driveway.

Straddling the cultures of two countries – American Anglo-Saxon and Croatian – only partly answers the question "Why." Only a small number of Croatians who straddled both cultures decided to join Croatia's Homeland War in 1991. So, while culture is a major factor, it's not the only factor.

Politics

The journey that took me from being a street activist gadfly, handing out anti-Yugoslav leaflets on the streets of Detroit, to rushing to the defense of a country in the midst of violent revolution, to becoming a Registered Foreign Agent for the fledgling war-torn Croatian State was a slow and evolving process. My political journey began in 1978, and each step in that journey would result in a psychological change. Normal feelings of fear would gradually be replaced with a sense of over-confidence and defiance. The idealistic political activity that was originally rooted in the belief that the Croatian people had a right to be free, slowly morphed into illegal activity in an attempt to realize that political objective. The transition was so gradual, over a period of so many years, that the change was imperceptible to me at the time.

However, there were personal events unrelated to politics that also shaped me. Although they had nothing to do with Croatian politics, they probably provided fertile ground for the phase of my life that I entered in 1978. Those earlier events included the Croatian culture that I was born into, the city in which I lived and worked, and finally, my early family life.

My friend Ivana likes to caution her husband Ante when telling stories, "You don't need to go all the way back to Adam and Eve." So, I'll try to keep her advice in mind as I write the pages that follow and attempt to answer the question, "Why did you get involved?" This will require me, however, to go back to some of my early personal experiences.

Early Years

My father was born in Detroit to a mother and father that came to America at the turn of the 20th century. My grandfather Franjo Palaić came from a town in Croatia called Petrinja and Grandma Ljubica came from a small adjacent village called Križ-Hrastovica. Grandpa was a butcher who learned his trade as

7

an apprentice working in the well-known meatpacking factory in Petrinja called Gavrilović. He would eventually own his own small grocery store on Riopelle Street in Detroit. Even today a number of butcher shops can be found on Riopelle Street. Grandma was a homemaker who gave birth to three girls (Ann, Helen and Rose) and one boy (Frank), my father. Grandma and Grandpa lived the remainder of their lives in the United States, never returning to the land they left so many years ago. Two World Wars, the creation of two oppressive Yugoslavias prior to WWII that were hostile to Croatians, and finally the creation of a Communist Yugoslav regime following WWII, made their return impossible.

Detroit, however, had a fairly large population of Croatians. So, while they left their homeland, they did not have to leave their people, language or culture. Being the owners of a Detroit grocery store gave my grandfather and grandmother constant contact with other Croatians in their community. English may seldom be used in such stores and the owners' children often work in them. Because of this, the children are immersed in their parents' culture simply by being in contact with people of their parents' nationality and selling the foods they eat. Even today, you can find similar stores and the children of recent immigrants working right beside their parents, just as my father did during his entire childhood. My father never questioned this, and there was no question on the part of his parents whether it was right or wrong to force their children to work, while other children played sports, or engaged in other after-school activities. That was just how it was.

Today's American parents, or perhaps parents from some Western European countries often engage in endless self-analysis and introspection, but not Croats, and certainly not Croats from a small town at the turn of the 20th century. I'm sure there are worse childhood offenses in Croatian culture than saying "no" to parents, but at the time I couldn't imagine what those offenses might be. I am confident that my father never refused to work in his parent's grocery store. I am second- (or

8

third-generation, depending on how you calculate it) and I cannot recall ever saying "no" directly to my parents. My mother may have been born to Irish parents, but we were raised in a Croatian home and saying "no" to them was not an option for me or my three siblings.

My mother worked outside the home, so until I went to school, I was with my Croatian grandmother all day, every day. My grandfather, Franjo, died when I was just a few months old. Grandma was sixty at the time. Although I am older than that now, she always seemed to be an old lady to me with her swollen legs, grey hair and a black dress with pink flowers, thick coke-bottle-like glasses and sausage-like fingers. She was also wonderful! The thought of her smile today, decades later, still warms my heart. I'm certain that my eventual love of Croatia and Croatians began with the love I first felt from Grandma, my Baka. Today she is my ideal of everything a good grandma should be. Every morning she would have a cold bowl of prepared Cream of Wheat cereal in the fridge waiting for me. She knew I liked to eat it cold, so she would prepare it the night before. It would be waiting for me when my mother dropped me off in the morning. She would talk on the phone in the Croatian language with friends and her sister-in-law for what seemed like hours to a young boy. I didn't understand a word she was saying, but I recall loving the melody of the language. I also found her heavy Croatian accent endearing when she spoke to me in her broken English.

Around the holidays I would sit with her in the kitchen watching her perform the lost art of making apple strudel. Even as a young boy, I was awestruck at the ease with which she shook and pulled on the strudel dough. There were times when the dough would extend two feet beyond the edge of the large kitchen table, enabling her to stretch, pull and shake it as thin as possible before rolling in the grated apples and baking it in the oven. As I recall the vision of my old grandma moving around the table, moving her arms up and down, back and forth, it was every bit like watching a graceful ballerina, except her theatre was the kitchen and her stage was the kitchen table. If God eats food in His kingdom today, I am completely confident that my grandmother's apple strudel is his favorite dessert.

Grandma was also a great cook and holidays at her house were really something special. When I look at old family photos, I can't understand how my father could have remained so thin growing up in a home with a mother that cooked as well as Grandma did. In later years I felt sorry for him knowing that my mother was not quite the cook of the same caliber: I imagine it was difficult for him to adjust to her limited culinary skills. Maybe it was because Mom worked all day and then came home to four hungry kids that she didn't have time to focus on improving her cooking and baking skills. Or, maybe it was because she thought all meat had to be burnt to a crisp to avoid salmonellosis. Whatever the reason, I'm sure it was a difficult adjustment for my father.

But, on Christmas it was Dad's turn to cook. After midnight Mass he would cook two types of kielbasa (smoked and fresh) and we would eat other foods and pastries given to us by my grandmother. This was at a time when midnight Mass really started at midnight and lasted over one hour. It was well after one in the morning when we returned home, and the cooking and eating would begin. The excitement of opening gifts, together with the hunger associated with fasting before Mass and then finally being able to eat, kept my three sisters and me awake till the early morning hours of Christmas day.

Special events like weddings and funerals were also great experiences. It seemed like every Croatian wedding reception was held at the Roma Hall in Detroit. I remember it being a large open hall with accordion-like doors separating one hall and function from another. We children would enjoy pulling the room dividers open and closed as the parties were underway. Unlike some other nationalities, children were invited to Croatian weddings and there were always plenty of other children to play and dance with on the dance floor.

Strangely, some of my earliest and fondest memories are of funerals. When I was young, there were many different Croatian customs associated with funerals, depending on what part of Croatia a particular family came from. One of my family's customs, when a close member of the family died, was to kiss the corpse of the deceased. Perhaps this custom was brought to America from my family's town of Petrinja. My wife, Sandra, who grew up in Croatia's capital, Zagreb, had never heard of this custom and grimaces at the thought of kissing a corpse. But my father would hold me up in his arms while I leaned into the coffin to dutifully kiss the lips of one of my deceased aunts. Yes, this seems strange to me now, but at the time it was the most normal thing in the world for me to do at a funeral. Besides, my father directed me and saying "no" was not an option. One would think that this experience would create negative feelings toward the funerals, but it didn't. Quite to the contrary: I loved many aspects of the Croatian funeral experience.

At a funeral I attended in Arizona recently, I was surprised to see attendees wearing shorts to the funeral Mass. Others were wearing white, red or any other colored clothes they had in their closet on that particular day. I guess it's because I can't shake my childhood experiences that this is unsettling to me. Everyone that came to pay respects to the deceased in my family knew they should wear black out of respect for the departed and their family. That tradition is still mostly adhered to in Croatia.

At Orlich Funeral Home, a Croatian-owned funeral home on Woodward Ave. in Detroit, women gathered upstairs in the parlor where the body of the deceased was laid out, and the men, after some respectable period of time, would find their way downstairs to the basement's smoking room. During what seemed to a child as endless praying of the Rosary by the women and priests, I was eventually able to slink away where the men were gathered in the basement. Once having successfully navigated my way down the narrow, dark, wood-paneled stairs and through the fog of cigarette smoke, I discovered that the men were standing or sitting on the benches by the wall smoking, talking and laughing. Invariably, one of the men would buy me a Coca-Cola from the old, red, metal Coke machine. This was also my first glimpse into the difference between the sexes. I don't ever recall seeing any of my three sisters downstairs, or any other female with "us men", or maybe I was just too enthralled by the smoky world of dark suites and deep voices speaking in a foreign language to remember.

From the funeral home the procession of cars would make its way the short distance down Six Mile Road to Mount Olivet Cemetery where the people stood around the coffin as it was lowered into the ground with one more prayer led by the priest from St. Jerome's Croatian Catholic Church. Then, one by one, people would walk past the open grave and toss in a handful of dirt or a flower.

Returning to one of the homes for the wake would be the most enjoyable thing for me. I recall making my way past all the legs, shoes and backsides to the wondrous site of the desert table set up in the basement. I couldn't imagine that there could be so many different types of pastries in the world. Each of the women would bring her specialty: cookies, poppy seed and walnut rolls, apple and chocolate pita (a kind of Croatian cake with pie dough on the bottom and top), strudels, a sea of cakes. I'm certain there was also ham and kielbasa on the table, but I was only concerned with the amazing pastries. The men would drink homemade wine and many types of hard alcohol referred to as *rakija* while they continued filling the basement with plumes of smoke that drifted from their cigarettes. The women would drink *bambus* which is a mixture of red wine and a soft drink. My grandmother's favorite *bambus* was made with a combination of red wine and "red pop", a type of carbonated strawberry soda. There was a general overload on my senses as I maneuvered through the sea of people, whose faces I could not see, while chewing one of many pastries of the day and listening to the crying and conversations spoken in the strange Croatian tongue.

Other than being among family members and attending St. Jerome's Church with my family, however, my contact with the wider Croatian community in Detroit was minimal. My father was the product of a time in America when foreigners from Eastern Europe were looked down upon. Even the public-school system encouraged the melting pot philosophy and discouraged students from taking pride in their family's heritage or speaking their mother tongue in the privacy of their homes with family members. This, I believe, is the primary reason my father had no interest in introducing his family into the culture found in the broader Croatian community or teaching us to speak Croatian at home.

The ironic thing is that we always took pride in our Croatian heritage. While we may not have learned how to dance the dances, sing the songs, or speak the language – with the exception of a few words – much of the culture was transferred to us in other ways. This transfer of culture was mostly through food and behavior. It was always clear to my sisters and me that we were Croatians and not Yugoslavs. We never heard our father refer to himself as a Yugoslav, even though in those days it was much easier for other Americans to understand the basic area your family came from if you told them you were from Yugoslavia. Dad never had to correct us on this topic, because we never said we were anything other than Croatian when referring to our nationality.

It was also always clear to my siblings and me that Dad was anti-Communist. As children we didn't fully understand what Communism meant. We did come to learn, however, that the Communists killed three of my grandmother's nephews. It wouldn't be until years later, though, that I would fully understand what that meant, or why they were murdered.

I was anti-Communist even as a teenager in high school. In tenth grade I received disciplinary action for a physical altercation with another boy at Salesian High School, the all-boys Catholic high school that I attended in Detroit. America was in the middle of the Vietnam War at the time and the young man came into the class one day waving the flag of Communist North Vietnam. When he sat in the desk next to me, I told him to put the flag away. In response he made the mistake of waving the flag in my face; I stood up, pulled him out of his desk and lifted him up over my head while he was still holding the flag. At that precise moment Fr. Moore walked in and yelled, "Palaich, put him down!" To the surprise of Fr. Moore and my fellow students, I put him down by throwing him to the floor. Fr. Moore calmly directed me to the office of the Vice Principal, Fr. Kelly, for disciplinary action. "Why did you throw the kid on the floor?", he asked. When I told him about the Communist flag waving, he chuckled and said, "Good! But I still have to give you detention on Saturday as your punishment."

A Trip to Communist Yugoslavia

My father passed away in 1977. It was at his death that I developed a sense that the link between our Palaich family in America and the Palaić family in Croatia had been broken.

However, my Uncle Ray and Aunt Florence Stojanić (really older cousins) had continued to remain in contact with the Palaić family in Croatia over the years. They had even been back on a couple of occasions to visit the family in the town of Petrinja. I was fascinated by the stories from their travels. So, in 1978, a year after Dad's passing, I made my first trip to Croatia. It was enlightening in many ways. At twenty-four years old, I finally met my family in Croatia, which in 1978 was still a captive nation within the Communist state of Yugoslavia.

My knowledge of Communism did not just come from history books, TV news and newspapers, or, for that matter, from stories about the communists murdering my relatives. Like anyone else living in America before the dissolution of the Soviet Union and their various satellite states in 1989, I was fully aware of the Communists' evil history of mass murder and oppression. In addition, while serving in the U.S. Navy's Communication Technician (CT) School in Pensacola, Florida, I received the highest security clearance possible (well beyond

14

Top Secret). Today, the Navy calls it the "Center for Information Dominance." At that time, the CT school was primarily concerned with training Navy personnel in electronic intelligence gathering. Part of that training involved learning about Communists and their various techniques for gathering information from American officials, citizenry and anyone else involved in American intelligence. Many of the operating techniques of foreign Communist agents working in the U.S., I would learn, were unsavory. For example, their tactics often involved entrapping Americans working in sensitive government positions who exhibited various moral weaknesses. Once the unsuspecting targets were compromised, they would then be blackmailed for the classified information they had access to. I had no illusions about Communists.

When I first landed in Zagreb, I was immediately struck by the contrast between the world I came from and the failings of a Communist state. Those contrasts could first be seen superficially on the façades of the city's buildings. If one could look past the decaying, unpainted stucco, the leaning fences and walls, and the cracked massive doors of the buildings, one could see the classic Austro-Hungarian architectural details similar to those found in cities like Vienna or Budapest. The unkempt stuccoed buildings in Zagreb, however, revealed to the tourist that paint had worn off the surface decades ago. What was left was a grey façade with soot imbedded in the recesses and chunks of stucco missing completely from the façade. The only fresh paint one could see were the tired and over-played Communists slogans thought up by men whose interiors mirrored the decaying buildings. Although Yugoslavia was run by the Communist Party, the slogans would have been very familiar to anyone growing up in Mussolini's Italy or Hitler's Germany. One only had to delete the name Tito in the painted slogans to see that they were in fact word for word translations of Fascist slogans used decades earlier. Slogans worshipping the former Communist dictator like: *"Tito je naš"* (Tito is ours) and *"Živio Drug Tito"* (Long live comrade Tito) were strategically handwritten with red paint on many buildings. It was obvious that the slogans were painted by Party hacks with Communist Party approval. To my eyes, the city's decaying buildings were symbolic of the decaying effects that Communist ideology had on the society as a whole.

Seeing soldiers and police saunter through bus and train stations also left an impression on me. It was disturbing to observe the attitude of those strolling authorities with machine guns slung over their shoulders: the police could barely conceal their contempt for the citizens who were walking by or simply standing nearby. Documents would be demanded without explanation. Machine gun-toting soldiers would arrogantly demand that elderly ladies open their bags for inspection. I would later learn that most of the police in Croatia and almost all of the police of senior rank were Serbian and not Croatian. This explained their harsh attitude toward the average Croatian citizen on the street. It wasn't that they simply had contempt for the citizens: they had a special contempt for the Croatian people they were entrusted with protecting.

Worlds Collide

In the summer of 1978, a bus pulled up to the front door of Ulica Matije Gupca 44 in Petrinja and stopped. My great-uncle was sitting in the window of his house. The driver called out to me, "There in the window is Dragan." After sixty-eight years, the Palaić family that had been separated by oceans, wars and politics was again united as I approached my family's house in the town of Petrinja. It was amazing that I was actually meeting the eighty-year-old brother of my grandfather after so many years of family separation. Uncle Dragan was wearing a collarless button-down white shirt under a sweater and a black suit. As I looked up at him in the window, I could see that his elbows were propped up on a pillow resting on the windowsill as many people do in Croatia while they observe the street below. As I introduced myself to him, my first impression was that he was a slim and dignified old gentleman with well-groomed grey hair and a thin mustache. A feeling of melancholy swept over me as I thought about my father who had never seen Croatia, let alone visited the family home that his grandfather and uncle helped to build and that I was standing in front of.

Grandpa Franjo first came to America in 1907, when he joined his father Antun in Detroit. According to notes that he wrote decades later, Grandpa made his way to U.S. shores while working aboard a sailing ship called *The Snowden*. The ship had sailed from Argentina where Grandpa lived for nine months. Grandpa left the ship after arriving in the Boston Harbor and entered the United States illegally to join his father in Detroit. Antun had come to America a few years earlier to find a better life, as did many from Petrinja in that period. His goal was to make his fortune and then return to his home in Petrinja. Antun did well for himself financially in a short period of time. He eventually bought a boarding house just outside today's Hamtramck, which is a small city surrounded completely by the much larger City of Detroit. Grandpa Franjo returned to Croatia one year later with the intention of never returning to America. However, he once again returned to America at his father's request in 1910, and again entered illegally by crossing the Canadian-American border at Niagara, New York. When grandpa Franjo left Croatia, he left his younger brothers and sister behind: one of those younger brothers was Dragan, the same eighty-year-old man whom I was meeting for the first time sixty-eight years later in 1978. The window that Dragan was sitting in was in the house that he and his father Antun built with their own hands after Antun's return to Petrinja in 1928.

In the U.S., Grandpa Franjo anglicized his name by changing it to Frank, and opened a butcher shop, raised a family and lived his entire life as an "illegal alien."

My grandmother, Ljubica Vidović, joined Grandpa in 1912, as an eighteen-year-old girl. The tattered letters that our family still has today are evidence of their youthful correspondence and indicate that they did not know each other well. They had only seen each other occasionally (and from a distance) when she would travel the short distance from her village of Križ-Hrastovica to a larger nearby town of Petrinja. Their personal letters with each other only began after the Palaić family in Petrinja and the Vidović family living in Križ-Hrastovica gave their approval to the marriage. Ljubica finally agreed to travel to America at the coxing of Franjo, and then only after Franjo's repeated assurances that they would be married upon her arrival in Detroit. That long and arduous journey in 1912 between Petrinja and Detroit would be the last trip across the ocean for either of them. Over the next several decades they only communicated with family members through letters. Neither ever saw their families again. My Grandfather died in 1954, the year I was born, and my Grandma passed away in 1970, when I was sixteen years old.

As I stood in front of the family home in Petrinja, I had the incredible feeling of satisfaction that the two worlds had been unified again. A grandson had returned to the family's hometown after sixty-eight years of family separation. And, while that first trip to Croatia ended with my arrival in Petrinja in 1978, the trajectory of my life over the next two decades had been subtly and unknowingly altered. The next time I saw Petrinja would be at the close of the Homeland War seventeen years later. Not only would the town look completely different in its devastation, but I would personally evolve into a person far different from the visitor standing in front of the family home.

My Baka

2

Šljivovica, Lamb and Politics

THE PALAICH FAMILY had roots in the only Croatian Catholic church in Detroit. St. Jerome's Church was situated on Detroit's famous Eight Mile Road. Prior to building a church at that location, Detroit's Croatian community congregated at the church located at 901 Melbourne Street. As we children got older, and attended Catholic schools, our parents would take us to other parishes closer to our home. I was baptized at Our Lady of Fatima Catholic Church, but our deepest roots were found at St. Jerome's Croatian Catholic Church.

I wish I could say that I returned to the Church in the late 1970s, after several years of not practicing my religion, because of a newborn faith in God. Unfortunately, my church attendance was the result of my newfound interest in the Croatian culture after my father's death and my trip to visit relatives in Croatia. Sadly, I was only a cultural Catholic at that time.

It was through the Croatian Catholic Church in Detroit that I made my first contact with a small group of local Croats committed to overthrowing Yugoslavia and creating an independent Croatian state. When I hear reports of Mosques serving as recruiting places for young Muslims to fight for a Caliphate, I'm not surprised. The Croatian Catholic churches throughout Croatian diaspora were also central gathering places where committed Croatian activists were always on the lookout for fresh young members to recruit to their various organizations – and there were many. All organizations, however, had the same common objective: they wanted to give birth to a Croatian state, and they wanted to see the dissolution of any Yugoslavia that held Croatia captive within it.

Every year St. Jerome's Croatian Church celebrated the Fourth of July (America's Independence Day) with a church picnic advertised as both Fourth of July and Hrvatski Dan Piknik (Croatian Day Picnic). I suppose the Croatian Day title was a response to a holiday called "Yugoslav Day" celebrated on November 29th by pro-Yugoslavs. I never heard anyone at our church refer to him or herself as Yugoslavian and I don't think anyone would have dared. Even prior to the official dissolution of Yugoslavia in 1992, the Croatians at St. Jerome's Church were Croats – at least publicly. The truth was, however, something different. The Yugoslav Secret Police, commonly referred to as UDBA, also knew that the Catholic churches in the Croatian diaspora were gathering places for fomenting political discord against Yugoslavia. It was common practice to use some members of the Croatian community to spy on other Croats in the diaspora. The willing collaborators would then feed the information back to their Yugoslav Agent handlers. It was through these collaborators that the Yugoslav intelligence agencies were kept informed.

The Croatian picnics were wonderful and unlike any American picnic. In fact, you could smell the picnic before you ever actually arrived at the picnic grounds that were next to St. Jerome's Church. Clouds of smoke billowed up and wafted through the air carrying mouth-watering aromas of various meats turning on spits over red and grey embers.

People say that at one time there were as many as fifty lambs, twenty-five pigs and dozens of chickens being served at the picnic. By the time I came back to church in 1978, however, they were down to about twenty-five lambs, ten pigs and a few dozen chickens. The lambs were my particular favorite and over several hours of spinning over the hot coals the skin would turn from pink, to white, and finally to a golden, crackling, crispy, salty goodness. When the man in charge, usually older, gave the word, two men would lift the lamb off the fire – one man on each end of the pole that the lamb was skewed onto. The lamb, dripping with juices, would then be placed onto a wooden table for cooling. Normally, this is when children, who were waiting patiently, would gather around the butcher block where the roasted lamb would be expertly chopped up with a meat cleaver. It was at this point that one of the men would surrender to the begging children by cutting off salty pieces of the crispy skin and give one to each of the waiting youngsters.

Men would stand around drinking and talking as usual – sometimes doing both excessively. Some would drink beer, but others would drink some variation of *rakija* that I had first witnessed being drunk by relatives at funerals and weddings. The general term of *rakija* covers almost any strong alcohol including a Croatian specialty called *šljivovica*, which is a hard liquor made from fermented plums. Younger men would engage in a testosterone-driven exercise of throwing a large rock as far as one could. The game wasn't very creative, but it resulted in a lot of joking and friendly banter. It also led to the consumption of large quantities of alcohol. While waiting in line to purchase beer, the men took pleasure in buying ice cream for any of the many children that passed by.

There was always a live band of four or five musicians playing standard Croatian folk music under the roof of a pavilion. The older men could usually be found around the pavilion dancing with their wives on the cement slab floor.

Children would take part in the festivities by mimicking the adults and spinning in circles to the music. One could also occasionally witness a father dancing with his small daughter who would try to maintain her balance while standing on his feet. The women could be found sitting on lawn chairs in small circles talking while tempting the passerby with the homemade pastries they had made the night before. Mrs. Barbara Kunce was my favorite baker, because she made the best apple strudel I had ever tasted – with the exception of my grandmother's. The dough on both grandma's and Barbara's strudel was so thin you could almost see through it. That thin dough, when baked properly, resulted in a crunchy, crispy skin wrapped around a golden filling of apple goodness.

It was at one such Fourth of July/Croatian Day picnic in 1979 that I first encountered the more militant, pro-Croatian and, therefore, anti-Yugoslav elements within the Croatian community. The men in question were only two of many scattered throughout Croatia's Diaspora, but these two were a force to be reckoned with. Their names were Petar Ivčec and Marko Stipaničić. Until that first encounter, I had never met any individual that lived with such single-minded dedication to any cause or ideology. Their politics had consumed their lives and developed into an almost religion-like devotion. Almost immediately, I saw a similarity between their commitment to freeing the Croatian people from the slavery of Communism and the Christian missionaries evangelizing the Good News of the Bible. They were unwavering and focused fanatics. I intentionally choose to use the word fanatic, because I have come to appreciate the purpose-driven life of fanatics in combination with a worthy cause. Like true evangelical disciples willing to give their lives for God and his Church, these Croatian freedom fighters thought of very little else other than the liberation of their people in Croatia. Whether they were at work or with their families they were consumed with the work of revolution (or more precisely, counter-revolution). In close to forty years, I can't recall spending time with either one of them when politics wasn't the main topic of conversation. Over the next few decades I would be privileged to encounter others with similar fanatical political passions as I was gradually introduced to the people involved and their lifestyle. It was a sub-culture within the Croatian community.

Croatians in the diaspora who were even minimally involved in opposition to Yugoslavia and Croatian self-determination, shared one common cross: they could never return to their homeland and their families. With the exception of those who were lucky enough to experience a Free Croatia in 1991, they were forced to live in a foreign country, and never return to visit a sick parent, or bury a deceased relative. My respect for those who chose to give up so much of their own life and happiness on behalf of those left back home never diminished over the decades. They would become for me living examples of prisoners who escaped bondage, darkness and ignorance in Plato's "Allegory of the Cave." They couldn't return to their homes to personally free others still held in bondage, but they could at least speak out on their behalf. They could be their voice in the West.

At this very first encounter with Marko and Petar (Pero for short), however, I could only sense the electric energy of two people who were deeply passionate about an idea that they were trying to share with me, each in his own way and style. Pero was more reserved and steadier in his approach. Some may say his personality reflected the area of Jastrebarsko in Croatia where he was born. He was about five-foot-nine with thick hair, a thick body and a Fu Manchu mustache, giving him a bulldog-like appearance. When we met, he had lived in Canada for less than ten years and spoke English with a heavy Croatian accent. I learned early in our friendship that it was unwise to misjudge his intelligence based on his occupation as a Chrysler Motors assembly line worker. Although he had some college education, he is primarily self-educated and well-read. Pero's method of winning over political converts entailed a steady, relentless approach involving the use of history, logic and reason. He gave the impression of not taking things seriously; and in part that was true. However, in things related to Croatian liberation politics he was unrelenting to the point of being willing to risk his life for the cause of freedom.

Marko Stipaničić, on the other hand, was a passionate man who tried to persuade his converts with an extremely high level of emotional rhetoric. Some would say Marko's delivery was the result of growing up on the Dalmatian Coast in a city called Senj. Dalmatians, in general, are known for having more explosive and passionate personalities than people from Pero's birthplace. Marko was about five foot ten inches. He had a solid athletic body when he was younger. Marko was masculine, good-looking, and sported a very full, chevron-style mustache, that tended to act as a strainer trapping beer foam when he drank. The young Marko that I met reminded me of a younger, thinner version of Lech Walesa (the Polish activist and later President). His large mustache, square angular face and jaw, in combination with the hotheaded and fiery personality, made me wary of him on our first encounter.

On this particular first encounter at the picnic, I was sitting with my Uncle Ray, Aunt Florence and cousin Richard when they first approached. Pero broke the ice with some humorous conversation that I would later grow to appreciate as a big part of his personality. The conversation very quickly turned political with a recitation of political facts regarding Yugoslavia and its oppressive nature. The topic then deviated into Croatia's right to self-determination and the American government's complicity in propping up Yugoslavia, etc. Uncle Ray enjoyed provoking people and would do so with very little prodding. This time was no different and the more passionate and louder Marko became, the more Uncle Ray would smile and joke. Then he prodded some more. I, however, found the conversation fascinating – even exhilarating. The passionate arguments that they were making seemed reasonable and logical. They also spoke about organizing a violent provocation against participants celebrating a "Yugoslav Festival" the year before at a city park in Detroit. I knew about the demonstration, because I had seen a photo of about thirty Croatian demonstrators lined up against the wall by Detroit police in the *Detroit Free Press*. I also remembered being surprised to read that those arrested were Croatians. I agreed to meet Marko and Pero the next weekend at the church rectory. They were planning to print hundreds of leaflets on an old printing machine that was in the basement of the church rectory. The pair of idealists intended to distribute the leaflets at yet another demonstration that they were organizing somewhere in the Detroit area. It was to be my induction into the movement.

Fr. Vincent Cvitković looked surprised when he opened the door and I explained that I was there to help Marko and Pero with their work in the basement. Fr. Vince directed me to the stairs leading to the basement where I was greeted warmly by both men. It was an uneventful meeting; by the time I arrived they were almost done with their printing of leaflets. What I most remember from that particular encounter was that Pero had been given press credentials by a Croatian émigré newspaper that he sold at various Croatian churches, clubs and events. The paper, *Budućnost* (Future), was a very anti-Yugoslav magazine linked to the Croatian Republican Party headquartered in Buenos Aires. Their president, Dr. Ivo Korsky, was a patent lawyer fluent in at least four languages. When I met him in Buenos Aires in 1989, I was shocked that his English was more sophisticated than that of many of the native speakers that I knew living in America.

Pero would eventually use those press credentials to wiggle his way into a press briefing with journalists from all over the world who were in Detroit for the 1980 Republican Convention. It was at that convention's press briefing that the Republican Party's Nominee for President of the United States – Ronald Reagan – called on Pero as a "member of the press" to ask his question.

I heard Pero's voice on the television before I saw him. On that particular day I stayed home from work with the flu.

While lying sick on my couch listening to the press conference on television, I heard a familiar voice: the journalist asking the question had a heavy Eastern European accent. To the best of my recollection it went something like this: "Mr. President," he said, "you are known for being an anti-Communist. What will your response be when small nations, like Croatia, attempt to free themselves from the Communist state of Yugoslavia? Will you support Croatia's right to self-determination?" I quickly sat up to see if that was who I thought was asking the question. I couldn't believe it. "Pero?" I said to myself. The fact that Pero Ivčec, a simple factory worker acting as a journalist, was on national television asking the next President of the United States a question about Croatia was so amazing that I didn't even hear Reagan's response. I was too focused on the image I was seeing on TV. But at that moment I understood the power of creative thinking when it was linked with persistence.

I learned afterwards from Pero that, as he was walking down Jefferson Avenue just outside of the convention center, a black limousine stopped, and the door opened. Pero was offered a ride by an aide of the future U.S. Vice President and former C.I.A. Director, George H. Bush. Apparently, Bush's aid had recognized Pero from the press conference. Pero wisely refused the ride.

Many years later, Pero's ingenuity came to mind and led me to create my own fake news agency called Pan National News. The phony news agency would eventually allow me to receive various press accreditations of my own during Yugoslavia's wars of aggression against Croatia and later Bosnia-Herzegovina.

In 1979, however, I was just in the beginning stages of my indoctrination and journey into the Croatian Liberation Movement. The journey that I began harmlessly enough at age twenty-five by passing out leaflets at local demonstrations against Yugoslavia with Pero and Marko, would eventually lead me down a path that entailed ever-growing risk-taking and danger.

27

1980 Republican Convention in Detroit

Petar Ivčec

Author, Marko Stipaničić, Božo Čačić

3

Down with Yugo!

LOOKING BACK at the early years of my political involvement, I see a young man full of naïve idealism. At that time, I focused on organizing and participating in various anti-Yugoslav demonstrations and campaigns. Those passionate early years were accompanied by persistent danger lurking around the periphery. Sometimes that danger took the form of threats, intimidation and physical confrontations with pro-Yugoslav people living in the United States and Canada. Today I see all those experiences from my political and personal life as part of the training that prepared me for more serious things to come.

The pro-Yugoslav factions we came into contact with saw us as a threat out to destroy what they viewed as good. Even though they themselves had left Yugoslavia for a better life in the West, their family members at home may have continued to personally benefit from the Communist regime as long as they continued to be good party members who didn't criticize the regime. We viewed pro-Yugoslavs as supporting a regime that was guilty of crimes against humanity, suppression of free speech, jailing of political opponents and suppression of religion. Serb-dominated Yugoslavia had given up any pretense of treating the Croatian Republic as equal long before its dissolution. The Croatians were vastly underrepresented in the courts, the police and the military compared to the Serbs who controlled all the major institutions in Croatia.

Some of the more serious threats came from people we identified as Yugoslav Secret Police or UDBA Agents who operated in North America. Americans were forced to face the reality of hostile foreign agents from Yugoslavia preying on American citizens after the release of a 1979 Senate Foreign Relations Committee report. The Senate committee report stated that U.S. Intelligence Agencies viewed the Yugoslav Agents as "Friendly Foreign Agents" and, therefore, allowed Yugoslavia to set up extensive spy networks in the U.S. The Senate report went on to say that the goal of Yugoslavia's spy network was "the penetration and destruction of anti-Communist émigré groups." Syndicated columnist, Jack Anderson, angered U.S. intelligence agencies, as well as President Carter's State Department, when he wrote in August of 1979 that the Yugoslav Secret Police were operating with impunity inside the U.S. against opponents of Yugoslavia. In an article published in the New York Times on August 10, 1979, the Carter Administration officials rejected Foreign Relations Committee findings "that Iran, Chile, Taiwan, Yugoslavia and the Philippines had maintained extensive spy networks in the United States to monitor and stifle dissent among their citizens here."

The content of that report became reality in my own life on November 13, 1982, in the form of a death threat the day after the Detroit Free Press published my letter to the editor in which I was critical of Yugoslavia. On that occasion I had just returned home as my wife was hanging up the telephone. She was shaking and in tears as she relayed the coward's message. "Tell Michael he is dead!" the caller said. Both her and I were familiar with the caller's voice, because he was often a television spokesman for the Yugoslav community in Detroit.

On another occasion on November 29, 1983 (a day celebrated as Yugoslav Day), I was playing with my two small children on the living room floor when my home was fired on by what sounded like a shotgun. I threw myself on my children and stayed on the floor for several minutes. When I finally got up to look out the small window in our front door, I could see that all the neighbors on my street had turned on their porch lights and had come outside to see where the shots had come from. Aware of the date, November 29th, I knew the gunshots were meant to intimidate me. The car carrying the shooters had sped away down the street. I filed police reports after each of those two incidents out of caution.

Justification

Somewhere around this time I seriously began to question if my involvement in this thing called Croatian liberation was justified. I had a family with two young children to consider. My only connection to Croatia was the blood connection through my paternal grandparents. Certainly, having sympathy or even empathy for oppressed people in various parts of the world was good. But there were many parts of the world that were facing political oppression, poverty or religious persecution. In addition, I barely spoke the Croatian language. It wasn't my mother tongue. The recurring question that I found myself asking was: "Is it unreasonable, or even delusional to link yourself so closely to this cause of Croatian freedom since you were born and raised in America? Sure, you are Croatian by blood, but is that enough?"

Intellectually, the question fascinated me. Political science and social psychology have been my interests for many years, and I received degrees in both disciplines. I also became fascinated with the subject of revolution and independence movements. Studying various revolutions became a passion.

Down with Yugo!

What struck me was how similar Croatia was when compared to events leading up to the creation of the State of Israel in 1948.

The Jewish people had an international diaspora and so did Croatia. From one perspective, this could be viewed as a negative. However, when the nation that is trying to achieve independence needs international political pressure and finances to realize that independence, having a diverse diaspora becomes an extremely positive factor. The Jewish diaspora became a major force in the formation of the Jewish state. I came to believe that one day the Croatian diaspora would also serve as a driving force for Croatia's liberation.

Jews had countless political organizations as did Croatia's diaspora. Prior to Israel's armed conflict upon establishing a state, the various Jewish political parties disagreed on most things (much the same as political parties in Croatia's diaspora). The political parties of Israel unified, however, once the actual fighting started. I came to the conclusion that Croatian political parties would also unify once the first bullet was fired in the fight for freedom from Yugoslavia.

The West supported the status quo in Palestine as they supported the status quo in Yugoslavia. The Jewish people had to convince the West, but especially the British government, that there would be no peace in Palestine until the Jews had their own state. The trend in the world by the 1970s was for an increase in the number of nation-states; it seemed reasonable to assume that the Croatian state would also be recognized in the future if that recognition would ensure long-term peace in Europe.

What finally settled my deeper question of whether I was justified in being personally involved in Croatia's liberation movement was learning of the biographies of two of Israel's founding fathers: Menachem Begin and Ben Gurion.

Both Ben Gurion and Menachem Begin were born and raised far from Palestine and their future Jewish state. Gurion was born, raised and educated in Poland. Begin was born on the border of Poland in what is today Belarus, but was educated in Poland. Both Begin and Gurion were raised as passionate

Zionists. Ironically, neither of them was raised speaking Hebrew at home which at that time was a language preserved primarily in written form for Jewish literature, poetry, commerce, etc. Hebrew was not revived as a spoken language until the Zionist movement of the 19th century. Yet, both men – I was amazed to learn – went on to not only support the State of Israel, but to fight for it as revolutionaries and eventually to lead it as Prime Ministers.

The lives of Menachem Begin and Ben Gurion, therefore, served as real-life examples of men who were born outside of their future homeland, did not speak their people's historical language and yet were passionate nationalists. The biographies of these two Jewish leaders resolved the questions and hesitation in being involved in Croatia's liberation movement. Their stories gave me the determination to move forward on my own journey.

Demonstrations

Demonstrations at various events inevitably led to conflicts with pro-Yugoslav people. Those demonstrations always involved passing out leaflets describing just how evil the Communist State of Yugoslavia was and how the Croatian people suffered as a result of that Yugoslav Communist oppression. The leaflets would encourage the readers to boycott the event and thereby show their solidarity with those speaking out against oppression and defending freedom. Sometimes we demonstrated at a concert when a singer or a musical group was brought from Yugoslavia at the invitation of one of the pro-Yugoslav organizations that cropped up in various North American cities. Ironically, one of the organizations that we very frequently demonstrated against indirectly was The Croatian Fraternal Union (CFU).

Croatians in Pittsburg, Pennsylvania, founded the Croatian Fraternal Union in 1894. Sometime over the years, however, the organization's by-laws were changed to allow anyone of Slavic descent to become a member, which also meant that non-Croats could become board members of the organization. The fact that the organization supported the Allied governments during WWII and opposed the Croatian government during the war was completely understandable since the Croatian Fraternal Union had its headquarters in America and Croatia was allied with the Germans. As proud Americans, as well as proud Croatians, they supported their adopted country by aiding American war efforts.

It was CFU's policies after WWII, however, that brought the organization into conflict with anti-Communist Croats. CFU continued supporting Josip Broz Tito and his regime after the war in ways that we found morally reprehensible. Because the Croatian Fraternal Union opened up membership to non-Croats after the war, the Yugoslav regime was able to infiltrate the leadership of various chapters of the organization. Ivo Smoljan states on page 293 of his book "*Tito i iseljenici*," that in a letter to the organization Tito himself praised the CFU for "spreading brotherhood and unity among our people."

The slogan "brotherhood and unity" became a laughable Orwellian cliché to Croats who experienced anything but brotherhood and unity under Tito. Therefore, this cozy relationship between the CFU and Yugoslavia didn't sit well with the more recent Croat émigrés – many of whom fled Yugoslavia for political reasons. Political émigrés of the 1970s had been left with two choices: flee the former Yugoslavia after the failed Croatian Spring, or be classified as "Enemies of the People" and be prosecuted at home. The Croatian Fraternal Union, on the other hand, seemed determined to be co-opted by Yugoslavia through various cultural exchanges that they enjoyed with the regime. Anti-Yugoslav Croats believed that working with Yugoslavia in any way gave the regime a legitimacy that it did not deserve.

What became most unacceptable, and at the same time most telling, was that neither the officials, nor the members of the CFU ever spoke out publicly against the many flagrant human rights offenses committed by Yugoslavia against its own citizens. Even the most naïve person would only have had to read reports from Amnesty International to learn the truth about Yugoslavia's crimes – including assassinations of many opponents living in emigration. Instead of speaking out, the CFU admonished us at demonstrations for having the "audacity" to condemn Yugoslavia's horrific human rights violations. Whether we were demonstrating against the Yugoslav Ethnic Festival in Detroit, or against various performers advertised as "Singers from Yugoslavia" like Lepa Brena, we could be certain of encountering very vocal pro-Yugoslav members of the CFU as we distributed leaflets in front of their venues.

One man who served as an exception to this rule, and will be covered more in future pages, was Ante Beljo. Ante Beljo would become a close confidant of the first elected President of Croatia, Dr. Franjo Tuđman. Beljo eventually moved back to Croatia where he was elected Secretary for The Croatian Democratic Union (HDZ) and later became a member of the Croatian Parliament.

When I first met him in the 1980s, Beljo was living a simple life in Sudbury, Ontario, working as a supervisor of electricians. I knew of Mr. Beljo through my various Croatian political friends – including Pero Ivčec. Pero had known him for years and described him as a solid Croatian who worked with members of many Croatian organizations including the Croatian Republican Party and the Croatian National Resistance better known as OTPOR. During a recent meeting with him in May 2019 in Zagreb, however, Beljo stated that he was never an official member of any of the political parties in the diaspora, because he believed he could be more effective working through cultural organizations. One of those cultural organizations was the Croatian Fraternal Union. At that time, Mr. Beljo was a contributing writer for *Zajedničar (*Fraternalist*)*, the CFU's official newspaper. Normally, being associated with *Zajedničar* would have tainted Beljo; however, because he enjoyed the trust of members belonging to the more militant Croatian political organizations, his membership in the CFU was not opposed. All members of the CFU were allowed to submit articles to be published in the organization's newspaper: it was hoped that by infiltrating the organization he could begin introducing articles into the *Zajedničar* that had a more pro-Croatian position than the CFU was ever accustomed to publishing. Many believe that Beljo was instrumental in facilitating the eventual shift in the CFU's paradigm from a pro-Yugoslav to a pro-Croatian organization. That paradigm shift began in the mid-1980s. With Beljo's persistent prodding, the CFU would eventually complete its political evolution by fully supporting Croatia's independence when Yugoslavia's dissolution was on the horizon. Croatia's future president Franjo Tuđman's personal diary indicates several private meetings with the CFU president Bernard Luketić in the late 1980s. For further reading on the Croatian Fraternal Union's transition process, the article "The Croatian Diaspora in North America" by Ivana Durić is a good place to begin.

Down with Yugo Campaign

The first Yugo automobile built by the Yugoslav company *Crvena Zastava* (Red Flag) came off the assembly line in the Serbian town of Kragujevac on November 28, 1980. It was first sold on the American market in the summer of 1985 to great fanfare in Yugoslavia. Within just a few years it became known as the worst car ever made. In some American markets, buyers were even given a free Yugo with the purchase of a more expensive American automobile. It reminded me of my childhood when gas stations in the U.S. would give customers a free glass for filling their cars with gas. The car had quite simply become a joke in most countries, America included. Jason Vuic, in his book *The Yugo: The Rise and Fall of the Worst Car in History*, highlights many popular Yugo jokes from the era. My favorite: "Q: What is included in every Yugo owner's manual? A: A bus schedule."

Yugo America Inc., a subsidiary of Crvena Zastava, finally filed for Chapter 11 under the American federal bankruptcy laws on January 31, 1989. But, in 1985, when the

Yugo was first introduced to the American market it looked as if the car might be a successful competitor to the inexpensive autos being sold in the U.S.

Since our strategy was to fight against Yugoslavia, both politically and economically, it was imperative that we do what we could to limit the success of the Yugo so that fewer revenues from Yugo sales would be available to the government. We found Yugo America Inc. especially distasteful because former U.S. Secretary of State, Lawrence Eagleburger – a lifelong supporter of Yugoslavia – was on its Board of Directors in 1985.

According to the Office of the Historian at the American State Department, Eagleburger joined the U.S. Foreign Service in 1957 and was assigned to the U.S. Embassy in Belgrade from 1961-1965. He returned to Yugoslavia as the U.S. Ambassador from 1977-1980. He is said to have been fluent in the Serbian language. According to an article published in the London newspaper *The Independent* on June 6, 2011, during Yugoslavia's dissolution Eagleburger developed a reputation for being so soft on Yugoslavia's war crimes that the European press began to refer to him as "Lawrence of Serbia." His defense of Yugoslav war crimes went as far back as 1981, when he traveled from Belgrade to Washington D.C. to warn the U.S. Congress not to impose sanctions against Yugoslavia for its human rights abuses against the Albanian minority in Kosovo.

Because influential Americans like Eagleburger had such strong political ties to the regime, it was very difficult for us to fight against Yugo America Inc. on a purely political level. Yugoslavia may have had a terrible human rights record involving murdering and jailing opponents, but they successfully cultivated their image of being an important non-aligned nation regarding the Soviets. According to the National Security Decision Directive (NSDD) on U.S. Policy Towards Yugoslavia, of March 19, 1984, even President Ronald Reagan continued to provide military aid and training to the Yugoslavs during his two terms in office. The only leverage that we had in our campaign to hurt Yugo auto sales, therefore, rested in the fact that we were located in Detroit, "The Auto Capital of the World" and the international headquarters for the United Auto Workers Union (UAW).

Our strategy was to use whatever means we could to bring negative attention to the Yugo, including jokes. Initially, we tried to get the support of the UAW. We naïvely believed the union's claim that they supported human rights and worker rights. They should have been a natural ally in our campaign against such a flagrant violator of those rights. Admittedly, the UAW and its members were very opposed to foreign car sales in the U.S. The UAW was so opposed to foreign cars that it was successful in forcing union members working in Detroit's auto factories who drove foreign cars to park in separate and distant parking lots far away from the entrances. Those workers who chose to violate these designated parking areas would find their imported cars vandalized when they finished their shift at the factory. Furthermore, other Detroiters who parked their foreign cars at Detroit area shopping malls also risked getting their cars vandalized by union workers while they were inside shopping. However, whatever the UAW's reasons were, they continued to refuse to support our boycott of the second-rate foreign auto built by underpaid workers in Yugoslavia.

We next used the obvious tactic of demonstrating directly against car dealerships that sold Yugo automobiles. A couple of years earlier we developed a relationship with the Albanian community in Detroit (which will be discussed later in this chapter) and sought their assistance in forming an alliance to oppose Yugo sales in America. The news media in the "Motor City" are always interested in auto-related stories. Our demonstrations received a great deal of attention, not only in the print media, but TV news outlets as well. They often showed up to film us for the evening news programs as we protested with signs outside the car dealerships. The slogans on our signs always carried the same basic theme: "DON'T BUY YUGO" or "BUY AMERICAN – NOT COMMUNIST CARS." Although we did not have the support of the UAW, two of our members were autoworkers and, therefore, we thought we were safe in displaying signs that also read: "UAW MEMBERS AGAINST THE YUGO."

Another approach we had in our strategy was to aggressively publicize the concept that Yugo America was dumping an inferior car with a questionable safety record on the American people. The Office of the United States Trade Representative defines dumping as: "Exporting a product at a price lower than the price it normally charges on its own market, or alternatively, lower than its cost of production or the price it charges in third country markets." We argued that Yugo America Inc. was in violation of World Trade Organization (WTO) agreements.

On several occasions we demonstrated with signs outside of General Motors World Headquarters on Grand Boulevard in Detroit in order to attract attention to our cause. The signs said simply: "YUGOSLAVIA DUMPING YUGOS ON THE U.S." In addition to the articles in Detroit's mainstream papers, the auto industry's most important publication, *Automotive News*, wrote on the subject and covered our demonstrations in their paper on more than one occasion. If Americans would not ally themselves with Croats because of Yugoslavia's human rights abuses, then surely they could, at the very least, be convinced to join us in boycotting the Yugo for patriotic reasons due to Yugoslavia's predatory pricing policy in America.

The North American Auto Show held every year in Detroit was another major event where we demonstrated against the Yugo. The protest took a bad turn one year when one of the Yugo cars that were on display was set on fire. Had I known in advance that there was a plan to set fire to the Yugo I would have tried to prevent it. Every year there were thousands of people – including families – at any given time inside Cobo Hall where the event was being held. There was a serious possibility of people being killed or injured because of this utterly stupid act. The foreign-made cars were always displayed on the lower level of Cobo Hall. It was on this level that the Yugo was set ablaze and thankfully extinguished before the fire raged out of control and injured someone, or worse. I never discovered who set the car on fire and remember being furious with whoever took it upon themselves to commit this illegal act without consulting anyone. If the individuals involved were not active in anti-Yugoslav politics, they would not have shown up on the police radar as persons to investigate, but we certainly would have been blamed. The Cobo Hall fire would not be the last time a Yugo car was set ablaze in the "Motor City." The next time was during the 1986 demonstrations against Detroit's annual "Yugoslav Festival."

Annual Yugoslav Festival Protests

In the late 1970s the City of Detroit began to highlight the many diverse ethnic communities of Detroit and the neighboring suburbs. Every major ethnic group found in the Detroit area would celebrate their culture by exhibiting their food, music and dances in the central plaza in downtown Detroit – Hart Plaza. The festivals would begin on Friday and end Sunday evening. They were a major attraction for many years. Yugoslavia was one of the countries represented every year. As reported in his book *The Yugo*, Jason Vuic writes about an incident in 1986, when someone foolishly decided to display a Yugo car at the festival. The car was prominently placed at the entrance to Detroit's Hart Plaza by one of the Detroit area auto dealerships. We were surprised that the organizers of the festival would act so provocatively since according to an article in the *Detroit Free Press* from August 29, 1986, the venue had already been bombed before the opening of the Yugoslav Festival in 1980. As stated previously, I did not hold the view that unprovoked violence against persons or property was acceptable, but occasionally some of the particulars became known to me after the fact. In this case, one individual threw a gasoline-soaked rag under the car and another followed shortly afterwards with a book of matches lighting the rag on fire. There was always a very large police presence at the Yugoslav festival, but the fire department was not present on that day. As a result, the car quickly became engulfed in flames and pandemonium ensued. Black smoke and flames from the car could be seen billowing up in the sky. It was the last time a Yugo would be displayed at the Yugoslav Festival in Detroit.

The earliest demonstration against the Yugoslav Festival was organized in 1977 by a handful of Croats. Of course, my friends Pero Ivčec and Marko Stipaničić were among the original instigators. That demonstration resulted in some punches being exchanged by Yugoslavs and Croats after the Croats stormed into the midst of the festival goers pushing and shoving as they went. The next day the local newspapers displayed a picture of them being lined up against a wall by police with their legs and arms spread apart. Another photo appeared on August 22, 1977 in the *Detroit Free Press* on page 33 showing demonstrators ripping and burning the Yugoslav flag.

The next day a handful of Albanian men from Yugoslavia's Kosovo region joined the protest outside the festival grounds after seeing the published newspaper articles. Being new to this type of protest, however, the Albanians brought machine guns and buried them under the grass in a park across the street from where the festival was being held. Pero and Marko were organizers of the demonstration and, therefore, felt it was their responsibility to persuade the Albanians not to act on their impulses. We were always leery when we came into contact with people that weren't known to us, especially if they advocated violence – or in this case men who came among us carrying Mac 10 machine guns. Could they be plants from either the American agencies or the Yugoslav UDBA? It was a serious concern, because many Croats in the '70s and '80s were prosecuted for committing terrorist acts after being infiltrated by agent-provocateurs working for Yugoslavia's UDBA. However, this initial encounter with Albanians would serve as the foundation for a long-term relationship that culminated in the founding of the Albanian-Croatian Alliance. Our alliance with

Down with Yugo!

Albanians, who were mostly from Kosovo, caught the attention of both the Yugoslav and the American governments almost from the very beginning.

As a result of this alliance, hundreds of Croatians and Albanians took part in the annual demonstrations against the City of Detroit's Yugoslav Festival. In the beginning it was enough to simply show up en masse and hold signs to attract the attention of the news media. Over time, however, reporting on demonstrations against the festival became "old news" for the media outlets. Our protests began to receive less attention even though the numbers of demonstrators increased every year. The eventual lack of interest meant that we had to find creative ways to draw attention to our protests. By the time the City of Detroit cancelled the Yugoslav festival in the late 1980s we had become pretty adept at finding innovative ways to create public interest in our protests.

Perhaps the most successful campaign was to spray-paint almost every freeway overpass in Detroit with the slogan "No Yugo Festival." For several weeks leading up to the "Yugoslav Festival" in September, Pero and I would spread throughout the city between 1:00 and 3:00 in the morning with spray cans in hand. Later the Albanians would also join us in the action. Detroit can be a dangerous place to be skulking about at 3 a.m. so I was often armed with a 38-caliber pistol (illegal to carry at the time). It was dangerous to risk getting caught by the police in possession of a handgun while painting graffiti; but it was even more dangerous to get caught by the one of the city's gangs with no way to defend oneself. Sometimes the slogans would be spray-painted on walls of the overpasses. Other times the spraying would be accomplished by hanging upside down and writing on the overpass while a second person held on firmly to the belt of the individual doing the spraying. Everyday people making their way in and out of the city were surprised to see yet another bridge covered with the slogan "No Yugo Festival" or "No Yugo." The message became so well known that when a Detroit newspaper called *Metro Times* asked readers to vote on the most popular street graffiti in the city, the "No Yugo Festival" graffiti won. We even spray-painted the message on the city's people mover structure just outside of the FBI headquarters in downtown Detroit.

Always trying to get media attention, we hired an airplane to fly around Hart Plaza where the Yugoslav Festival was held one year. The plane also flew around Detroit's Federal building where the F.B.I. had offices on the twenty-sixth floor. The plane pulled a banner which read "No Yugo Festival." Although it drove the Yugoslav Festival organizers crazy, I later learned that the F.B.I. agents working in the building found it hilarious. One agent who was assigned to the Counterintelligence Unit, William Noonan, would jokingly ask me later, "How is the Croatian Air Force doing?"

In September 1985, Pero Ivčec and I decided it would be both funny and newsworthy if he were to climb the one-hundred-foot flagpole at Hart Plaza and rip down the Yugoslav flag where it flew for the entire weekend of the festival. We had no idea how dangerous that stunt would be for Pero, but he simply couldn't tolerate seeing the Communist country's flag, complete with the red star, flying proudly over a major American city.

Pero imprudently decided to climb the pole in shorts and a T-shirt. We didn't consider that the stainless-steel pole would be extremely hot after being exposed to the sun for hours. Second, according to some individuals who were milling about among the festivalgoers, some men were talking quietly among themselves about shooting Pero off the flagpole with the handguns they were carrying. That option quickly faded, however, when the first large contingent of police arrived on the scene, followed by a fire truck. The fire truck pulled up to the plaza and began extending the truck's ladder into place above Pero to prevent him from reaching the top and, therefore, the flag. Newspaper reports from that day (*Detroit Free Press*, September 9, 1985) document that the pro-Yugoslavs below were screaming at the firemen, "Stop him!" The firemen began ordering Pero to descend the pole, but the problem was that he could not come down even if he had wanted to. The leather belt that we purchased with the intention of preventing him from falling was also preventing him from descending. He was stuck, unable to go higher or lower himself down. In addition, he was exhausted, and his skin was burning from the intense heat of the stainless-steel flagpole. The firemen eventually noticed that Pero was in trouble and began to move the ladder into place under him so that he could climb onto it. Pero could have fallen to his death that day. We were both grateful that the fire truck that first showed up to stop him was helpful in getting him down. He admits today that he was so exhausted that he almost fell in the process of moving from the pole to the firemen's ladder. The police later handcuffed him and laid him down in the police car where they repeatedly banged the door against his head as it hung outside the car. While he was being transported in the backseat of the car to a precinct station for booking, an obese female officer sat on top of him. Seeing that he was in distress while bouncing up and down on uneven roads, she began to laugh at him. This bouncing, together with the effects of heat exhaustion, caused Pero to vomit in the officer's hat that she had placed upside down on the floor just under Pero's head. When Pero arrived at the police station the officers stood him up against the wall in the garage and began to hose him down with hot water from a large water hose. The extremely hot water scalded him, and the police were subsequently forced to take Pero to the local hospital for emergency medical treatment. While Pero's flagpole incident resulted in tremendous media coverage, it was not the best thought-out plan and it could have easily resulted in his accidental death that day.

The Yugoslav festival was the gift that just kept on giving. Every single year it provided us with the opportunity to highlight both the evils of Yugoslavia as well as the Croatian and Albanian desire to be rid of the regime once and for all. As much as we demanded that the City of Detroit put a stop to the festival, it was in fact the last thing we wanted.

The Albanians came up with a unique approach to draw attention to Yugoslavia's oppression at the beginning of one of the final years of the festival using performance art in their protest. One of the Albanian leaders with whom we worked closely was a man named Gjok Martini. Mr. Martini and his brother Marko owned a van conversion company in Detroit and came up with the idea to convert a car into a Yugoslav tank – complete with a gun barrel and turret. The entire shell of the full-sized tank was constructed out of wood and fabricated to fit over an automobile that was hidden within the tank. The tank was then painted green and the necessary Yugoslav Communist stars were painted on the side. The wooden tank then exited Mr. Martini's shop, travelled south down the Lodge Freeway, exited at Jefferson Avenue and stopped at Hart Plaza. It arrived just in time for the opening of the Yugoslav Festival. When the tank came to a stop, Albanian men in the national costume of Kosovar Albanians climbed on top of the tank and began yelling: "Down with Yugoslavia! Down with Yugoslavia!" The Albanians were arrested, and the tank and car were confiscated and transported to a city impound lot located on Michigan Avenue next to the Federal Building where it would be used as evidence in the subsequent court case. However, before the case could be brought to court, the Albanians broke into the parking lot at night and stole their tank back from the police. They returned it to Gjok Martini's shop in the middle of the night the same way they came into the city – this time driving Northbound on Detroit's John Lodge freeway.

There were other occasions when our demonstrations at the Yugoslav Festival resulted in potentially dangerous situations. The Yugoslav factions became increasingly more physically threatening in their attacks against us. The result was that we also became even more defiant and bold. In retrospect, it is clear that the violent confrontations we experienced in Detroit were preparing us for the real war in our future. Likewise, my earlier days living and working in Detroit prepared me for the life of potential violence in which I then found myself.

Down with Yugo!

As an adolescent in Detroit, I very seldom left home without carrying a knife of some type into the streets because of the sometime-unsafe neighborhood in which I lived. I preferred carrying a dagger that I would strap to my left forearm when I was able to wear long-sleeve shirts. This gave me quick access: I wouldn't have to take the additional time to open it if it was necessary to use it. In later years, but before my political involvement, I often carried a pistol. I am ashamed to admit today that in my younger days and prior to my return to the Catholic Church, I was prepared to use it on several occasions. In most cases it was anger over some perceived act of disrespect that precipitated my impulse to take revenge on the supposed offender.

My father became addicted to prescription drugs (i.e. Darvon, Percodan, Percocet) when I was around eight years old. This probably had a dramatic effect on my phycological development. His addiction to drugs proved disastrous to not only him personally, but to the whole family because getting his drugs seemed to be the driving force of his life. As a result of his drug use, he was often without employment during much of my developing years. When I was eleven years old, he overdosed on drugs requiring my sister, Marie, to call the ambulance to save his life. He barely survived that night; subsequently he was forced into the psychological ward at Pontiac State Hospital in Pontiac, Michigan. As I watched the emergency medical crew carry him past me with foam coming from his mouth that night, I recall clearly to this day making a vow to myself: "I'll never be weak like him." That vow made by an eleven-year-old boy would be a major controlling factor for a large portion of my life prior to my return to Christ. It became impossible for me to back down from any fight with that childhood vow always echoing in my head: "You can't be weak."

The same year that my father overdosed and almost died, I was sent to an all-boys' camp for underprivileged kids called Camp Ozanam on Michigan's Lake Huron. The camp was owned and operated by the St. Vincent de Paul Society. It was the first time that I was either away from home or in the country. The feeling I had on my first morning at the camp was similar to what I felt on my first day in military boot camp. As soon as I entered the mess hall of the camp, I thought I died and went to heaven. There were all kinds of foods to choose from for breakfast and as much juice and milk as a kid would ever want to drink. We hiked in the woods, slept on the beach one night in sleeping bags, and practiced our skills at archery.

One day, there was even a boxing competition in a real boxing ring with real boxing gloves. A number of boys were paired off and the goal was to eventually have a run-off among winners resulting in a final champion being proclaimed. I never made it past my first fight, but not because I lost the fight. When the bell rang and the referee called for us to commence fighting, I attacked my opponent with a series of blows to his face. He didn't have a chance against my pent-up anger. When he fell to the mat, I jumped on top of him and began to further pummel him. I guess I was more familiar with the rules of street fighting than boxing. The referee had to pull me off the poor kid and began to berate me for my overly aggressive behavior. I seriously didn't understand what I had done wrong. We were told to fight, and I fought in the only way I knew. The referee looked at me like I was crazy as he disqualified me from the competition.

I guess you could say that I was a tough kid who became a tough adult. In the mid-1970s when I was in my early twenties, I worked as a theatre manager in several of Detroit's theatres. Being the only white guy in the dangerous downtown Detroit theatres forced me to be tough. My proclivity towards using violence to solve problems only intensified during that period. In the 1970s, Detroit was getting the reputation for being the murder capital of America. With an increase in crime, gang violence and scarce police presence in downtown Detroit, there were plenty of opportunities to find violent confrontations. Sadly, it was not uncommon for me to put a loaded and cocked pistol to a person's head; on one occasion I even attempted to attack the Mayor of Detroit's niece during a confrontation in the Grand Circus Theatre. I will describe that distressing event later.

With this past as a background, there was no way that attempts by pro-Yugoslavs to intimidate me during our demonstrations against the Yugoslav festival could ever be successful. Detroit's Hart Plaza, where the Yugoslav festival was held, is sandwiched between Jefferson Avenue to the North and the Detroit River to the South. Since we always demonstrated and passed out leaflets on Jefferson Avenue, it was there that most of our encounters occurred.

On one Sunny Saturday afternoon, one of our Croatian demonstrators, Miro Komšić, was passing out leaflets when he was surrounded by six to eight pro-Yugoslav Albanians known to carry guns. They began to threaten Miro saying that he should leave or else. I was on Jefferson Avenue about five hundred feet east of him when I heard Miro yelling for help. I was carrying a thirty-eight-caliber pistol in the inside pocket of my jacket that day and began running in the direction of Miro who I could see was surrounded by a large group of men. Being concerned that the pistol would fall out of my pocket while running, I instinctively reached inside the left side of my jacket to hold it in an attempt to prevent it from flopping out of my pocket. It was only later that I came to realize why the menacing group surrounding Miro began to flee as they saw me running down the middle of the busy boulevard responding to Miro's calls for help. I can only imagine how I looked to the Yugoslav Albanians threatening Miro and to the other bystanders who were watching the crazy man running right down the middle of Jefferson Avenue with one hand inside his jacket. It was in fact both stupid and crazy. It is incredible that none of the many police officers stationed around the event who must have seen me did not arrest me. Thankfully, the men chose to flee upon seeing me. Knowing my temperament at the time, I am certain that there would have been a shoot-out had they decided to stay and challenge me rather than flee.

Another memorable incident that occurred on Jefferson Avenue involved Marko Stipaničić as we were passing out leaflets. A man we identified as Nino Barishaj, a local travel agent dealing in charter flights to the former Yugoslavia, led a group of pro-Yugoslav Albanians to where we were standing. Barishaj attempted to rip the pack of anti-Yugoslav leaflets from Marko's hands. Even though Marko resisted, I could see that he was afraid. I stepped in between Marko and Nino saying, "Don't touch the leaflets again, or I'll kill you right here." The thought that I was willing to kill someone over a handful of leaflets is disturbing to me today, but it serves as an example of how my impulse to respond with violence was transitioning into its use for political purposes. On that occasion, though, I didn't have my pistol on me, but I had trained in karate for several years and was getting fairly accomplished. I was certainly capable of killing him with my hands if I wanted. Nino reminded me that all the guys behind him – and there were several – also had guns and were willing to kill me, too. When he said that, the Albanians pulled back their jackets to proudly display the pistols that were stuck inside their belts. Thinking he had us intimidated, Nino once again reached for Marko's stack of leaflets, but Marko resisted by holding onto them even tighter. "If you don't let go, I'll rip your throat out," I said as quietly and menacingly as I could. "They will kill you." Nino replied as he motioned to his guys. "Yeah, but I'll have your throat in my hand by that time." Nino gave up and sheepishly walked away with his crew in tow. Marko kept his stack of leaflets.

The Croatian-Albanian Alliance

Kosovo declared its independence from Serbia in 2008. Prior to Kosovo's independence it was a province of Serbia. According to Wikipedia, Kosovo has received diplomatic recognition as an independent state from 116 states including the United States, Canada, Australia, Great Britain, Germany, France and Croatia.

Down with Yugo!

The Albanians living in Detroit prior to 1981 were not particularly active in their political opposition to Yugoslavia. That all changed, however, when Serbs in the region of Kosovo stepped up their brutal campaign of suppression against the Albanian Kosovars, when the latter began demanding human rights and independence for Kosovo. In 1982 we were successful in creating an alliance with the Albanian community in Detroit using contacts we developed in 1977 during our first demonstrations against Detroit's Yugoslav Festival. Prior to 1981 – and even later in some cases – it had been very difficult to motivate the Albanians from the former Yugoslavia to work with Croatians against the Serbian-dominated Yugoslav government. The reason for this was partly because many Albanians had pro-Yugoslav allegiances prior to Serbia initiating pogrom-like attacks in Kosovo, and partly because they tended to view both Croats and Serbs as coming from the same Slavic race and, therefore, as untrustworthy.

Consistent with the ancient maxim, "The enemy of my enemy is my friend," we were finally able to convince Albanians to join with us in an organization called the Albanian-Croatian Alliance. The meeting to establish the new organization was held in a conference room at the Pontchartrain Hotel in downtown Detroit. The first Croatian members were Marko Stipaničić, Pero Ivčec, Ante Čuvalo (who came from Columbus, Ohio to attend the meeting as a founding member), Roko Juričić and myself. On the Albanian side was Marash Dushaj, Preng Gruda, Kol Mihilli and Qazim Rrushaj. Ironically, one of our contacts tipped us off that one of the Albanians present was wearing a wire for the F.B.I., but since we were not advocating violence, we weren't worried. Neither did we let on that we were aware our meeting was monitored by the American federal agents. It was a tactic I had picked up in Naval Communications Technician School. If someone is "bugging you," never let them know that you are aware of it. Because the federal agents underestimated our sophistication in this regard, this practice gave us the advantage over those doing the eavesdropping. The practice allowed us to feed misinformation to the listening agency when we wanted.

The Albanian-Croatian Alliance would never have been realized had it not been for Marko Stipaničić. Marko was a dynamic and charismatic speaker and a close bond developed between Marko and the Albanians. They seemed to relish in his passion and his single-minded desire for freedom for Croatians. The rest of us were more laid back in our approach, but Marko was always traveling at full speed and the Albanians loved him for his dedication and his passionate delivery style. Years later I encountered an Albanian from the old days named George Mihilli who had moved to Arizona from Detroit. He is the son of Kol Mihilli, founding member of the Albanian-Croatian Alliance. We had many conversations in years past, and on several occasions, I stopped in to talk with him over coffee in a small restaurant he owned on St. Antoine Street in Detroit's Greektown. Thirty years later in Arizona, he immediately asked about Marko by name – even though he had long forgotten my name or Petar Ivčec's name.

During the 1970s and 1980s Croats were becoming more and more involved in violent activities around the world (i.e. bombings, airplane hijackings, assassinations). Some of these people, such as Marijan Buconjić, Drago Sudar and Miro Barešić, would return to Croatia after spending years in prison to work for the Croatian government in various capacities. Buconjić and Sudar would later become acquaintances of mine. Barešić would be killed during the Homeland War under questionable circumstances. While in Croatia, I often drive by the statue erected in his honor in the small town of Drage.

I first met Marijan Buconjić at a Croatian Republican Party conference in Long Beach, California, around 1984. Jozo Brekalo, Vlado Dizdar and Marijan Buconjić attended the conference, because they were members of the Croatian Republican Party. I was at the conference, not as a member of the Croatian Republican Party, but as a visitor. The three had recently been released from prison for their involvement in the takeover of Yugoslavia's Mission to the United Nations in New York City on June 14, 1977. A banquet was held on the last day of the conference with about 200 people in attendance. Buconjić, Dizdar and Brekalo were the last to enter the banquet room and as they did all 200 people stood in complete silence in their honor. The display of respect for the three revolutionaries had a profound effect on me.

According to an article published by the *New York Times* on June 16, 1977 the three men were charged with "burglary, possession of a deadly weapon and attempted murder." During the two-hour siege, a Yugoslav mission guard was shot. Buconjić is reported to have told reporters on his way to arraignment: "We're going to fight until we realize our objective, an independent state of Croatia." The *N.Y. Times* also quoted a State Department official's response to Buconjić's statement in the article: "The United States opposed the Croatian demands for independence."

Buconjić was the last of the three to be released from prison after serving a sentence of seven years' imprisonment. It would have been possible for him to be released on probation earlier, but when the parole board demanded that he refrain from further political activity as part of his probation, Buconjić stoically refused and spent an additional year in prison.

The Detroit area was not immune from similar violent activities. Several businesses became the targets of a bombing campaign in the years between 1981 and 1986. With the exception of Detroit's Hart Plaza, which police believed was bombed in an apparent message to Yugoslav Festival organizers and City of Detroit officials, it was thought that the Detroit businesses targeted for bombings were owned by people who collaborated in one way or another with the Yugoslav government. The *Detroit Free Press* published an article on August 28, 1981 describing one of the bombed buildings as a travel agency that primarily booked flights between the U.S. and the former Yugoslavia. Their customers were mostly émigrés from the former Yugoslavia. Travel agencies that focused on visitors to the former Yugoslavia, as well as airline offices belonging to *Jugoslovenski Aerotransport* (JAT), were targeted by extremists because they were thought to be providing unofficial cover for Yugoslavia's intelligence agency UDBA. It is fairly common knowledge today (since the airing of the popular television show *The Americans*) that many governments used travel agencies to provide such cover for "illegal agents" operating abroad. I learned early on, however, not to make any inquiries into who may be involved in the bombings or other serious illegal acts. The concept of "need to know" was something I was very familiar with since my days in U.S. Navy training. Asking questions, like who and how, would only create suspicions. It was naturally believed that the only people who asked such questions were working for American or Yugoslav intelligence in some capacity. If one expressed too much curiosity they would forever be viewed with suspicion. I was already aware that some believed I worked for the American government, simply because I was born in America. Not knowing if anyone I knew was involved in the illegal activity, and unable to ask, I continued to forcefully voice my opposition to this type of illegal activity. Acting in self-defense was one thing, but bombings were indefensible. In this way, if people I knew were involved, I would at least be on record regarding my opposition to these illegal acts.

My ignorance of who may have been involved also made it easy for me to deny any knowledge when I was questioned by an F.B.I. Agent assigned to the Counterintelligence Department in Detroit named William Noonan. At one point early on, Noonan did attempt to recruit me as a Confidential Informant (CI). I responded to his offer by refusing and telling him I'd bring a lawyer next time we met.

The Albanian-Croatian Alliance and the Detroit bombings did catch the attention of at least one member of the Senate Foreign Relations Committee in the U.S. In the 1980s the Foreign Relations Committee published a report on Yugoslavia by Senator Jesse Helms. In the footnotes of the committee's report was a reference to the Albanian-Croatian Alliance and the Detroit bombings. In the report, written by two aids at the request of Senator Helms, it was prophetically stated that the Albanian-Croatian Alliance and the bombings were a sure sign of things to come in Yugoslavia. It was an indication, the authors wrote, that the various ethnic groups were not pleased with the Communist regime of Yugoslavia and that our organization in Detroit and the bombings were a prelude of things to come in Yugoslavia. Within a decade of this prognostication, the former Yugoslavia would in fact dissolve.

The Case of Pjeter Ivezaj

One occasion that gave me great satisfaction was being involved in the release of a thirty-year-old American citizen named Pjeter Ivezaj from a Yugoslav prison in 1986. On August 19, 1986 the Yugoslav government arrested the Albanian-American when he returned to Yugoslavia to visit family members.

He was charged by the Yugoslav government with taking part in an anti-Yugoslav demonstration in Washington D.C. in 1981, according to a *Detroit Free Press* article dated October 11, 1986. Many newspapers, including the *Lansing State Journal* on September 30, 1986, reported that he was tortured and beaten while in jail. Furthermore, the Yugoslav government officials refused to allow the U.S. Ambassador to Yugoslavia to speak with Ivezaj. Ivezaj was found guilty on October 6, 1986 by a court in Titograd, Yugoslavia. He was sentenced to seven years in prison.

A small blurb appeared in the *Detroit News* on September 30, 1986 describing his arrest. I contacted the journalist who wrote the small article and chastised him slightly. It was my experience that this aggressive approach was often the best way to handle journalists who are always on guard against being used by people with an agenda. "You missed the whole point in Pjeter Ivezaj's arrest in Yugoslavia," I said. "What's the point that I missed?" the journalist asked defensively. "Look," I said, "he took part in a demonstration in Washington D.C. in 1981, but he was arrested in Yugoslavia in 1986. Ivezaj was an American citizen when he protested in Washington." I continued, "You have to ask two questions: how did the Yugoslav police in Montenegro know that Ivezaj demonstrated in Washington D.C. five years previously? The next question is this: should Yugoslavia be allowed to arrest and imprison American citizens who exercise their free speech while on American soil?"

It was evident that I caught his attention based on the silence on the other end of the phone. After a pause, he asked, "So, how did they [Yugoslavia] know?" It was the opening I was waiting for; and I believe it was what eventually led to a great deal of publicity about Ivezaj's arrest, because it forced the press to look at the Ivezaj case from another perspective. I explained the role of the Yugoslav secret police in America and other Western countries. The journalist was directed to a 1979 Senate Foreign Relations Committee report published in the *New York Times* on October 10, 1979. In the article, the *N.Y. Times* quoted a Senate report stating that "a confidential source had advised the United States Government that the goal of the Yugoslav intelligence agents based here [in America] was the penetration and destruction of anti-Communist émigré groups."

"Do you have any proof that the Yugoslav government has committed these acts against any émigrés here in the Detroit area?", he asked. I anticipated this question as well and had the answer available. I gave him the name of a man from Windsor, Ontario, Ilija Jakšić, who had also been brought into police headquarters for questioning the year before while he was visiting relatives in the former Yugoslavia. Yugoslav secret police agents wanted Jakšić to spy on fellow Croatian émigrés once he returned to his adopted home in Canada. To my joy, one of the first articles that appeared the next day questioned how Yugoslavia knew that Ivezaj took part in the demonstration against Yugoslavia in 1981, which led to his arrest in 1986. Then on October 2, 1986 the *Detroit News* published an editorial titled

Down with Yugo!

"Free Pjeter Ivezaj." The editorial strongly condemned Yugoslavia for the arrest of Ivezaj. They also began to question how the regime knew the names of people demonstrating peacefully in the U.S. in opposition to Yugoslavia? We had developed a close relationship with a reporter for the *Detroit News* named Armand Gebert over a period of several years; and on October 10, 1986 he published an article titled "Immigrants Fear Homelands' Secret Police." Gebert also questioned how the Yugoslav government knew of Ivezaj's involvement in peaceful demonstrations in the U.S., and how that knowledge led to his eventual arrest and imprisonment.

Politicians like the former Congressman William Broomfield were already involved in the Ivezaj case prior to me interjecting myself. However, I can say that the reporting took on a whole new dimension once the activities of Yugoslav spies operating in America were highlighted. It began a journalistic feeding frenzy that moved from the newspapers to the local television and radio stations. Once elected officials like Congressman Broomfield and U.S. Senator Carl Levin realized they were receiving favorable publicity, they sought even more involvement in the case. The increased involvement by politicians resulted in increased media attention and louder demands for Ivezaj's release. Within a few days, the story of Pjeter Ivezaj began making national and international news with U.S. politicians promising to do everything in their power to free Pjeter Ivezaj. In today's lexicon, the story of Pjeter Ivezaj went viral.

The Yugoslav government only fully understood the ramifications of their bad decision to jail Ivezaj when U.S. Congressman Broomfield kept his promise and introduced a bill in U.S. Congress to suspend Yugoslavia's "favored nation" trade status on October 9, 1986. These new trade restrictions on Yugoslav goods would have dramatically affected the importation of Yugo cars and other products into the U.S. The whole Yugoslav economy was going to pay the price for the continued imprisonment of one Albanian-American citizen.

The very next day, on October 10, 1986, the Yugoslav government succumbed to U.S. pressure and released Ivezaj from prison. U.S. Ambassador John Scanlan contacted the Michigan congressional members on that day to say that Ivezaj had finally been released from Titograd jail where he was being held. The *Detroit Free Press* asked Congressman Broomfield on October 11, 1986 if congressional pressure helped gain Ivezaj's release from prison. Congressman Broomfield responded, "There is no question about it."

First Meeting with Franjo Tuđman

In May of 1988 Pero, Marko and I met with a former political prisoner recently released from a Yugoslav prison who was visiting Detroit. His name was Franjo Tuđman. On May 30, 1990 he would be elected President of Croatia. Tuđman originally planned on simply coming to Detroit and speaking to Croatians in the social hall of St. Jerome's Croatian Catholic Church on Eight Mile Rd. We were concerned with both his personal safety while in Detroit and in limiting his possible exposure to prosecution by Yugoslavia when he returned home. For these two reasons we carefully selected the people who would have private access to him, drive him and provide lodging for him and his wife. The people we chose would have to be dependable and known to us, but we didn't want Tuđman to be seen (or photographed by UDBA) keeping company with any of the more radical Croatians. If UDBA had photographed Tuđman standing next to a known radical at a public lecture, for example, that could have been explained. However, the concern was that Yugoslavia would have prosecuted Tuđman, yet again, if he was seen in the private company of known revolutionary types bent on Yugoslavia's destruction.

It was also important for us to maximize the public relations benefits of Tuđman's visit to Detroit. Amnesty International had adopted Franjo Tuđman as one of their "Prisoners of Conscience" while he was in Lepoglava Prison and we decided that I would present the representatives of Amnesty

International with a plaque on behalf of the Croatian community. Dr. Tuđman made a notation of this presentation and his speech on page 262 of his personal diary.

Tuđman also made an entry for the previous day, July 4, 1988, indicating a dinner in the home of Mirko Kovač. A very small group of us that organized his speaking event in Detroit had dinner with him in the Kovačs' backyard. In attendance were Tuđman, his wife Ankica, Mirko's wife Ana, Marko Stipaničić, Pero Ivčec, Miro Komšić and me. Of course, we could never have dreamed that within two years of our meeting with him that evening, the regimes of Eastern Europe would begin to crumble one by one and that Franjo Tuđman would become the first ever democratically elected leader of Croatia. The subject of the Senate Foreign Relations Committee report, discussed earlier in the chapter, came up after dinner. Marko began telling Dr. Tuđman about the report that Marko believed had been written by Senator Helms. Marko's reason for talking about it was to show Tuđman how Croatians in Detroit were so effective that our actions even caught the attention of the Senate Foreign Relations Committee. I knew that Marko was wrong, because I was the one who accidently discovered the report. Two of Helms' aids had written the report – not Helms – but I chose not to embarrass Marko by correcting him publicly. I was in complete shock, however, when Dr. Tuđman immediately contradicted Marko. "No!" Dr. Tuđman said emphatically. "That was not Senator Helms, that was two of his aids." Marko turned to me to verify what Tuđman just said, because he knew I had found the report. "Dr. Tuđman is right," I said. "Two of Helms' aides wrote the report." I was utterly amazed. "How could Tuđman have possibly known about this very obscure report among a very large collection of other reports written by various U.S. Senators on the Foreign Relations Committee?" I wondered to myself as I sat there stunned. "How did he even know about the report? How did he know with such certitude that the report was written by aids of Senator Helms and not Helms himself?" It was one thing for me to know these things. I lived in America. I had access to a large public library in one of America's major cities. But this man lived in a Communist country a continent away; I was amazed at the depth of his knowledge. The conversation also revealed something of Dr. Tuđman's character. He was extremely confident about what he knew and how he knew it. He also lacked patience for people who – in his view - did not know as much as they believed they knew. In the face of such powerful and authoritative confidence, even Marko Stipaničić was forced to quietly back down. It was rare for Marko to retreat from any verbal confrontation regarding politics, but I learned that day that Franjo Tuđman was an unstoppable force when he thought he was right!

I found it easy to support Franjo Tuđman when he ran for President of Croatia against many other well-known and qualified opponents. I had witnessed his personal charisma and confidence that was rooted in knowledge and an amazing attention to detail. Some of the hardline Croatian groups opposed Tuđman for the very reasons that made him a good choice in my eyes. Since he was a former Communist partisan, he would be the best candidate to make the transition from Communism to democracy. Because he had fought as a Yugoslav partisan during WWII and later rose to the rank of Major General in the JNA, he could not be seriously linked with anyone from the NDH government of WWII. In addition, he was arrested and incarcerated twice by the Yugoslavs. First for "subversive activities" following his pro-democracy activities during the Croatian Spring of 1972 and again in 1981 for spreading "enemy propaganda." These arrests added to his bona fides in our eyes.

Planning for another project was already underway before my first encounter with Dr. Tuđman in 1988. The project involved documenting the post WWII war crimes of Yugoslav communists. I chose our private meeting with him that evening to ask him for an interview on the subject. Tuđman indicated during dinner that he was familiar with the massacres as a former partisan. I explained that I wanted to record the eyewitness testimony of the survivors of Bleiburg. Most Croats in diaspora had heard of it, but inside Yugoslavia the situation was quite different: those who did know, didn't talk about it for fear of prosecution. As the evening was concluding I pulled him aside and asked him directly. His answer was short and emphatic: "No! Now is not the time." Although I would meet and speak with Tuđman on several subsequent occasions, I was, unfortunately, never able to interview him on film concerning the Bleiburg Tragedy and the subsequent death marches organized by Tito. Tuđman mentions our encounter and my work in a diary entry dated July 6, 1988: "Palajic [sic] who is collecting, actually working on a degree about the problem of victims."

Once Tuđman became president, however, he strongly supported events aimed at educating the Croatian public more thoroughly about the Bleiburg Tragedy. In May 1995, at the fiftieth anniversary of Bleiburg, Tuđman authorized a series of events throughout Croatia and Herzegovina beginning with lectures in Croatia's Parliament building. I was invited to join the historian Nikolai Tolstoy and two other Brits to take part in the speaking tour. When I approached Tuđman in 1988, I couldn't have possibly imagined that my project would end up being a full-length documentary and that I would have the opportunity to present it in the Croatian Parliament one day.

For Baka's Homeland

One of thousands of bumper stickers distributed

Down with Yugo!

Police Report: December 1, 1983

Police Report: November 15, 1982

Anti-Yugoslav Demonstration, Detroit

Down with Yugo!

Albanians on fabricated Yugoslav tank being arrested

North American HRS Congress, California 1984

Petar Ivčec attempting to remove Yugoslav flag from city flagpole

Down with Yugo!

Marko Stipaničić firing up Croatian and Albanian demonstrators (2 federal agents among crowd)

For Baka's Homeland

Many immigrants fear governments they fled

Gannett News Service

As national attention focuses on the plight of a Michigan man arrested while visiting his native Yugoslavia, many immigrants in the United States still fear the regimes they fled.

Croatians, Albanians and others with roots in Yugoslavia said fears that the old country is watching are very real. They claim agents of the Yugoslav communist secret police are active in Detroit.

Those worries were dramatized this week when a Sterling Heights, Mich., man who immigrated from Yugoslavia was convicted by a Yugoslav court, apparently for taking part in a peaceful demonstration in 1981. Albanian descendant Pjeter Ivezaj, 30, demonstrated in Washington against Yugoslavia's treatment of its Albanian minorities.

"It's nothing new," West Bloomfield, Mich., businessman Ekrem Bardha said of the Ivezaj case.

Bardha said, "It is incredible how lives are being interferred with and how our constitutional rights are threatened. ... There are Yugoslav agents in this country who keep records of former Yugoslav citizens who are outspoken dissidents against the Yugoslav government.

"Pjeter Ivezaj is an excellent example," said Bardha, who fled penniless from his native Albania in 1953. He believes such Yugoslav reprisals have increased in recent years.

Yugoslavia is a non-aligned communist nation dominated by Serbo-Croatian Christian Slavs but with many different nationalities. There are about 2 million Albanians within Yugoslavia. They mainly are Muslim, speak a non-Slavic language and often feel discriminated against.

Croatians, another Yugoslav ethnic group, also have run into trouble with the Yugoslav government. Some Detroit-area Croatians say Croatia, now a republic within the Yugoslav federation, should be an independent, non-communist country.

Michael Palaich, spokesman for the Croatian Inter-City Committee, said, "Croatians here and elsewhere in the country and the free world have long felt the pressures of Yugoslav agents."

El Paso Times, Oct 11, 1986, page 12

68

Author with Pjetar Ivezaj (left) after his release from Yugoslav prison

Franjo Tuđman with Amnesty International representatives, Detroit 1988

4

The Bleiburg Tragedy

I FIRST HEARD of the atrocities committed by Tito's Yugoslav regime from my Grandmother long before I ever heard the term Bleiburg Tragedy, or the subsequent death march called the Way of the Cross (*Križni Put*). When I was very little my Grandmother told me about her family members whom the Communists killed after WWII. I never knew it at the time, and still don't have all the facts regarding their deaths, but I recall that they were her nephews. However, a book published in 1995 by Matica Hrvatska Petrinja titled *Petrinja's Book of Victims* might provide answers and help corroborate her story. Three men who share my Grandmother's maiden name, Vidović, and who lived in her small village of Križ-Hrastovica outside of Petrinja, are listed on page 168 of the book. All three are documented as being killed by the partisans, with one being killed in the death marches conducted by Tito's henchmen following WWII. Grandma told me the story of her family members being hung from telephone poles by the Communists during their post-war killing spree. The combined feelings of horror and disbelief at hearing her story left a lasting imprint on my young mind.

The first book I read on the terrible historical event that became known as the Bleiburg Tragedy was *Operation Slaughterhouse: Eyewitness Accounts of Postwar Massacres in Yugoslavia*, by John Prcela and Stanko Guldescu published in 1970. The book relates many horrific eyewitness accounts documenting the inhuman brutality perpetrated on Croatian men, women and children by the partisan forces of Josip Broz Tito.

Then in 1986 Count Nikolai Tolstoy wrote a book titled *The Minister and the Massacres*. Pero Ivčec, Marko Stipaničić and I drove to the book presentation by Mr. Tolstoy at Hillsdale College in Hillsdale, Michigan, shortly after the publication of the book.

Although Tolstoy did not focus solely on Croatian victims and Yugoslav war crimes, he did seem to find some former WWII British soldiers of the 8th Army who were willing to come forward after over forty years to talk about what they personally witnessed and how they had acted as co-conspirators in the war crimes of the Yugoslav partisans.

Growing up in America and being exposed to the dominant Anglo-Saxon culture, I found it difficult to believe that the British were capable of the things described in Tolstoy's book. They were too cultured, I naively thought, not capable of such brutality. As a young boy I had watched my share of British documentaries and entertainment films depicting the British as a cultured people incapable of deception, let alone acting as co-conspirators in the massacres of thousands of men, women and children. They had honor; they were civilized; they protected the innocent, I believed. They were, after all, part of the Allied Forces following WWII that prosecuted war criminals. My own father was stationed in England during WWII as a member of the U.S. Army Air Corps. How could they possibly be responsible for committing war crimes at the end of WWII in Europe? I was sure that the British involvement in these war crimes depicted in *Operation Slaughterhouse* and *The Minister and the Massacres* were exaggerated and I wanted to find the truth and research the subject with my own objective eye.

If I was naïve about the possibility of British soldiers being involved in the Bleiburg Tragedy and subsequent death marches, I was not naïve about the possibility of Yugoslav partisan involvement. There was no doubt in my mind that the Communist government of Yugoslavia was capable of such atrocities. Communist regimes throughout the world had the uncanny ability to justify or simply deny the slaughter of millions of their own citizens. It started with Lenin after the Soviet revolution and Stalin continued the murderous tradition. The subsequent Communist dictatorships of other Eastern European countries (like Yugoslavia) simply continued the practice of murder. The slaughter was always followed by the same denials and by expunging the crimes from history books. I was certain that Yugoslavia was no different in this respect.

It was also clear to me at this point in my political involvement, that pursuing the truth about the Yugoslav massacres was not without some personal risks to my family and me. By this time, I had already had my life threatened and shotguns fired at my home for activities that were far less threatening than exposing the truth about mass murders. I was also fully aware of Amnesty International's 1985 report documenting the political assassinations committed by Yugoslavia's UDBA entitled "Yugoslavia, Prisoners of Conscience." But there was something about the importance of the project that compelled me to disregard the personal threat.

My research on the Bleiburg Tragedy first began around 1985 when Yugoslavia was still a powerful force. Many Yugoslav citizens who personally took part in the massacres were still deeply entrenched in that regime. Others were reaping benefits (i.e. free apartments and pensions) that the Yugoslav regime doled out. There was, therefore, no hope of getting any of the former partisans involved in the massacres to speak with me.

Nor was there any chance in 1985 of exhuming the mass graves strewn throughout Yugoslavia. That process would not begin until Croatia's independence. The existence of many mass graves was well-known thanks to eyewitness testimonies of survivors documented in *Operation Slaughterhouse.*

My earliest concept for the project was not to produce a documentary film, but simply to video tape the memories of Croatian soldiers and civilians that survived the events of Bleiburg and subsequent death marches. There was a sense of urgency in getting the project off the ground. Forty years had already passed, and the survivors of the massacres were old and beginning to die off. I knew that documenting their eyewitness accounts would be especially important in the future after they had all passed away. As important as the written testimonies in *Operation Slaughterhouse* and *The Minister and the Massacres* were, it was my belief that it would be invaluable for future generations to actually see the elderly survivors relive their emotional experiences and tell their stories in their own voices.

With this as a starting point, it was first necessary to get the various Croatian communities around the world to become involved in the project through fund raising. Initially, I found myself in the uncomfortable position of begging for donations from Croatians of Detroit, Chicago, Windsor and Toronto. Later, I had to expand my efforts to include the Croatian diaspora in Australia and South America. Australia was particularly important for raising funds due to its very large and active Croatian population. Two very active and influential Croatian men in Australia, Tomislav Beram and Fabian Lovoković, graciously organized a speaking tour in the cities of Sydney, Melbourne, Canberra, Geelong and Adelaide. Tomislav Beram also arranged for me to interview several survivors of the Bleiburg Tragedy while I was in Australia. Tomislav and I remain dear friends and we are able to see each other in Croatia on occasion. I am forever indebted to the Croatian diaspora that helped make the eventual documentary possible. Without the funding and their assistance in arranging interviews with subjects, the film would never have been realized.

During my fundraising, I came across Croatian survivors in all the cities I visited, as well as in Buenos Aires, Argentina, and one in London, England. But, unfortunately, I discovered through this process that there was at least one Croatian man living in Mississauga, near Toronto in Canada who was alleged to have personally murdered hundreds of Croatians at the mass grave of Jazovka in Croatia. Smičiklas was a former Yugoslav partisan from the Karlovac area of Croatia. An eyewitness to the killings who lived in the same Canadian city as Smičiklas, identified him as someone who took exceptional joy in shooting Croatians in the back of the head before throwing them through a small hole that was the mouth of the large cavern several meters below ground called Jazovka. The witness, whom I knew personally, was nine or ten years old when he witnessed Smičiklas murdering men and women brought by a truck to the small opening in the ground outside a Croatian village of Sošice. The witness, Janko Popović, stated that the road leading to the cave opening was strewn with identification documents. Mr. Popović stated that everyone in the area around Jazovka knew about the murders that took place in 1945. The captives threw the identification documents from the moving trucks as they were being transported to their deaths. Popović theorized that the victims hoped that their documents (if found) would help bring peace to family members who otherwise might believe that their loved ones had simply disappeared. Mr. Popović recalled watching from up in a tree as Smičiklas slaughtered his victims one by one. His gun would often overheat and malfunction after scores were killed. When that happened, Smičiklas would resort to bashing the helpless victims in the back of the head with a hammer and throwing their lifeless bodies into the deep vertical cavern. Sadly, Smičiklas would later immigrate to Canada where he would freely walk among other Croats of Mississauga at various lamb roast, parties and weddings. The Croats of

Mississauga never knew there was a mass murderer in their presence.

Although Mr. Popović refused to allow his story to be recorded on film out of fear, his testimony confirmed for me the importance of the project. It further compelled me to move forward with interviewing survivors.

The project began by filming Croatian survivors who lived in the cities of Windsor, Toronto and Chicago. All of the cities were within driving distance of Detroit. During one weekend of filming in Toronto I discovered that Nikolai Tolstoy would be giving a speech on his book *The Minister and the Massacres* in a conference room inside Toronto's City Hall building. As luck would have it, Ante Beljo organized Tolstoy's speaking engagement.

I filmed Tolstoy's lecture at Toronto's City Hall where fewer than twenty people were in attendance. Afterwards Beljo, Tolstoy and I went to have lunch at a small restaurant in downtown Toronto. It was at that lunch that Tolstoy and I exchanged contact information. There was no way of knowing at the time how instrumental that initial meeting would be to the success of my project. Tolstoy would become an important source for contacts with several former British soldiers quoted in his book and eventually used in my documentary film.

Therefore, in August 1988, using Tolstoy's information, I made contact via mail with most of the former British 8th Army Officers. Some of the British witnesses I hoped to film were reluctant at first, but they eventually accepted me into their homes with the help of Tolstoy's introductions.

Nigel Nicholson

Nigel Nicholson initially said that he knew very little about the repatriations of Croats from the part of Southern Austria known as Carinthia. He stated in letters and eventually in a phone conversation, that he primarily dealt with the Cossacks at the end of WWII while stationed in Southern Austria as an Intelligence Officer with the British 8th Army. I told him that that was OK and that if he did not object, I would still like to speak with him. He invited me to his well-known family home called Sissinghurst Castle outside of Cranbrook Kent, England. The former British Officer, Member of Parliament and author had willed the castle over to the British government in exchange for being allowed to live in the home for the duration of his life. In exchange Britain's National Trust would maintain the house and its extensive grounds and gardens.

In 1945, as an Intelligence Officer in the British 8th Army, Nigel Nicholson was instrumental in carrying out (if not devising) the duplicitous scheme to ship tens of thousands of Croats to Yugoslavia. As he stated in a contemporaneous report from May 1945, the Croats were being sent to a "known fate of murder."

The 30,000 – 50,000 Croats who came into his jurisdiction had arrived in Southern Austria after the May 15, 1945 surrender of a much larger mass of 200,000 Croatian soldiers and 500,000 civilians at the fields of Bleiburg in Austria.

That larger group had hoped to surrender to General Scott of the British 8th Army in an attempt to avoid the wholesale slaughter that the Croats knew would take place if they were forced to surrender to Tito's partisans. General Scott, however, would not accept their surrender and instead brokered a meeting between the Partisan General Milan Basta and Croatian negotiators General Herenčić and Professor Danijel Crljen. It was at that conference that General Scott informed the Croatian representatives that the British soldiers under his command would compel the surrender of the Croatian soldiers and civilians if the Croats did not comply and surrender to the Communists voluntarily. The so-called "negotiation" sealed the Croats' fate. Within two days the entire contingent of men, women and children was marched back to Yugoslavia in what Croats would forever refer to as The Bleiburg Tragedy (*Bleiburška Tragedija*) and The Death Marches (*Križni Put*).

In his role of Intelligence Officer, Nigel Nicholson was to gather the 30,000 to 50,000 soldiers and civilians making their way north toward Austria after the larger mass of 200,000 Croatian soldiers and 500,000 civilians had been forced back to Yugoslavia from Bleiburg. The British would detain the stragglers in various Austrian camps until the men, women and children could also be forcibly repatriated to Tito's partisans. And this is where Nigel Nicholson's involvement gets interesting.

The Croats had already experienced the bloodthirsty brutality of Communist partisans under Tito since 1941. They knew from first-hand experience that the partisans killed and tortured those who surrendered to them. If there were women in villages overrun by the partisans, they would very likely be raped first and then killed. Age made little difference: children and old people would also be killed as the partisans overtook a Croatian town or village. The Croats that were fleeing towards Southern Austria in May of 1945 had travelled there from different parts of Croatia and as far away as Bosnia and Herzegovina in an effort to escape the barbarous tactics of the Yugoslav Partisans. These scenes of slaughter, rape and mass graves would be repeated once again by Serbia's next generation during Croatia's Homeland War (*Domovinski Rat*) from 1991-1995.

Nigel Nicholson admitted during filming that the British 8th Army knew full well that these men, women and children who made their way to Southern Austria seeking safety would refuse to turn around and place themselves into the savage hands of Tito's Partisans. No; the British would have to come up with a viable story in order to clear the ever-growing refugee camps strewn along Austria's southern border. So, a bloody deception was concocted, and the Croats, unfortunately, bought it.

According to Nicholson and supported by contemporaneous documents, the Croats were told that if they voluntarily boarded the train cars – which were nothing more than cattle cars – they would be taken to Italy where they would be offered protection by the Allied Forces. The deception served several purposes. First, it would rid the British of the nuisance that an exodus of tens of thousands of people presented to them. They would no longer have to use British resources to feed and protect the people from the marauding bands of partisans. Second, in spite of the fact that at this period in May 1945 most of the fleeing people were civilians, Tito (an official ally of the British) was demanding that the British repatriate them into his hands. Third, and perhaps most important, the use of deception in getting the people onto the cattle cars would relieve the British of the need to use force. Convinced by the false narrative, the Croats simply complied with the British request in an attempt to save their lives and the lives of their children. The official Situation Reports (SITREPS) that Nicholson still had in his possession, and which I surreptitiously photographed in his home, indicate that British Intelligence was concerned that forcing non-compliant civilians by beating or bayoneting them onto the cattle cars would affect the moral of the average British soldier who would be left to carry out the orders of his superiors.

In the interview, Captain Nicholson explained that in the end the Croats bought into the story of deception. They willingly boarded the cattle cars that they were told would take them to Italy. According to Nicholson and the intelligence reports he submitted in May 1945, eighty to ninety people were loaded onto each cattle car. Once all the cars were completely filled with the duped Croats, padlocks were placed on the doors. Nicholson stated that the partisan forces which were present in the area were directed to stay away from the trains: the British knew that the deception would unravel if the Croats saw any soldiers with the familiar red star of Communism on their caps. They would simply refuse to board the trains.

For the most part, the Croats continued to believe that the trains were going to Italy until they reached the Rosenbach train station. The Rosenbach station was – and still is – the last train station on the Austrian side of the border before the trains continued to their destination: Yugoslavia. Nicholson went on to explain that only when the trains stopped at Rosenbach did the British troops disembark, and Tito's partisans come out of hiding from behind the walls of the train station. Nigel Nicholson calmly told me that it was only at that moment that the real deception was discovered by the Croats. They finally realized that they had been duped.

He stated that the Croats, by looking through the wood slats of the cattle cars, could see that the control of the train was being turned over to partisans. He stated that screams of horror could be heard from inside the locked cattle cars as the Croats saw the red stars on the partisans' caps and finally realized that the British had lied to them about their destination. Captain Nicholson related that many Croats committed suicide inside the cattle cars right there at the Rosenbach station. With their helpless cargo inside, the trains were then boarded by the partisans and transported through the Rosenbach tunnel and into Yugoslavia where more Yugoslav partisans were waiting for them.

As if this treachery by the British 8th Army was not bad enough, Captain Nigel Nicholson stated in his interview that he and all the British involved knew that the men, women and children were being sent to a "known fate of murder." He recalled that on at least one occasion a man was able to escape the slaughters from the Yugoslav side of the border and find his way back into the waiting arms of the same British forces that sent him over the first time. The man informed Nicholson that the partisans were slaughtering everyone across the border. "What happened to the man who escaped and relayed this story to you?" I asked. "We sent him back again too," Nicholson calmly explained.

Colin Gunner

Another former British officer who found himself in Southern Austria with the British 8th Army in May 1945 was Colin Gunner. When I interviewed him in Banbury, England, in August 1988, Gunner was a wreck of a man. He lived in a tiny camper on a farm where he worked. I interviewed him there as he chain-smoked and drank whiskey. In the beginning of our discussion he was very obtuse and defensive. But as we delved deeper into his story, I could see that he began to mellow. His alcohol consumption must have also helped to loosen his tongue a bit. By the end of the interview I finally realized that he would never completely let down his guard while the camera was running, regardless of how much alcohol he drank. I gave him the impression that I had shut off the camera and began to put my equipment away. Thinking that the camera was off, his demeanor changed immediately. In a matter of a couple of hours Gunner had transformed from a combative and non-apologetic loyal Brit, to a remorseful old man who was reliving the terrible Yugoslav crimes he had witnessed forty years before. I felt sympathy for the old man sitting in front of me who as a young man had shown no compassion for the thousands of Croats that he and his fellow soldiers forced across the Lavamund bridge and delivered to the partisan executioners. As though he had finally and fully realized his own role in the terrible and bloody event, he began to cry.

Captain Gunner recounted his involvement in the mass exodus of Croats beginning on May 15, 1945. Unlike Nigel Nicholson, Gunner was involved in forcibly repatriating the largest group of Croats that had been stopped by the British in the fields of Bleiburg. Official British 8th Army documents which I discovered in British Archives at KEW Gardens estimate that there were 200,000 soldiers and 500,000 civilians in this exodus of people seeking British protection. We know that those figures are fairly accurate, because they were estimated with the help of photographs taken from high above by British Spitfire airplanes. Gunner was directly involved in the Bleiburg Tragedy. He recalled not only watching as tens of thousands were driven to their deaths, but witnessing the murders of Croat men, women and children while they were still on the Austrian side of the border.

The enormous mass of people camped in the Bleiburg field was divided into two groups by the partisans after the Croatian military was forced to surrender. One group was marched directly from the Bleiburg field to the Dravograd bridge. The second group of mostly soldiers, but some civilian women and children too, were marched across the Drava River bridge at Lavamund.

Captain Colin Gunner's orders were to take a position on the North side of the Lavamund bridge with a jeep to ensure that all the prisoners were successfully driven across the border by the partisans. When asked how long it took to march the enormous group across the bridge Gunner replied, "One night, one day and one night." Next, I asked, "And how many people would you estimate were forced over the bridge?" After some thought Gunner stated, 'Three hundred thousand." It is interesting to note here that Gunner estimated this number without having access to official British estimates. In fact, I would not discover the document estimating the total number to be 700,000 in the British Archives until the following year. If we divided the 700,000 figure from the document into two separate death columns, Colin's estimate of the number that passed by him in Lavamund was eerily accurate. Colin Gunner stood by as people were beaten and killed by the partisans: he specifically recalled watching from his position as Croats were killed and thrown into the ditch, or into the swiftly moving Drava below.

"Did you witness civilians being killed too?" I asked. His matter-of-fact reply was: "Babes in arms!" Throughout the interview Mr. Gunner insisted that he was just following orders as a low-level soldier. That response struck me as ironic, because it was the same defense that Nazis who were put on trial by The Allied War Crimes Tribunal attempted to use as a defense. Years later I would hear the same defense uttered by a Serbian soldier and convicted war criminal that I interviewed in Sarajevo in March 1993 named Borislav Herak. Herak was tried, pleaded guilty and initially sentenced to death in Sarajevo in September 1993. His death sentence was rescinded twenty years later, but he too gave the same response that all war criminals give: "I was just following orders."

In 1991, Gunner authored a biography of his days serving in the British military during WWII titled "Front of the Line." His involvement in the Bleiburg Tragedy in May of 1945 is barely mentioned in the book.

Gerald Draper

Gerald Draper was the last former British officer I interviewed in England that year. In many ways, he was the most important witness that I interviewed. Frankly, I was shocked that a principled and honorable person of his stature could be found in England. Prior to my interview with Draper, the deeper I dug into the British involvement in the Bleiburg Tragedy and the forced repatriations, the more defensive and recalcitrant the British witnesses became. They became incredulous at any suggestion that the British had acted dishonorably regarding the events in Austria in May and June of 1945. With the exception of Draper, they would all run down a list of extenuating circumstances that left the British 8th Army little choice in what they did. They would say that they did what they had to do under very difficult conditions. Almost all of them used the classic excuse of following orders. Nigel Nicholson in particular continuously reminded me – and himself, I believe – that he did make his "protest known" to those in command, and maybe he did. However, I reminded him: "You still carried out unlawful and immoral orders." That, of course, did not go over well with Mr. Nicholson.

But Colonel Gerald Draper was cut from a much different cloth than the others I interviewed. Gerald Draper had not been involved in the Bleiburg Tragedy, or the forced repatriations of Croats. He did, however, know a lot about war crimes and what constituted a war crime and crimes against humanity.

Mr. Draper was Prosecutor for the Allied War Crimes Tribunals including the famous trials of Nuremburg following WWII. He was also the War Crimes Prosecutor who took the confession of Rudolf Höss, the Commandant of Auschwitz, found guilty of crimes against humanity and hung from the gallows on the grounds of Auschwitz. In addition to his qualifications as an expert on war crimes and crimes against humanity, Draper was a Professor of Law at the University of London's School of Economics until his retirement. For the remainder of his life, until his health issues prevented travel, he was an honored guest speaker at the annual Holocaust Memorial in Tel Aviv, Israel.

I could not imagine a better person to answer the following questions: first, were the Yugoslav partisans guilty of war crimes, crimes against the peace, or crimes against humanity, if they committed the acts they were being accused of committing? Second, were the British guilty of war crimes, or crimes against humanity for refusing to protect the hundreds of thousands of Croatians that fled Communist forces in Yugoslavia and were seeking safety from the British 8th Army? Third, former British Soldiers admitted that they knew in 1945 that they were sending men, women and children to a "known fate of murder" when they sent them to Yugoslavia under partisan control. Were individual British soldiers who were "following orders" guilty of war crimes, or crimes against humanity when they carried out the deceptive scheme of locking thousands of Croats into cattle cars and sending them to their slaughter?

The former Nuremburg Prosecutor's answer still surprises me many years later. Professor Draper insisted that the British officers who were involved in denying protection to the Croats in Bleiburg (i.e. General Scott) as well as the British officers (i.e. Captain Nicholson, Captain Gunner) involved in the forced repatriations could be prosecuted as war criminals. He insisted that a soldier is only obligated to obey lawful orders and the orders resulting in the murders listed above could not be construed as lawful in nature. But he added that he did not think there was a political will in England to prosecute British citizens for crimes they had committed outside of Great Britain over forty years earlier.

It may also be interesting to note here that, with the exception of Draper, all the former British officers admitted in one way or another that their prejudice towards the Croats as "Eastern Europeans" made it easier for them to hand them over to be murdered. When I asked how Captain Gunner viewed the people being marched to their death, he replied, they were "foreign people." Major General H.E.N. Bredin, who I did not use in the film, responded by admitting more emphatically that the British were influenced by "racism" in organizing the forced repatriations of Croats and other Eastern Europeans.

The British government has (unofficially) acknowledged its involvement in the Bleiburg Tragedy and the forced repatriations of not only Croats, but also Serbs and Slovenes. Several of my interviews with survivors and with the three former British officers above, can today be found in the archives of the British Imperial War Museum in London. But they have yet to acknowledge their role in a "crime." Yet, if we look at the actions taken by members of the British 8th Army's 5th Corps objectively, we can only come to the same conclusion as the former WWII War Crimes Investigator Gerald Draper: the British who were responsible could have been charged with committing war crimes and crimes against humanity in Southern Austria in May and June of 1945.

The Documents

The third leg of the project was the documentation that would be required if I was to corroborate the statements of Croatian survivors and former British 8th Army participants. The three major official sources for documents were the Imperial War Museum in London, the British National Archives at KEW Gardens and the Britain's Ministry of Defense. I found my way to these great archives on two separate trips to England, the first time in August 1988 and the second time in May 1989.

Tolstoy had already done quite a lot of research in the archives when he wrote *The Minister and the Massacres*. His book dealt with the more general topic of British forced repatriations. The groups repatriated were Cossacks, Serbs, Slovenes and Croats. I wanted to focus entirely on the forced repatriations of Croatians at Bleiburg.

The British Archives hold a tremendous amount of material regarding this subject. Researchers to this day have only scratched the surface of what is available. Perhaps the most important document that I discovered, which I do not think was ever previously published, was a Situation Report (SITREP) from May 1945 estimating the size of the Croatian mass exodus that made its way from Croatia to Southern Austria in May 1945. It was important to find a document (other than Croatian sources) estimating the size of the exodus. First, because Croats at the time had no way of knowing just how many soldiers and civilians were in the exodus. During my interviews with Croatian survivors I asked many times, "How many people would you estimate were in the exodus?" The answer was always the same whether it was concerning the exodus, or the later death marches: "There is no way of knowing, because I couldn't see the end of the line, or the beginning of the line." Even when Colin Gunner was asked to estimate how many people had crossed in front of him through Lavamund he could only estimate 300,000. Second, even if it were possible, nobody would accept a Croatian estimate as objectively reliable. Therefore, when I discovered the British 8th Army document that estimated the size of the exodus as 200,000 soldiers and 500,000 civilians, I was thrilled. The contemporaneous document used aerial photographs captured by British Spitfire planes to support the British estimate. This would corroborate the story of more than one Croatian survivor who told of watching Spitfires flying overhead and photographing the Croats in the fields of Bleiburg. I thought the Bleiburg survivors had exaggerated when they first began telling me of being photographed by the British pilots. The documents together with the reports found in the Imperial War Museum proved that they had in fact been photographed as reported. Photographs, as we know, are an excellent way for estimating crowd size.

The notebook that Nigel Nicholson had kept in his possession forty years after the event was also very important. The former Intelligence Officer for the British 8th Army gave me access to the notebook following my interview with him at his home at Sissinghurst Castle. He placed the notebook in front of me at a desk in his home while he went to a separate building in the back of his home where he had a writing office on the second floor. I was fascinated by what I read on the worn and tattered pages of the old notebook. Some of the entries in the notebook from May and June of 1945 were in his own handwriting. Other pages were typed and used for official Situation Reports that were forwarded by him up the 8th Army chain of command.

In the documents the reader could see the whole scheme of deception laid out: they remove any doubt that the British used a disgusting ploy of deception to get the Croats to board the cattle cars that would take them to their death. The documents specify that locks were placed on the doors of the cars to prevent the Croats from escaping. Nicholson went on to write that the partisans were asked to stay out of sight of the hapless Croats until the trains reached the Rosenbach tunnel in Southern Austria. The partisans were only allowed to board the train at Rosenbach, permitting them to take over the final stage of the duplicitous scheme. There are far too many entries in the notebook to list here, but suffice it to say that they are as detailed and accurate as one would expect from an Intelligence Officer.

Knowing that the valuable time that I had with the documents was limited I began to film the pages of the Situation Reports with the same video camera that I had used in our interview just moments ago. It was fortunate that I chose to film the notebook while having access to it. When I returned to the states, I wrote to Mr. Nicholson asking him to copy pages of the notebook and forward them at my expense. Nicholson refused saying the print on the pages was too light to provide legible copies and therefore it would make little sense to attempt copying them. But, by that time it was too late. The words that he wrote on those pages, and which are now on film, would forever serve to document the British involvement in the forced repatriations of men, women and children to their certain death using a bloody scheme of deception.

As was stated previously, my earliest idea for the project was to focus on interviewing Croatian survivors, British participants and accumulating as many documents, photographs and historical videos as fast as possible. However, the historical events unraveling across Eastern Europe in 1989 changed the direction of the project. The winds of freedom that first started blowing in Poland had finally reached the borders of Croatia as well. Even the Croatian people were beginning to believe that they might be able to throw off their Communist oppressors in Yugoslavia.

It became increasingly clear to me that Croatia could not rely on Western governments to take their side when Croatians too would eventually begin to demand freedom. It was a fairly common view of most of the Croatians directly involved in the liberation movement that the Western countries would never willingly support the dissolution of Yugoslavia. Yugoslavia was viewed by the West as serving its purposes ever since the signing of the Yalta Agreement by Roosevelt, Churchill and Stalin in 1945. Yugoslavia's position as a geopolitical buffer zone was further cemented when Tito broke from direct Soviet control in 1948 and created the Non-Aligned Nations Pact. Simply stated the West still believed it benefited from the existence of Yugoslavia. Even the normally anti-Communist U.S. President Ronald Reagan openly supplied Yugoslavia with military aid and training, because he viewed it as being outside the Soviet sphere of influence. This support for Yugoslavia is best exemplified in an address to the House Foreign Affairs Committee dated June 10, 1981 by then-Assistant Secretary for European Affairs, Lawrence Eagleburger: "We firmly support Yugoslavia's independence, political unity, and territorial integrity." Eagleburger went on to say, "We are engaged with Yugoslavia's military authorities in a modest program of visits, arms transfers, and training."

Croatia would very shortly join the other Eastern European countries in freeing herself from the yoke of Communism despite the Western countries' support of Yugoslavia. It was also my deep belief that once they began the process of breaking away from former Yugoslavia, there could be no return without Croatia experiencing the same genocide that she had experienced after 1945. There was also no doubt in my mind that history was about to repeat itself – as it always seems to.

I reached the conclusion that the best way to avoid a future bloodbath on the same scale would be to educate the Croatian people at home about what had happened to the previous generation of Croats that surrendered in May and June of 1945. Although I had absolutely no experience making documentaries, I decided that the best way to reveal that terrible history was through telling the story as only a full-length documentary could.

It was a history that the Yugoslav regime successfully hid from most of the Croatian citizens prior to 1991. Even today there are many former hardline Communists – who now call themselves Anti-Fascists – that refuse to believe because of some sort of cognitive dissonance, that the government of Yugoslavia that they loved and that their parents loved could have ever been capable of mass slaughter on such a scale. It was also important, in my mind, that all of the potential political leaders of Croatia that were emerging (most of them former political prisoners) be made aware of the dangers, if they already were not. They had to understand that once independence was declared there could be no going back – no retreat and no surrender. They had to be made aware that by declaring Croatian independence they would cross the proverbial Rubicon.

In 1991, the completed documentary with a letter from me expressing the views stated above found its way into the hands of many of the potential leaders in Croatia: Franjo Tuđman, Gojko Šušak, Ante Beljo, Dobroslav Paraga, Marko Veselica, Zvonomir Čičak.

It is clear when viewing the history of Croatia's Homeland War and the war in Bosnia-Herzegovina that my initial impressions were correct and justified. The methods used by the Yugoslav Army and the Serbian Chetniks are well documented by various governments and non-governmental organizations that employed people on the ground during Croatian and Bosnian wars of independence. Yugoslavia, the fourth largest army in Europe, would go on to slaughter thousands of its own citizens and dump them in mass graves throughout Croatia and Bosnia-Herzegovina exactly as they had done following WWII. Furthermore, Croatian and Bosnian women would come to be treated as tools of war and objects of rape by the same Yugoslav regime that had for decades propagated the slogan "Brotherhood and Unity" at every opportunity. While the death toll in Croatia during that terrible war of 1991-1995 is estimated to be around 20,000 and in Bosnia-Herzegovina 200,000, it certainly would have been much higher had Croatia and Bosnia-Herzegovina failed to achieve their goal of independence. Surrender by Croats and Bosnians would certainly have resulted in much higher post-war retaliatory massacres. It is possible that those numbers would have exceeded even those following WWII and the surrender at Bleiburg.

After the completion of the 1½ hour documentary, I made the decision to smuggle about five hundred VHS tapes into what was then still Yugoslavia. This was not a decision that I made lightly. Croatian citizens had been prosecuted and had received long jail sentences for simply bringing one Croatian émigré newspaper across the border into Yugoslavia. Non-Yugoslav citizens like Julie Bušić were arrested and imprisoned for throwing anti-Yugoslav leaflets from a high-rise building overlooking Jelačić Square on November 29, 1970. Large crowds, who had gathered in the square below on that evening to celebrate Communist "*Dan Republike*," were surprised when they were bombarded by the leaflets sent flying from atop the building to the square below. I was uncomfortably aware that my future would not be very pleasant if I were caught smuggling hundreds of video tapes that documented one of its best-kept secrets into Yugoslavia. With the serious risks in mind, I made a nighttime crossing of the Yugoslav border in May 1991 on a train from Klagenfurt, Austria, to Zagreb, carrying four large suitcases filled with the videotapes.

On May 19, 1991 Croatia was holding its plebiscite on independence titled "Referendum for Croatia." My goal was to be in Croatia with the tapes before the momentous occasion. So, when I made the crossing, the Yugoslav Army still had a very strong presence on the Yugoslav border. While still on the Austrian side of the border the train stopped at the border crossing station of Rosenbach. It was there that I encountered a Yugoslav solider with the red star emblazoned on his hat and uniform. The Austrian police left the train and the Yugoslav soldiers boarded for our next leg of the journey into the former Yugoslavia. It was on that same border crossing that Yugoslav partisans, forty-six years previously, had boarded the trains carrying Croats to their deaths. Sometime after our departure from Austria, but before arriving in Yugoslavia, a soldier entered my train compartment. With the usual discourteous attitude offered civilians, the soldier first looked at me and then at the four large pieces of luggage that I had stored on the luggage racks just above my seat. "What do you have in the bags?" he asked me in Serbian. Although I understood his question, I responded by saying, "I only speak English." He repeated, this time in English. "What do you have in the bags?" "Clothes." I said. He gave me a questioning look as if he was trying to understand why this thirty-seven-year-old guy would have four large suitcases with him. I quickly handed him my American passport hoping it would deflect his attention from the bags. I knew at that point in my political education that I would have a much better chance of being ignored when he verified that I was American. I knew from my earlier trip to Croatia in 1978, that the border guards going in this direction on the train were mostly concerned with citizens of Yugoslavia who smuggled goods from abroad. Since I was an American there was little chance of me smuggling in clothing or other Western goods. As he looked at my passport, I wondered what I was going to do if I had to open up one of my suitcases. Thankfully, he simply handed the passport back to me without saying a word and left my compartment. I was relieved until the passport control agent arrived demanding my passport again. This time he was not interested in what I had in my suitcase and simply stamped the passport and handed it back to me. It would be my first smuggling attempt, but not my last.

When I arrived in Zagreb, I immediately looked up Ante Beljo, who at that time was the Secretary for *Hrvatska Demokratska Zajednica* (HDZ), the leading political party in Croatia. He knew about my film and at that time asked if I would like to show my movie in the most prestigious museum in Zagreb, The Mimara Museum. I could not help but wonder what my grandmother and grandfather would have thought if they had seen the grandson they held as a boy premiering his movie in the capital city they knew so well in their youth.

The film was shown in a salon just to the left of the museum's entrance to an audience of seventy-five to one hundred people. I was still nervous, because I knew Yugoslav agents were still very active in plain clothes in the city. Ante Beljo, however, was Mr. Cool. In fact, he was always Mr. Cool. Whether it was years previously when we drove Tolstoy around Toronto looking for a restaurant to have lunch, or later when I was with him crossing the Sava River from Croatia into Bosnia during the war, I never saw Beljo get excited or flustered. His calm demeanor gave me confidence. During the film presentation there were the expected disturbances that confirmed for me that some in the audience had ulterior motives for attending. At various parts of the movie, mostly from the back of the salon, pro-Yugoslav hecklers would yell, "*Laži! Laži!*" (Lies! Lies!). With that exception, the showing went well and was received with some polite applause until the lights came on. We were, after all, still in Yugoslavia in May 1991. As I walked back to the Palace Hotel where I was staying, I passed by several Yugoslav soldiers standing in the doorways along the street with rifles slung over their shoulders. The Referendum for Croatia on May 19, 1991 was only days away and there was a palpable nervousness in the city. Croatia was getting ready to vote for its own sovereign country after centuries of foreign domination. The war for independence was just a few months away: life in Croatia would never again be the same.

To my knowledge, Franjo Tuđman never sat down with any historian or filmmaker to reflect on what he knew about the Bleiburg Tragedy as a former Yugoslav General. However, as discussed in the previous chapter, Tuđman would be the first official to use government resources in an attempt to educate the Croatian public regarding the truth about Bleiburg. He was the force behind organizing the fifty-year commemoration of the Bleiburg Tragedy. It was hard to believe that only seven years had passed between my initial meeting with him in Detroit and the speaking tour he organized in May of 1995. Under the direction of Tuđman, Ante Beljo invited me to go on a speaking tour throughout Croatia and Herzegovina with Nikolai Tolstoy, Ante Beljo and a couple of Brits who had worked as conscientious objectors in the various repatriation camps used by the British military in Southern Austria in the spring of 1945.

The speaking tour began in Zagreb at Croatian's Parliament building. What I said that day standing at the podium in the parliament building caused a minor disturbance among the British participants at the event. After years of research and interviews concerning British complicity in the forced repatriations of men, women and children, I was confident in stating: "Not only do the British have blood on their hands, but they have blood up to their elbows." The Brits were under the impression, when they accepted the invitation to play a role in the event, that the focus would be on partisan war crimes. Needless to say, they did not appreciate the condemnation of their countrymen who were guilty of acting as co-conspirators with Tito's partisan war criminals. What really created an uproar, however, was when I mentioned Nigel Nicholson by name. Gerald Draper, the WWII Allied War Crimes Prosecutor, stated the same thing in answer to a hypothetical question. When I said he should be tried as a war criminal for the role he played in the forced repatriations as an Intelligence Officer for the British 8th Army, I was only identifying one of the perpetrators by name. One of the British participants, John Corsellis, threatened to leave the speaking tour that day in response to what I had said. Tolstoy and Beljo were successful in talking him out of leaving, and after the event at the Parliament building, we were then transported by bus to the Presidential Palace to meet and have lunch with President Tuđman.

John Corsellis, who was assigned to the refugee camps in Viktring in May and June of 1945 as a conscientious objector, was still fuming on the bus on the way over to the presidential palace. After accusing me of working for Croatia's Intelligence Services he said, "I transcribed the interviews you taped with Nigel Nicholson for the Imperial War Museum." He screamed, "I know that Nicholson told you of the occasion where he saved thousands of civilians from being repatriated. He [Nicholson] has also been instrumental in bringing much of this information out into the public." I tried to explain to him calmly my reasons for saying what I did about Nicholson: "Yes, all that is true. But if you have listened to my interviews with him, you will also remember that he admitted being instrumental in sending tens of thousands of Croats to a known fate of murder. Furthermore, the fact that he has helped reveal the truth can only affect his case at sentencing if he were put on trial and found guilty. It would have no effect on whether he should be indicted for war crimes." Corsellis was hearing none of it and continued berating me while still on the bus. Finally, as we were approaching the portico to the Presidential Palace, I had had enough of listening to his Anglo-Saxon outrage. I turned and reprimanded him in a very harsh tone, "Look, what you have to remember is that you are not in England now. You are in Croatia – and don't forget it."

We didn't exchange another word during the next several days of touring the country with Beljo and Tolstoy.

It would be difficult today to find someone in Croatia who has not heard of Bleiburg. Memorials for what has become known as the Bleiburg Tragedy are held annually in May in the small Austrian town that will forever be linked to the tragic events of 1945. Smaller memorials are also held in various places around Slovenia and Croatia, like Macelj, where both victims of the death marches and other local civilians would eventually be murdered and buried in mass graves. Often these mass graves are at the bottom of natural caves that are scattered throughout Croatia and Slovenia. It is common for some communities to hold annual processions to various mass graves and hold a Catholic Mass during which both Fascism and Communism are condemned as systems of government that deny the God-given dignity of the individual.

There is still interest in the original interviews that I conducted with Croatian Survivors and British Army Officers even after many decades. Filmmakers and historians routinely contact me regarding the original interviews from thirty years ago. It was especially satisfying to be contacted by Laudato TV in Croatia requesting permission to use the primary source material still in my possession.

Laudato TV produced a film called *Magnum Crimen* that dealt with the Bleiburg massacres and death marches. This film was unique, however, because it was produced by Croatian filmmakers living in the Republic of Croatia. In addition to some of my original interviews, the young filmmaker Nada Prkačin would use new footage gathered at excavation sites throughout Croatia. Prkačin would also use various historians, Croatian political figures and Bleiburg survivors living in Croatia to tell the tragic story from a uniquely Croatian perspective. I was thrilled that these young Croatian filmmakers, living in Croatia, were continuing to expose the truth as new facts about Bleiburg and the death marches continued to be uncovered.

It is important to remember, however, that Croatian independence was far from being a certainty at the time of my film's premier that evening in May of 1991. A long and bloody war was still on the horizon. While it was not clear that war was inevitable, I was convinced that failure to achieve nation-state status was not an option once Croatia did declare independence. If Croatia wished to avoid a genocide that could dwarf the one experienced following WWII, she would first have to win her freedom.

Michael Palaich
44890 Kemp
Utica, Mich 48087
U S A

Imperial War Museum
Lambeth Road
London SE1 6HZ

Telephone 01-735 8922
Fax 01-587 5197

PS/FILM/TS
17 July 1989

Dear Mr Palaich

With reference to your interview material - video recordings
and transcripts - of those involved in the repatriation
of Croatians in 1945 and deposited with us.

This material remains your copyright and will only be made
available for reference purposes within the Museum. If any
other use is requested then they will be referred to you and
nothing will be released without the Museum first obtaining
your permission in writing. If copies of the material are
released with your permission, then the Museum reserves the
right to charge the user an appropriate access fee.

Yours sincerely,

Paul Sargent
Deputy Sargent
Department of Film

Survivor interviews archived in BIWM

Memorial to Croatian victims in Bleiburg, Austria

Bridge crossing River Drava at Lavamund, Austria

Captain Colin Gunner, British 8th Army, witnessed the murder of surrendered Croatians in May 1945

5

War Comes to Croatia

COUNTLESS BOOKS have been written about the dissolution of Yugoslavia by journalists, politicians and diplomats. Some are better than others. Since this is my personal account of the events, I will intentionally avoid addressing all the factors that led up to the eventual end of the Yugoslav regime and primarily focus on my personal experiences at the time.

The dissolution of Yugoslavia appeared to have come as a surprise to many politicians and journalists alike. This baffling reality becomes clearer if we know the biases that were at play for decades before the regime fell apart.

As stated earlier, even the anti-Communist American president Ronald Reagan made accommodations for Yugoslavia because of its geopolitical position in the world. Reagan simply did not view Yugoslavia as a threat, because he did not view it as being part of "international Communism" like the Soviets and their puppet states. America, and I think most Western governments, viewed Yugoslavia as an independent Communist state since Tito's break with Stalin in 1948.

Stalin had summoned Tito to come to Moscow in 1948 but, believing it to be a ruse to assassinate him, Tito refused. In retaliation, Tito began purging pro-Stalinist enemies within Yugoslavia by incarcerating those he perceived as being loyal to Stalin. The West, and the United States in particular, saw this as an opportunity to establish a buffer zone between the West and the Soviets, and they encouraged Tito's break with Stalin.

If Western governments loved the idea of Yugoslavia acting as a buffer zone with the Soviets, then Western journalists and academics treasured it even more. Those of us who knew the real Yugoslavia suffered through newspaper articles referring to Yugoslavia in glowing terms for decades. A skeptical reader would simply need to research the archives of any Western newspaper - especially after 1948 - to read the gushing reports describing how much freer Yugoslavia was than its more tyrannical Communist neighbors. Singing groups dressed in the local traditional peasant garb would greet journalists the moment they arrived on Yugoslav soil, and the happy spectacle would enthrall them. Articles would be written explaining to citizens of Western countries that all the people of Yugoslavia loved their leader Josip Broz Tito. Sure, he was a bit of a "strong man" even a "dictator" of sorts, they would admit, but they would explain his dictatorship as necessary to keep the "feuding" nationalities from continuing with their "age-old ethnic conflicts." Tito kept the peace, they would write, and the "Yugoslav people" worshipped him for it. They would often insist that shopkeepers showed their affection for Tito by displaying his picture in the front window of their stores. This was all the evidence they needed to prove the people's adoration for their dictator.

Of course, they had never learned, nor did they want to learn about the slaughtering of Croats and other internal enemies after World War II. They never attempted to learn about the political prisons of Lepoglava, Goli Otok or Stara Gradiška where prisoners were beaten, starved and killed. Citizens could find themselves in one of these notorious prisons for simply repeating a disparaging joke about Tito in public or singing a patriotic Croatian song.

When the citizens of Croatia declared their independence from Yugoslavia in a plebiscite titled "Referendum for Croatia" on May 19, 1991 it was an exhilarating moment for those who had been fighting for Croatia's independence for decades. But it was also a moment fraught with trepidation. Yugoslavia had spent decades cultivating an international image among politicians, journalists and academics, and Yugoslav exponents had also established personal and political relationships with the related organizations. Croatian freedom fighters, on the other hand, had been successfully labeled as fascists and terrorists by Yugoslavia with the assistance of the Western journalists. Some of the blame for this image can be laid directly at the feet of Croats themselves. But, the vast majority of Croats who demanded more freedom from Yugoslavia were simply people who wanted to practice their inalienable rights as human beings. They wanted to enjoy the same right to self-determination that other free people enjoyed. They wanted the right to declare themselves Croats and speak their own language without being labeled an "enemy of the state." They wanted their own courts, their own judges and their own police force. And, finally, they wanted their own army to defend them without having to beg a foreign government to come to their aid.

Those of us who had fought against Yugoslavia's propaganda machine for years knew that winning the war of ideas would be, perhaps, as important as winning the violent war that would ultimately be forced upon Croatia. We knew that Yugoslavia would unleash its vast political and propaganda resources in a parallel war of ideas against Croatia. Their propaganda war would be led by their central news agency, the Telegraphic Agency of the New Yugoslavia or TANJUG with offices worldwide. In addition to TANJUG the Yugoslav intelligence agencies would enlist the help of Serbian citizens in its diaspora to influence Western politicians in the countries where they resided. Two such organizations in America were SERBNET, headquartered in Chicago and Serbian Unity Congress (SUC) with headquarters in the San Francisco Bay area. Those Yugoslavs and Serbs involved in the propaganda wing of the war would also prove to be agile opponents in the war against Croatia.

To most people living in the West, it was soon clear that Serbs and Yugoslavs were not justified in their genocidal aggression against their neighbors. Their preemptive attacks across Croatia to "protect Serb minorities" were clearly nothing more than a land grab strategy that the world would witness decades later perpetrated in a similar way by the Russians in Crimea. When this strategy became transparent even to Western politicians and journalists, it was changed.

The propaganda arm of the Yugoslav war machine began referring to the wars of Yugoslav/Serbian aggression as "civil wars" and "wars of age-old ethnic conflicts." Yes, the Yugoslav spokesmen would reluctantly admit, "It is a terrible and bloody war, but it is, after all, a war in which everyone was equally guilty." They would insist that everyone "had blood on their hands." The logic of the strategy was that if there was no perpetrator of genocide, there could be no victim. They used this shift in strategy effectively to quell the mounting outrage against their genocidal practices.

As we were preparing for the propaganda war, we also needed to help Croatia defend herself against the military aggression of the Yugoslav National Army (JNA): experts claimed that the JNA had the fourth largest army in Europe at the time of Croatia's referendum for independence.

Sending Weapons

A friend asked me recently how I managed to gain the trust of the various political groups involved in the Croatian liberation movement. I had never thought about it before, but I think the answer is simple: I was effective, I didn't ask questions and I kept my mouth shut.

For example, while I am personally aware of some aspects of the smuggling of weapons and night vision equipment into Croatia, I am only superficially aware of other details. I may know how weapons made their way from the United States into Canada, but I do not know the name of the individual baggage handler at the Toronto Pearson Airport who loaded the weapons onto planes for us. I also cannot say for certain who was responsible for organizing our working arrangement with the Croatian Minister of Interior prior to Yugoslavia's demise. The fact is, I developed the practice of not asking questions long ago. Early on, I took the position that I only needed and wanted to know about the action in which I was involved. In my earlier days in intelligence training while serving in the U.S. Navy we would refer to this as "need to know." That discipline (along with a healthy dose of paranoia) served me well over the years. I never spoke of questionable activity over the phone unless it was to disseminate false information to those agencies I believed were listening to my conversations. I would never speak about anything serious in my house for fear of listening devices being planted in my home. Taking walks around a neighborhood was preferred, always being aware that even these conversations could be monitored using parabolic microphones. Today's listening devices are so sophisticated and so unobtrusive that a person would not recognize the listening device even if they saw it. The days are over when technicians had to enter your residence to install an electronic device in order to hear private conversations taking place inside. And, when listening devices are planted, they may be deactivated remotely when not in use, making them impossible to detect with the old practice of "sweeping for bugs."

In addition to not knowing all the details of the activity I was involved in, I also did not know and still do not know all the particulars of other smuggling operations that were under way throughout the world in order to give Croatia a fighting chance of success in the war. One of the boldest smuggling operations in which I was *not* involved (but which was conducted by some

Croats) involved the transfer of thousands of tons of armaments from Argentina to Croatia between 1991 and 1995. *The New York Times* reported on July 5, 2001 that the successful smuggling operation even resulted in an indictment of former president of Argentina, Carlos Menem, in 2001. He was charged with violating the United Nations arms embargo against the republics of the former Yugoslavia, but I never inquired into the operation and only have suspicions as to which friends of mine may have been involved.

The operation of smuggling weapons and night vision equipment in which I was involved prior to 1991 was relatively small in comparison to the shipments from Argentina. It was only one small story among many other larger ones that were occurring concurrently world-wide. One unsuccessful episode in Germany that ended badly for me will be discussed later.

Shortly after Croats voted for independence on May 19, 1991 weapons began to flow into Croatia's capital through the airport in Zagreb. Mind you, this was all happening even while the Yugoslav Army and Customs Department still maintained control over the airport. Croatia might have declared independence, but the full-blown war for that independence was still in the future. The Yugoslav regime still controlled all aspects of Yugoslavia's federal government – including the airports. There was, however, cooperation between those of us who were sending weapons and those inside Croatia who gladly welcomed them. The transfer of weapons could only be successful if they could somehow bypass baggage inspectors at the Zagreb airport. This was accomplished by offloading weapons from the aircraft with the cooperation of Ministry of the Interior (MUP). The general agreement for this assistance was that for every three weapons sent through the Zagreb airport, MUP would keep one. This was acceptable to us since we knew every weapon, no matter who used it, would be used against the JNA in support of independence. We viewed the confiscation by MUP as a donation to the cause. It was a practice that would later continue on a larger scale when arms destined for Bosnia-

Herzegovina would be sent via Croatia from governments like Saudi Arabia. According to a *Washington Post* article from February 2, 1996 those shipments were made with "the knowledge and tacit cooperation of the United States."

In our case, one way in which this worked was by having someone in the airport baggage department load the weapons destined for Zagreb on a plane in Toronto without going through the usual official declarations. The bags were marked with some identifying symbol that only MUP officials in Zagreb would recognize once they arrived. We had just such a person working in the baggage department at the Pearson airport in Toronto. The man working at the airport was a Croatian and, although it was very risky, he was willing to help transport weapons and night vision equipment in this manner. We would purchase weapons in the United States for cash. Among gun enthusiasts, gun shows were - and still are - very popular in America. This is where manufacturers and distributors showcase their merchandise and private sales can be made without the usual paperwork.

One early way of transporting the guns from the United States to Canada that I am familiar with was very dangerous. It involved putting weapons in the trunk of a car and driving across the border separating Detroit from Canada. There are two border crossings from Detroit, one via a tunnel under the Detroit River and the other via the Ambassador Bridge. These are official border crossings with federal customs officers on both sides of the border. One can drive across the border several times without ever being pulled over by a suspicious Customs Agent for a random vehicle check. On other occasions several cars may be pulled over at the same time for inspections. In addition, Canada has very strict gun laws and being caught smuggling a trunk full of AR15 or AK47 rifles would certainly result in long jail sentences. This dangerous practice is hardly advisable for any reason, but especially if one is not able to remain calm under pressure. The trouble is that in this kind of situation there is no way for an individual to learn how to control the body's natural reactions to stress and fear. An individual can learn to lie effectively. A person can even anticipate every probing question a customs official may ask. But there is no quick-and-easy way to learn how to control all the telltale biological reactions that are produced by the body when you are slowly approaching a customs checkpoint with a trunk full of rifles destined for Europe. Without all my prior experiences dealing with questions from F.B.I. Agents, or without the experience of smuggling suitcases full of video tapes across the Yugoslav border just a couple of months earlier, I'm not sure I could have been successful in masking my nervousness going into Canada with the weapons. As if this was not dangerous enough already, on one occasion some of the rifles were fully automatic machine guns. These weapons were even illegal to own in the United States where gun laws are more liberal. Persons found guilty of possession of automatic rifles would face very long jail sentences. It was determined by all of us that it was just too risky to continue smuggling items destined for Croatia in this way forever. Everyone understood that luck would eventually run out.

We discovered a less dangerous approach to smuggling items into Canada. The new method involved smuggling the items from Detroit to Windsor across the Detroit River using boats. Decades earlier, prohibition-era bootleggers smuggled alcohol across the same Detroit River from Canada to Detroit using high speed motorboats. We used a different twist to this smuggling method by renting motorboats on each side of the river from legitimate boat rental companies. These companies would customarily rent boats to sports fisherman that could often be seen fishing along the river. Each boat, however, was identified with letters and numbers and those letters and numbers identified which side of the river the boats belonged to. It would be far too suspicious for a smuggler to rent a boat in Detroit and drop off his goods on the Canadian side using the same boat. Since it was an international border, the river was often patrolled by Coast Guard ships and police whose job was to prevent smuggling.

Therefore, there would be two groups of Croatians dressed as fisherman and completely outfitted with traditional fishing equipment. One group would rent a boat on the Canadian side of the border, while the other group rented one on the American side. At an agreed-upon location (like Detroit's famous Belle Island), and after actually fishing for some time, the boats would pass each other, and the items destined for Croatia would be passed from the Detroit boat to the Canadian boat. After continuing to fish for some time, the boats were returned to their original rental locations and the smuggled items would continue making their way to Croatia via the Pearson Airport in Toronto.

In one operation the Croatian Ministry of Defense specifically requested two types of night-vision devices. The first type needed was "third-generation night-vision" goggles. These goggles are commonly seen in movies today, but were rare items in 1991. They were not only very expensive, but illegal to export outside of the United States without a license. The second type was a night-vision scope that could be fitted onto a sniper rifle making it possible to identify and shoot an enemy in the total darkness of the night. On one occasion, the request was accompanied by around seventy-five thousand dollars in cash. I recall this particular bundle of cash because the first bill in each bundle of money had Arabic writing on it. Although I was curious as to why Croatia would send cash with Arabic writing on it, I did not ask any questions as usual. We purchased as many items as possible with the cash provided. The night-vision equipment was then smuggled via boat as described, sent by plane to Zagreb and then forwarded by MUP to the fledgling Croatian Army. We were later thrilled to learn that Croatian soldiers successfully used the sniper scopes and goggles in the defense of Croatian cities of Osijek and Vukovar.

On September 1, 1991 all smuggling operations came to a very abrupt halt. That was the day that a Croatian Canadian businessman from Toronto named Anton Kikaš attempted to charter a plane carrying 18 tons of weapons and secretly land at the Zagreb airport. Not surprisingly, the Yugoslav Secret Police caught wind of the operation in advance and were tracking the plane long before it arrived inside Yugoslavia's airspace. Mr. Kikaš was arrested immediately and spent three months in jail before the Croatian government could arrange a prisoner swap between Kikaš and the highest-ranking Yugoslav Army prisoner in Croatian custody named General Milan Aksentijević.

The Yugoslav regime's response to the smuggling fiasco was to close the Zagreb airport to all non-military flights. While we sympathized with Mr. Kikaš and his arrest, as did all patriotic Croats, the capture of Kikaš and the closing of the airport could not have come at a worse time. Until the airport reopened, the only way to get arms into Croatia would be through neighboring countries.

I didn't know Anton Kikaš well. In fact, I only met him once prior to his arrest at a meeting in the high-rise offices of an attorney in Manhattan, N.Y. My good friend Ante Čuvalo called the meeting; there were about ten people present representing various patriotic Croatian political organizations. Kikaš was introduced as a Croatian businessman from Toronto, but he was the only one that was present who was not, to my knowledge, openly active in Croatian politics. I assumed that he was a good Croat otherwise Čuvalo would not have invited him to attend the meeting. At the same time, however, it was my belief that Kikaš was invited because he was known as a wealthy businessman. There were probably hopes that he would finance whatever plan was being discussed that day. Again, these were all assumptions on my part. Since I learned not to ask questions, I never inquired as to the reason he was invited to the New York meeting. Frankly, I spoke very little to Kikaš before, during or after the meeting. I knew that historically men with money were a necessary part of any successful revolution, but I personally wasn't comfortable associating with them. In my view, Kikaš should have simply financed the operation and then entrusted those with experience in this arena to actually carry it out. I believe Kikaš had good intentions, but he was just naïve to think he could land an Angolan 707 airplane full of weapons in an airport that is 95% controlled by the enemy you are trying to overthrow. We were successful in bringing in small quantities of weapons and material through the airport, because we were dealing only with the 5% of the authorities we had control over. Kikaš was literally not able to fly under the Yugoslav radar with a Boeing 707 plane full of arms.

In any event, after September 1, 1991 the international airport in Zagreb was closed and this had a major effect on all arms shipments into the country. It also affected how Croatians - and foreigners who wanted to fight for Croatia's independence - would have to enter the country afterward.

So when Pero Ivčec, Marko Stipaničić, Ante Pranić, Božo Čačić and I felt compelled to travel to Croatia on October 21, 1991 to help Croatia more directly in the war of independence, we would have to fly into another country in Europe first, and then make our way into Croatia by bus carrying the weapons from North America. Of the five of us that were travelling with weapons that day in October, three were arrested in London and I was arrested in Frankfurt after disembarking from Northwest Airlines flight 51 from Detroit. Ante Pranić was the only one who made it to Croatia with his weapons; the rest of us arrived in Croatia empty-handed. I would, however, be the only one to face the long-term consequences for smuggling weapons into Europe. The German police arrested me on October 22, 1991 on arms smuggling charges, triggering the U.S. government's own series of legal actions against me. I would spend the next 7 ½ years facing the consequences of that arrest.

German police photo: one of the confiscated rifles with night-vision scope

6

Arrest in Germany

"VHAT DO YOU have to declare?" the German customs official asked as I approached the counter. "I have two hunting rifles and ammunition," was my naïvely arrogant response. I was so certain that I was within my legal rights to bring the weapons into Germany that I made no attempt to hide the fact that rifles were inside: they were even in proper hard rifle cases with a foam interior to keep them protected.

"Vhat?" he asked again. This time it was evident in his voice and demeanor that he was not going to let me process smoothly through customs. Still, I tried to keep my cool and repeated myself confidently, "Two rifles and ammunition." "Open up!" he yelled nervously - and so I did. I'm sure there were no alarms going off in the airport, but at that moment there was tremendous confusion and the only alarms that were going off were probably inside my head. The customs official began yelling in German for help. The other passengers around me began gasping and looking at me as if I was a dangerous madman.

A supervisor and a couple of other scruffy looking guys in civilian clothes suddenly appeared, gathered all my belongings and proceeded to direct me to another room just off to the side of the baggage and customs area. One by one all my luggage was opened, thus revealing the contents.

"Vhy are you bringing in zese tings?" they asked. "I'm going hunting." "You are going hunting with camouflage uniforms?" they asked. I was surprised by this sudden interest in my camouflage uniform. I was expecting them to ask more questions about the weapons and ammunition. "Yes," I answered. American hunters often use camouflage outfits when hunting. Then they shifted their questioning. "Vit whom are you travelling? How many of you are there?" I explained that I was by myself. This led to other questions like: "Vhere are you going to hunt in Germany? Who is going to pick you up at the airport? Vhat does he look like?" By this time, I knew that they wouldn't be releasing me anytime soon so I made the decision to protect my friend Ante hoping that he would not also get arrested. My responses were intentionally meant to throw them off track. "I'm travelling alone," I repeated. "I am supposed to go hunting in Germany with these rifles, but I do not know where, or with whom I'm hunting. Someone is supposed to be waiting for me in the terminal with my name written on a placard. The driver with my name is supposed to drive me to a hunting lodge. That's all I know." With that said, the two scruffy customs officers in plainclothes ran off. I assumed they went out looking for someone holding my name written on a sheet of paper. Twenty minutes later they returned, but this time they were pissed off and out of breath. After searching the airport terminal, they found nobody holding a sign with my name on it. They began rifling through my luggage more aggressively now. "You go hunting vit bullet proof helmet?" they asked. "Vhy do you need night-vision scope to hunt? Vhy do you need night-vision goggles? Bayonets! You go hunting vit bayonets too?" he asked sarcastically. I could see how ridiculous my explanations were beginning to sound.

They must have called someone from the U.S. military to come in and take a look at the rifles and talk to me, because suddenly there appeared two young non-commissioned officers from the American Air Force behind the counter. "What's going on?" they asked. "I don't know. I just came to Germany to do some hunting and these guys are treating me like a terrorist because I have some camouflage clothing. Can you just explain to them that hunters in America wear camouflage clothing and that it's not a uniform?"

They explained that they were stationed at one of the nearby bases and didn't have much to do with this sort of thing. "The Germans just wanted us to look at your weapons and talk to you." With that said, they left.

Following those discussions, I was handcuffed and placed in the backseat of a small European police vehicle by the plainclothes customs officers. My luggage was placed in the trunk and I was taken to another office, but still within the grounds of the airport. They placed me in a small holding cell with a wooden bench and one blanket. I sat there in the cold cell for hours hoping I would be given more blankets.

Finally, the customs officers returned, pulled me out of the cell and placed me in a chair in front of their desk in the adjacent office. They had my address book in front of them, and as one of them leafed through the pages, he said, "Vee are not stupid. Vee know vhy you are here." This did not come as a surprise since anyone with any knowledge of wartime Croatia in 1991 would have recognized some of the names in the address book, which included Franjo Tuđman, Gojko Šušak and Dobroslav Paraga. It was clear to me that they knew why I was travelling though Germany. They knew that I was on my way to Croatia to join the war efforts. What I had no way of knowing at that moment was what they were going to do with me. At the time of my arrest I was convinced that I was going to be held in a German jail and eventually put on trial in Germany for smuggling weapons. I envisioned that process taking months. With that in mind, I was also determined not to volunteer any further information that would help them make a case against me in court. At this time one of the officers took my AR-15 rifle and began to install the night vision scope on the rail on top of the rifle. "You need dis night-vision scope for hunting?" they asked. "And dis bayonet, you need this bayonet also?" They asked, as they snapped it into place over the muzzle of the rifle. I responded by shrugging my shoulders. "And, vhat are zese for?" They asked holding up some metal parts. "They are spare typewriter parts that a friend asked me to bring for him," I responded. They were in fact some of the more nefarious gun parts that I knew would get me into serious trouble if their purpose was discovered. The parts were used to convert the semi-automatic AR-15 and the M1A1 paratrooper rifle into full-auto machine guns. As the questions became more specific in nature, I refused to say anything more to them. With each subsequent question asked, my response was the same: "I refuse to say anything further without an attorney present." They became more and more agitated with each refusal. However, by this time I knew that remaining silent was the best strategy for survival. I knew not to be intimidated by police questioning. After about one-half hour they brought in a woman translator to assist in the interrogation. The translator was young and attractive, and I was a fairly handsome thirty-seven-year-old at the time. Attempting to earn myself some advantage in the precarious position that I was in, I began to flirt a little with her as we spoke. She began very professionally by asking me questions in English as instructed by the customs officers, who were getting angrier as I continued to refuse answering the questions. Finally, when the police were talking among themselves, the translator told me quietly in English, "You know, you do not have to say anything without a lawyer if you do not want to." At this the officers began yelling at her in German. I don't speak German, but I could understand that they were telling her that she was to ask only what they told her to ask and nothing more. She was not supposed to tell me anything; and she was dismissed from the room. With that, the interrogation stopped, and I was put back in my cell for another long period of time.

When they finally pulled me out of the cell the second time, I could see that their demeanor had changed. They had a lengthy typed piece of paper in front of them and told me to sign it. "It's all in German," I said. "I don't understand German. How can I sign it?" "You have to sign it, or vee cannot release you. How much money do you have vit you for bail?" they asked. I was carrying about six thousand U.S. dollars at the time, but most of it was not my personal money. Most of it had been donated to the group that I was to meet up with in Frankfurt. I certainly did not want to give them all the money, so I told them that I had only three thousand U.S. dollars. I was still surprised at this point that they did not know what I had in my pockets, because they never searched me when I was arrested. I had enough familiarity with arresting officers in the U.S. to know that a full body search would have been the first thing they would have done when a suspect was arrested. So, they agreed to take three thousand dollars if I signed the document, which they said was a list of charges and an order to appear in court. Still not knowing what I was being charged with or agreeing to the charges I signed the document with hopes of clarifying things with the Germans at a later date.

With the document signed and the money handed over to the arresting officers, my confiscated bags were brought out to me. One of the officers led me to a vehicle. My bags were placed in the vehicle and I was driven back to the main terminal of the airport. Upon exiting I retrieved my bags and shook the officer's hand. "I want to thank you for your professionalism." I said. He replied, "That is right, vee are professionals. Vee are not stupid. Vee know why you are here." "Well, thank you again," I responded - quickly walking away before he changed his mind.

But, along with my surprising release from custody I was faced with another dilemma. What if I was being followed? How could I meet up with the rest of my friends? I had no way of knowing if Marko, Pero and Božo made it to Germany. In addition, I didn't know where Ante Pranić was, and even if he made it safely out of the terminal following my arrest. I decided that the safest thing for me to do was to walk around the terminal checking to see if I was being observed. I believe I walked around for several hours stopping to see if I was being followed, all the while keeping in mind that the police may be tracking me with video surveillance from inside the airport. I boarded a train after several hours and again tried to discover if I was being followed. After passing through many towns, I finally got off the train at a small town and took a cab to a local hotel. It was my intention to make calls back to the U.S. in hopes that the others would also call back home to discover where I was and arrange to meet somewhere in Germany. In a thinly coded message, I told the person in the U.S. to call the families of the others and explain to them that I had arrived in Germany and after being arrested I was free, but without some of my weapons and ammunition. The not-so-clever message was: "The bird has landed safely, but it lost a couple of feathers."

I was thankful that the other guys had the same idea and contacted their homes in Canada to see if there were any messages from either Ante or me. Ante was the first to show up at the hotel where I was staying just outside of Frankfurt. I was very happy to see him. His big smile greeted me as I opened the door of my room. I was also happy that Ante made it to Germany unscathed and in possession of his weapons and other equipment. He brought a friend with him that lived in Karlstruhe named Ivan Vidović. Apparently, Ante called Ivan once he got out of the airport and Ivan took him to his home for the evening. The three of us sat in the hotel room as Ante related his airport experience the day before when I got arrested. As Ante related the story, it became clear to me that there had been a tremendous commotion as a result of my arrest. He said that he watched from inside the terminal as the police kept running back and forth as if they were looking for something. But he managed to keep his cool and called his Croatian friend Ivan to pick him up at the airport and get out of there as quickly as possible.

Ante was a very unassuming man and it is understandable that he never raised the suspicions of the customs officers, or the police running around the airport terminal. He was already in his mid-fifties when we made this trip; he was about five-foot-eight with a very slim build and a head full of wavy grey hair. But, if he was small in physical stature, he had a huge heart and contributed much of his hard-earned money to various Croatian causes. He had become almost a father figure to me by the time he died of cancer in 1996. I first met him when I interviewed him as part of my filming for the Bleiburg documentary.

He related an unimaginable event that he experienced while living in the town of Banja Luka in Bosnia during WWII. It was a day like any other during the war. His father and older brother were away from home fighting on the Croatian side. His mother and his brother's pregnant wife stayed home with Ante who was only nine years old at the time. On that day - etched so vividly in Ante's memory – several men that he described as Chetniks burst through the front door of their home. Ante instinctively scrambled under the bed as the men asked in harsh voices, "Where are the men?" "They are fighting in the war," the women answered. "On whose side?" the men asked. "With the Croatians", she answered. "Why don't they fight with the Chetniks?" the men persisted. "Because they are Croatians, for the same reason you fight with the Serbians." With that, the intruders grabbed Ante's mother, cut off her head and threw it across the floor as Ante watched from under the bed. Next came his sister-in-law. "Where is your husband?" they asked her. "I told you, he is at war!" she said. As Ante watched in horror, the intruders then killed his brother's wife and proceeded to cut the unborn baby out of her womb while laughing and saying, "Look how the Ustaša baby cries!"

I understood that Ante's going to war with us in 1991 was as much about retribution for what happened to his family in WWII as it was about achieving Croatian independence. He was determined to fight in Croatia's war despite finding a good life in

Chicago after immigrating to America. In spite of my countless attempts to persuade him to stay at home with his wife Ana, he was determined to come with us. "I'm going with or without you," was his response.

Within a few hours of meeting with Ante, I received a phone call from Pero Ivčec in my hotel room. Pero related that Marko, Božo and he were stopped at Heathrow Airport, that their weapons were confiscated, but that they were released without being charged and were also somewhere in the Frankfurt area. We gave them the directions to the hotel, where they came that same day.

Once we were finally all together in Frankfurt, Ivan picked us up at the hotel and took us to his family's apartment in Karlstruhe where we spent the next couple of days hoping that things would quiet down. When we arrived at Ivan's I started taking inventory of the contents of my bags more thoroughly to see what I had and what the German police had confiscated. The AR-15 rifle and the M1A1 rifle were of course missing, as was the night-vision sniper scope that I hoped to bring to Croatia and several hundred rounds of ammunition. I was surprised, however, to find two night-vision goggles worth $6500 each along with the bayonets, riflescopes, camouflage clothing, boots and helmets. What I was most relieved to find were the two seemingly innocuous items that caused me the most concern from a legal perspective: the automatic rifle conversion kits that I had explained to the unsuspecting customs officer as being typewriter parts. I knew I had to be concerned about the confiscated weapons and ammunition being used as evidence against me in court regardless of whether my eventual trial would be in Germany or America. It was comforting at least to know that the conversion kits would not be used as evidence in any future trial.

Ivan was letting the five of us sleep on the floor of his apartment at considerable personal risk to himself and his family. We discovered how much of a risk he was taking when Ivan's daughter went out of the apartment and into the town one evening. She returned a short time later and was very excited as she relayed the news: "There are police all over the town." She had never seen so many police before in her neighborhood. We spent the next couple of days cooped up in Ivan's apartment waiting for things to cool off. When we believed things had settled down, Ivan dropped us off at the local bus station and we finally made our way to Zagreb. Even though all of us except Ante had been stripped of our weapons, we hoped that we could still contribute something to Croatia's war of independence.

Ante Pranić and author in HSP headquarters

Bringing supplies from Croatia to Bosnia via pontoon

7

Subterfuge and Subversion

WE DEPARTED the bus station in Germany and headed for Zagreb somewhere around October 16, 1991 on a bus that was only half full. It was surprising under the circumstances that there were even that many passengers who wanted to enter Croatia at the most dangerous period of the war. Nobody was sure that even Zagreb was safe from Serbian occupation at that time. There were constant air raids in the city and citizens were directed to take cover in basements when there was either a risk of bombing from jets, or from surface-to-surface missiles. The capital city of Zagreb had already been bombed several times and there were occasional firefights around the city and even at the Yugoslav National Army Headquarters in the center of the city. Zagreb certainly wasn't the most dangerous Croatian city at the time, but it was not a safe haven either. I respected the passengers on the bus that chose to join family members at such a precarious time.

With the exception of Marko, we attempted to be rather low key on the bus, not talking to the passengers and certainly not acknowledging that we were going to Croatia to join the Homeland War. Marko, however, began telling everyone he came across that we were travelling to Zagreb to join the war. This caused some arguing among us when we repeatedly asked him to refrain from telling everyone our business since we did not know any of the passengers or their allegiances. I recall Ante turning around several times during the trip and asking Marko, "Do you need some chewing gum?" Ante meant it as a rebuke with the clear implication that Marko should keep his mouth busy in other ways instead of talking to the passengers.

Once we got into Croatian territory it was clear that Croatia was a nation at war. The first obvious sign was that there was a complete blackout of the city. The darkened streets had an eerie appearance as our bus travelled on them. The homes were also without any visible light coming through the windows, as would normally be the case. Entering Zagreb across the Sava River we could see the tank traps strategically staggered across the bridge. The tank traps were something one might see in a movie: three pieces of steel I-beams welded together in order to deter any tanks that may try to cross the bridges. From a distance they resembled jacks that a giant child might play with. The bus was forced to drive around these tank traps, passing groups of Croatian soldiers acting as check points on the bridge. Referring to them as "Croatian soldiers" at this early period during the war generously describes anyone fighting for the Croatian side. The new untrained volunteer "soldier" was lucky if he had a rifle to call his own.

The absurdity of using the term "soldier" in this case became all the clearer as we entered Zagreb's main bus station at around one o'clock in the morning. Men acting as soldiers could be seen walking all around the bus station and streets. They were dressed in a strange variation of what served as a uniform in those early months of the war. Some of the soldiers were wearing camouflage trousers. Others were wearing camouflage shirts with blue jeans. I do not recall seeing any soldier wearing a proper military cap and only rarely did a volunteer soldier wear anything on his feet other than tennis shoes. Some of the new recruits would wear a sort of Rambo-style bandana around their heads as an homage to the 1982 Sylvester Stallone movie. A few had AK-47 rifles, but most of them carried no rifle, or had an old hunting rifle slung over their shoulders. These were no doubt the hunting rifles of family members given to the young man to defend his country against the entire Yugoslav Army. Looking out the window of the bus I thought to myself, "My God, how are they going to fight the fourth largest army in Europe with tennis shoes and hunting rifles?" Two other things left a lasting impression on me, however. First, some of them had a faraway blank stare that I had only heard about from veterans of our Vietnam War in America. It was a look that is difficult to describe unless you witnessed it yourself. It was the unblinking glare from an unshaven young man's face that appeared to look through you, rather than at you, as though he was unable to focus on objects close to him. It was clear that these young men had already spent time at the front. In many cases the front was just a few kilometers from Croatia's capital. I would later learn that in some cases they were sent to occupy some supposedly strategic empty house on the frontlines with only a Kalashnikov rifle and one magazine holding thirty bullets. Equipped this poorly, they were asked to defend a town from the encroaching well-armed enemy until their replacements arrived to relieve them. It was hard to imagine how they did it; but this information helped me understand the vacant look of someone who had experienced the hell of war while defending his homeland in such surreal circumstances.

The second thing that caught my attention was just how many of the Croatian defenders were wearing the Catholic rosary around their necks. Over the next few weeks, this took on added meaning for me when I saw Croatian defenders march to the front to fight against the army whose soldiers were wearing the all-too-familiar symbol of the state religion of Atheism on their uniforms – the Communist red star. The battle lines of the war could not have been drawn more clearly than by the symbols displayed by the soldiers of the opposing armies.

We must have been quite a sight walking from the bus station to what was then the Astoria Hotel on Petrinjska Street through the dark lightless streets. The only occasional light we saw was from the passing cars whose headlights were covered with tape, while leaving a small slit exposed for safety reasons. Although most of our weapons had been confiscated on our arrival in Europe, we still had duffle bags full of uniforms, gun cleaning equipment, boots, helmets, riflescopes and, best of all, two night-vision goggles that we were certain would be useful in the war. As we checked into the Hotel Astoria, we were greeted by smiling desk clerks who took our foreign passports. They knew immediately why we were in Croatia. Over the years to come I would develop a good relationship with them. This meant asking them to hold my bags behind the desk for several days at a time while I made various missions through Croatia and later Bosnia-Herzegovina. Often times the bags I asked them to hold contained grenades and although they never admitted to looking inside, I believed that they did. That realization came to me after the Homeland War when I returned to Hotel Astoria on a visit. I laughed as Ivan, one of the clerks that I knew from the war, asked smilingly in broken English, "Do you have any boom booms this time?"

Making Contact

The first thing on our agenda that first day was to make contact with acquaintances from previous years. Their names were Josip Jurčević, Davor Butković and Pavle Vranjican. We first met the trio as they were travelling across North America promoting a short documentary that they made regarding their discovery of a natural cave in Jazovka used by Tito's partisans and secret police to dump the bodies of hundreds (if not thousands) of Croatian soldiers and civilians following WWII.

I had also been in contact with Davor Butković nicknamed Žu after our initial meeting. He was given the name because Žu is short for *žuti* (yellow), describing the blonde-red hair and beard that made him stand out among Croats. Žu had called me several weeks prior to our arrival in Croatia asking if I could arrange another tour for the group. I could sense in his voice that he was very nervous about remaining in Croatia while it was being attacked and occupied by Yugoslav/Serbian forces. I sensed that he was just looking for an opportunity to flee Croatia. Since he was broke, a paid trip was the only option left for him. My response was that it was really impossible now for the Croatian diaspora to focus on anything other than organizing fundraisers for Croatia's defense. Every dollar collected – and there were millions collected – was being sent to Croatia for defense purposes. Second, I explained that I myself would soon be coming to Croatia and that all my efforts now were going into making that possible.

It was ironic that I (a second-generation Croat born in America) knew Zagreb better than my travelling companions who were born in Croatia. I was in Zagreb for the premiere of my film and for Croatia's referendum for independence in May of that year, so I still had a feel for the basic layout of the city. Božo, Pero, Marko and Ante had all left Croatia in their youth, so it appeared that they did not know the city at all.

Our first contacts upon our arrival were with Žu and Pavle. Josip Jurčević was not there at our first meeting in Zagreb. That was a little disappointing, because when we met them all in Canada it was clear that he was the designated leader of the trio. He was also the one who in later years would become very active in politics and would write a book on Bleiburg that received poor reviews from the Croats in the diaspora. He would also admit to me years later that he worked for one of Croatia's Intelligence Services. Although Jurčević was not at that initial meeting, our paths would cross again several times over the upcoming years. But for now, we were with Žu and Pavle and they proved to be welcoming and willing to help us establish ourselves. Someone at the meeting let it slip that we still had two night-vision goggles and we all noticed that their interest was immediately piqued. They didn't know that the two small items were worth about $13,000 in 1991, but they knew they were valuable. We agreed that we would all keep their whereabouts a secret. It was wartime after all, and we hardly knew our new acquaintances.

Žu and Pavle soon put us into contact with a soldier nicknamed Pika who described himself as the bodyguard of Tomislav Merčep. Ironically, I remembered Pika as a waiter who worked in the Korčula restaurant in Zagreb's center before the war. Every Croat during the war years knew the name Merčep, but even more importantly, the Serb paramilitary forces knew his name as well, which resulted in a bounty being put on his head by the Serbian-led Yugoslav Army. His name carried such weight and elicited such fear that often times simply the rumor that Merčep and his men were coming to a village was enough for the Serb forces to flee ahead of his arrival.

The five of us met with Merčep's men on several occasions. At the time we all believed that Merčep's unit was the one we wanted to join: we came to go to war and we were sure of getting that opportunity by joining Merčep's group. All his guys were emphatic that Merčep would only allow us into his group after speaking with us personally. At a meeting with them at the Pula restaurant we asked them to arrange a meeting with Merčep. Within days of our arrival in Croatia, we were on our way to speak with one of the leading military commanders in Croatia.

Merčep was recovering from a wound (I believe he was shot in his arm, or shoulder) and was recuperating in Zagreb's Rebro Hospital with his arm in a sling. As the five of us entered the hospital we were directed to his hospital room. Sitting in front of his room and holding an AK-47 on his lap was our new acquaintance and Merčep's bodyguard - Pika. He went into the room and a few minutes later returned to tell us it was O.K. and that we could go in. There he was, Tomislav Merčep in a private room lying in bed with his left arm in a sling.

In private life, before the war, Merčep was an engineer living in Vukovar and entered the war with a sense of patriotic duty to protect his nation. In 1991 he was arrested by the Croatian police, but later released. It is believed that his arrest at that time was related to the transferring of arms and explosives to another Croatian wartime hero named Branimir Glavaš in 1990. The arrest was also possibly related to Serbian homes being blown up in the Vukovar/Osijek area of Croatia. It should be remembered that at the time of his arrest Croatia was still under the control of the Yugoslav federal government. Shortly after Merčep's release from prison he came to Zagreb and was given the position as an officer in the Ministry of Internal Affairs (MUP) after joining the leading political party, the Croatian Democratic Union (HDZ). He was also given command of Croatian fighters that were most notable for their military activities in and around the towns of Gospić and Pakrac. Tragically, several of his men were put on trial in later years and convicted in the Hague for committing war crimes against Serbian civilians in the area of Pakrac. Merčep was himself put on trial by the Croatian County Prosecutor of Zagreb and found guilty. In 2017, after losing an appeal, he was sentenced to seven years in prison for failing to prevent the murders of 43 Serbian civilians in Pakrac by military units under his command.

As we were standing in his hospital room in October 1991, however, all we knew was that his men respected him, and his enemies feared him. We all felt it was an honor just to be considered for his unit.

Merčep was an unassuming thirty-nine-year-old man when I met him. He was only two years older than me and even though he was lying in a hospital bed I could see that he wasn't very tall in stature. He was soft spoken and had an unusual way of gently coughing as he talked. His controlled throat clearing became more pronounced as the subject of conversation turned to violence. His manner of speaking reminded me of Hyman

127

Roth from the movie *Godfather II*. On the rolling hospital table next to him was a box with the name Smith & Wesson written on it. Inside the box was a brand new 38-caliber five-shot J-frame aluminum alloy pistol. Merčep took it out explaining that it was a gift from a friend. I knew the pistol well since I owned the exact same weapon back home in Detroit. It was the same pistol that I often carried during demonstrations against the Yugoslavs. It was a very common pistol in America, but I knew it was fairly rare to see one in Croatia.

Merčep was very interested in our story and peppered us with many questions trying to get a feel for why we were in Croatia and why we were willing to fight for Croatia's freedom. He saw me as a young American guy who would be valuable because of Americans' reputation for playing video games – even though I was thirty-seven at the time and never played a video game in my life. Apparently, he was in possession of some wire-guided missiles that required the manipulation of a joystick-like device commonly used in video games. After about one-half hour, Merčep agreed to allow us to join his unit and told us to arrange things with his bodyguard, Pika. Before we left, however, he warned us: "The first time you make a mistake, or you are late, I'll consider it a mistake. The second time I'll consider it deliberate and you will be eliminated." We knew what he meant by the not-so-subtle threat and accepted the terms. We all made a mental note: don't make any mistakes with this man. We said our good-byes, left the hospital room and made arrangements to use Žu as a liaison between Pika and us. Pika agreed to transport us from Zagreb to Pakrac where Merčep's unit was stationed. He would arrange to pick us up a few days later.

Apartment on Račkoga Street

Within the first couple of days of our arrival in Zagreb, we also found more stable lodgings in a good-sized apartment on Račkoga street that we used as a kind of "safe house." The apartment was within view of the Muslim Mosque that the

Communists had confiscated after WWII and turned into the so-called "Museum to the Revolution." A wealthy Croatian émigré living in California with ties to the Croatian Republican Party owned the apartment. A Croatian Republican Party member from Buenos Aires named Mario Ostojić was living in the apartment for free as a guest of the owner. I had known Mario since 1989, when he helped me by arranging contacts with Bleiburg survivors living in Buenos Aires for my documentary. He was also generous enough to let me stay with him and his parents in their home in Buenos Aires. I saw him a couple of times in Toronto and at least one more time in Buenos Aires. Pero and Marko also knew him from one previous encounter in Toronto.

Mario's trip to Zagreb, his living accommodations and all his original contacts with government officials were organized by the President of *Hrvatska Republikanska Stranka* (Croatian Republican Party) Ivo Korsky, who lived in Buenos Aires ever since he was forced to escape Yugoslavia following WWII. Korsky knew Mario well and was confident of his abilities.

Like many Croats living in Buenos Aires, Mario's parents fled Yugoslavia after WWII in order to escape certain death under Tito. Mario was five years younger and two or three inches shorter than me. When I first met him in 1989, I was struck by his long hair and very full beard. It gave him the look of someone trying to imitate the look of Argentine revolutionary Che Guevara. I thought it was a curious look for an avowed anti-Communist and wondered what would motivate him to embrace an image that was so easy for others to misinterpret. To make things even worse, by 1991 the beard and hairstyle had also been taken by Serbian Chetnik forces that were known for killing and raping civilians in Croatia and later in Bosnia-Herzegovina. Many must have confused Mario's look with that of a Chetnik; I was surprised to see him still sporting the same beard and long hair in Zagreb in 1991. In any event, Mario had been living in Zagreb for almost a year when we arrived in October 1991.

Mario's political mentor Ivo Korsky had very close contacts with many people in the new government, including the recently elected President of Croatia, Franjo Tuđman, with whom Korsky was on a first-name basis. Mario had used many of the contacts made for him by Korsky to build additional contacts of his own. It is just coincidental that the main offices for the HDZ and the headquarters for the National Security Office (UNS) were both only a couple of blocks away from the apartment on Račkoga street that we were now living in.

Within a few days of arriving at the apartment, tensions started between Mario and the rest of us. First, Mario had changed since the last time I saw him. We all felt he was acting aloof and dismissive toward us. In later years I understood this to be the result of wartime stress. Pero, Božo and Marko, who were members of the Republican Party long before Mario, were forced to sleep on the floor with the rest of us non-members. This was especially upsetting, because there was a large bedroom with several cots being used by friends of Mario from Buenos Aires. His friends were also Croats, but they were not members of the Party – nor were they active in anti-Yugoslav politics. Since I was not a member of the Croatian Republican Party, I had no misgivings about sleeping on the floor, but Pero, Marko and Božo felt that their years of loyal membership should have given them priority over the other visitors who shared a friendship with Mario in Argentina.

Žuka

Another visitor to the Račkoga apartment was a former Argentine military officer named Rodolfo Barrios Saavedra, whose nom de guerre was Žuka. Žuka had previously been a Captain in the Argentine army and had a checkered past. In addition to being trained by the Argentine army, he received additional U.S. military training at the School of the Americas at Fort Benning in Georgia. According to what we were told by him at the time, he was a former member of the notorious Carapintadas (Painted Faces) group. The Carapintadas was a military group dedicated to fighting the Communists of Central America, but he was also involved internally in what has been called Argentina's "Dirty War" against government opponents – most notably the Left and Communists operating in Argentina in the 1980s. Their name "Carapintadas" is due to their practice of applying black grease paint to their faces before some "military action." Mohammed Alí Seineldín led his Carapintadas group in three rebellions against the Argentine leadership. The last coup attempt by Seineldín and his group to overthrow Argentina's President Carlos Menem was in December 1990. That coup attempt resulted in fourteen deaths and was unsuccessful. Seineldín was sent to prison and Rodolfo Barrios Saavedra was forced to flee to Uruguay with his family.

Barrios personally showed me the injuries he received in his battles with the leftists in Argentina and Central America, which included at least five bullet wounds clearly visible in various parts of his body. Barrios was asked by the Croatian government to come to Croatia to assist in training the fledgling Croatian Army. Certainly, Mario's contacts in Argentina helped to arrange for Barrios to come to Croatia and give his military assistance by first training soldiers in Split and later taking over military leadership in Livno, Herzegovina, from the now famous General Ante Gotovina.

Žuka received his orders from Croatian Military Headquarters within days of his arrival in late October of 1991 and was assigned to training Croatian soldiers in and around Split, the country's second largest city. This new development (together with logistical problems with Merčep's people) led to a disagreement among our small group of five volunteers.

Since we were already accepted into Merčep's unit, we were simply waiting to be notified when we would be picked up and transported to the town of Pakrac, where Merčep's units were at the time. After waiting for over one week we were finally notified by Žu what the hold-up was. According to the story we were given, Pika had been arrested outside Zagreb's main train station and taken into police custody. He was charged with killing a man described as being with Yugoslav Military Security Service (KOS). Even though he was one of Merčep's bodyguards and Merčep was in the Ministry of Interior, we had no idea if or when Pika would be released from police custody.

We were all given the option of staying and waiting for somebody from Merčep's unit to pick us up or joining Žuka's unit and accompanying him to Split. My preference was to wait in Zagreb until we were contacted in order to eventually join Merčep's unit as we originally planned. The other four in the group had other thoughts, and that finally led to us going in different directions.

Since Marko Stipaničić was born in Senj, he chose to take a bus to Senj the next day and join a military unit in that town. Ante Pranić decided to join the Croatian Defense Forces (HOS), which at the time was a paramilitary force under the leadership of Dobroslav Paraga. Paraga was also the President of the Croatian Party of Rights (HSP). Ante knew Paraga well, as did I, so he went to see him the next day at a building Paraga had occupied across from Zagreb's train station and which was serving as his headquarters. The building was appropriately named after the father of Croatian nationalism, Ante Starčević. Pero Ivčec and Božo Čačić made the choice of joining Žuka's new unit and travelled with him to Split within a couple of days of their decision.

Drago Pilsel (who I had known since 1989 in Buenos Aires, but few people outside of Croatia have ever heard of) was one of the Argentines who were occupying the cots in the Zagreb apartment at that time of Žuka's arrival. Always the opportunist, it seems that Pilsel calculated that it would serve his purposes to accompany Žuka, who spoke only Spanish and English, down to Split and act as an interpreter for the new commander. Pilsel, the self-described "human rights activist," has - to my knowledge - never publicly disclosed that he traveled to Split with Žuka to serve as a translator for the former Carapintada and fellow Argentinean. Petar Ivčec (who was also under Žuka's command) alleges that after just a few months, Pilsel would quit his role as translator following several disputes with Žuka's soldiers over his misperceived authority. One can only wonder if this rejection by honorable patriotic Croatian soldiers in 1991 led him on a revenge-seeking career of caustic attacks against everything patriotic Croats hold dear. One can only empathize with the deep loss felt by Pilsel's mother whose one son, Branko, died heroically in Croatia's Homeland War, while her other son became a pariah to Croatian patriots.

Žuka would continue to honorably serve the Croatian military during the Homeland War. He eventually replaced Ante Gotovina as commander of Livno and was instrumental in Croatia reclaiming all occupied Croatian territory in 1995. Despite his checkered past in Argentina, the Croatian men under his command love him to this day.

But back to Zagreb in October of 1991: it was still my desire to join Merčep, so I remained in contact with Žu as I continued to inquire into the whereabouts of Pika. While I waited and waited, the days went by and so did the war. I was getting tired of waiting and increasingly antsy. Continuing with my plan to eventually go to Pakrac, I decided it would at least be productive to document the war photographically, with an emphasis on establishing proof that the Serbs and the JNA were targeting civilians in their bombing campaigns of Croatian towns and cities. It was my belief that such documentation could be used after the war in future war crimes trials. I also knew that in order to get free access to various locations I would need some sort of press credentials.

Ante Beljo

It was at this time that I decided to once again contact my friend Ante Beljo, who, as I explained in previous chapters, I knew from emigration as well as from earlier in the year when he arranged for the showing of my documentary film *The Bleiburg Tragedy* in the Mimara Museum in Zagreb.

Ante was more than helpful. He made a few calls to the Foreign Press Office in the Hotel Intercontinental, and I was issued a press pass as a correspondent for what was at that time called the Ministry of Information and later the Croatian Information Center. Those press credentials gave me the ability to attend the various press conferences in Croatia. But, more importantly, I had access to official Croatian events and buildings around the country. It also gave me authorization to photograph events when stopped by the police. The police routinely stopped me and demanded documentation from me; the press accreditation listing the Ministry of Information as my employer never failed to help me with the police.

I accidentally found a niche that I thought was perfect for me while waiting for Merčep's guys to pick me up. Foreign journalists, who knew nothing about Croatia, or the war, were arriving daily to cover the war. Their first stop was Zagreb's Intercontinental Hotel to acquire press accreditations issued by the Croatian government's Foreign Press Bureau. Without those credentials they could not work in Croatia. My goal was to meet as many of them as I could while they waited for their credentials to be processed. They were not hard to pick out and they all spoke English, which was fortunate for me since my Croatian was limited. Typically, I would simply approach them and make small talk: How long have you been here? Have you ever been to Croatia? What do you know about the war? I found that all of the journalists that I spoke with were astonishingly ignorant about the war and Croatia. If they really took their job seriously, they could have read a brief history of Croatia or the former Yugoslavia. Of course, the problem in those days was that most of the current information they might have read would have been written and disseminated by the Yugoslav government in Belgrade, or one of the government's sycophants.

Certainly, they knew I was American since I spoke English with an American accent. The identification badge I wore had my photo, my name and the word PRESS in big bold letters on it. The journalists never took a closer look to see that I was also a correspondent for the Ministry of Information. I was fortunate to have had many encounters with journalists prior to the war. That previous experience gave me valuable insight into how they tended to think. I also knew how little they could digest at any one time. The mistake many people made in speaking with the news media was that they would bombard them with too much information all at one time. In my early days of activism, I would stand on the sidelines and watch as the journalists' eyes would glaze over at a never-ending history lesson from a well-meaning Croatian or Albanian spokesperson.

The best approach, it seemed to me, was to treat the journalists as the uninformed and intellectually lazy people that they tended to be. My approach was to give them a different way to look at things so they could appear to be intelligent when they wrote their articles or spoke with their colleagues. It was necessary to be very delicate, however. It was possible to scare them away by coming on too strong, and yet it was necessary to redirect their thinking and focus so that they might see the war from a different perspective. If they were from America or Great Britain, I would direct them to the archives of the *New York Times* or *London Times* for a broader historical view of Croatia. The Serb/Yugoslav propaganda machine liked to focus on Croatia during WWII, so I found it effective to direct journalists to their own country's historical archives prior to WWII. I knew what was written in those old *New York Times* and *London Times* articles dating as far back as 1918, because I had read them.

One suggestion that seemed especially compelling was the condemnation of the Yugoslav government by Albert Einstein following the murder of Croatian nationalist and scientist Milan Šuflaj in central Zagreb on February 18, 1931. On May 6, 1931 the New York Times printed a letter addressed to the League for the Rights of Man and signed by Einstein and Heinrich Mann. In the joint statement the two men urged a protest against the "horrible brutality which is being practiced against the Croatian people" by the Yugoslav government. Their letter of protest continued to say: "Murder as a political weapon must not be tolerated and political murderers must not be made national heroes." This condemnation of Yugoslavia by Einstein in 1931 was compelling to highlight in 1991 for a couple of reasons. First, the author of the letter was Albert Einstein (hardly a Croatian nationalist). Second, both the murder of Šuflaj and the practice of murdering opponents by the Yugoslavia government occurred long before the Homeland War of 1991-1995 and prior to WWII. This reinforced the Croatian position that Croatia's demands for freedom from any form of Yugoslavia was not a new phenomenon, nor was the Yugoslav government's use of murder to suppress political opponents a new tactic.

If the journalist seemed open to looking at that line of research, I would also point him to articles in their own newspapers documenting the shooting of a Croatian leader named Stjepan Radić on the floor of the Yugoslav parliament on June 20, 1928. Once again, the historical facts demonstrated that neither Croatian demands for freedom, nor Yugoslav oppression, were something new.

"You don't have to take the information you hear from the government of Croatia as fact," I would say. "Just look in OUR own archives beginning in 1918 and moving forward to present time. These people who are at war now are fighting for their lives. They fight for the same thing we Americans and every other freedom-loving people fought for: freedom of speech, self-determination, freedom of religion, the right to elect their own representatives. Oh, and by the way, they are fighting within their own borders. Not one Serbian soldier has been killed within the borders of Serbia. It is a defensive war fought entirely within the borders of Croatia." Since I knew they hated to be accused of thinking simplistically, I would use that against them whenever I could. "That's just an overly simplistic way of viewing this war," I would say. "When I first got here, I thought like you. But the more you learn the more you'll find that our view is too simplistic and perhaps even racist." I would also say things like, "You are missing the big picture," or "You are viewing this war as a foreigner." Then I would go on to explain how they should view it from a different perspective.

On at least one occasion I went a little too far and was discovered by a journalist from an Israeli radio station. He said that he was in Croatia to see events first-hand. Later he would travel to Belgrade to learn from a Serbian perspective. Understandably, he was primarily focused on the part of Croatian history from 1941 to 1945 when the Croats had allied themselves with the Germans during WWII. I was probably a little too strong in imploring him to look at Croatian history both before and after the Second World War. "You know that many of those who are fighting for Croatian forces today are children and grandchildren of the same anti-Fascist partisans that fought against Hitler. Just because they are Croats does not mean that they come from fathers who sided with the Germans during the war. In fact, Tito exterminated most of those who sided with the Nazis after the war. We can't condemn all Croats as if they share some genetic guilt. That would be both primitive and racist." After the journalist graciously listened to my standard monologue, he responded by giving the following advice: "If you want to be effective in the future you should try to be a little more objective when talking about this." In those days Croatia was full of foreign agents from every conceivable country. Intelligence agencies have always used the cover of journalist in their clandestine work. I believed that many of the so-called "journalists" that I came into contact with were foreign intelligence agents acting under the cover of "journalist." I assumed that this was also true for the middle-aged man who stood before me representing a radio station in Tel Aviv. Knowing that my cover was blown I responded directly and harshly. "I can no more be objective about the slaughter of Croatian civilians, the rape of Croatian women, the ethnic cleansing of Croatian villages and using Croatian civilians as hostages than a Jewish person can be objective about the Holocaust. You must know that Croatian history does not begin or end with WWII." It was the one time that I knew I had come on too strong, but I hoped that he at least left with a different view of Croats and their war for independence.

Another prime location for speaking with journalist was in the bars and restaurants. Since there were no tourists in Croatia during the war, the hotels were primarily occupied by refugees, journalists and diplomats. The journalists were easy to pick out and they loved hanging out in the bars, sharing rumors and experiences, but mostly rumors. I had lost whatever respect I had for journalists long before the homeland war. That is not to say that they were all flawed, biased and lacking basic intellectual curiosity. John Burns with the *New York Times* and Pulitzer Prize winning journalist Roy Gutman were two reporters that really stood out as examples of what a journalist should aspire to.

The typical journalists I met would pool their money together, even though they worked for competing papers and agencies, then drive to areas outside of Zagreb that had been badly bombed by Serb forces. The nearby town of Karlovac was a favorite destination for these day excursions, because there were always damaged buildings to photograph for their papers and it was close enough to Zagreb that they could be back in the hotel bar by early afternoon to continue their alcohol-fueled gab sessions. It was then that the spinning sessions began. If there happened to be a journalist who strayed as far as Slavonia, on Croatia's Eastern border with Serbia, he had the attention of all the others. He was viewed as an expert on the war simply because he chose to veer a little farther off the path than the others sitting around the bar and drinking until late at night.

Several American, Canadian and British journalists were sitting in the Chinese restaurant of the Hotel Astoria late one evening loudly discussing how terrible the Croatian soldiers were and how corrupt the politicians were. This was another common attribute I found among Western journalist during the war. First, they were always too loud. Second, they didn't fully appreciate that they were in a war zone away from home when they pontificated about the war. They just finished falsely accusing General Branimir Glavaš of selling guns to the same Serbs who were attacking the city of Osijek and neighboring villages – as if the JNA was lacking weapons – when they moved on to accuse Dobroslav Paraga of some violation they thought he had committed. What the journalists did not notice was that a group of three soldiers came in with military patches on their shoulders that identified them as members of the Croatian Defense Forces (HOS). As stated previously, HOS was the paramilitary group that was organized by the same Dobroslav Paraga that these journalists were condemning. For the most part the HOS guys loved Paraga. Many young Croats understand and speak English and, unfortunately for the journalists that night, these soldiers understood everything. In those early days of Croatia's war, it was typical to see Croatian soldiers walking around the city, as well as sitting in bars, with fully loaded rifles. These soldiers had Kalashnikov rifles propped against the table where they sat. After some time listening to the monologue of the loudest "expert" journalist (whose last name was Akerman) ranting against Croatia, one of the HOS soldiers began to yell expletives against the journalists' mothers and threaten to kill them all. These verbal threats would have normally been taken in stride, but I suddenly became aware that I was sitting directly between the HOS soldiers and the journalists when I heard the familiar sound that an AK-47 makes when a bullet has been chambered. Not wanting to get caught in a crossfire, I turned in the direction of the now loaded AK-47 and simply said to the soldier in Croatian, "Watch out for my head!" I said it with a smile in an attempt to bring some levity to the dangerous situation, but it didn't appear to help. The soldier became more and more enraged as the journalist became more and more oblivious to the danger simmering around him. I had already moved to a safer location in the bar and out of the direct line of fire, when Ivan, the hotel desk clerk, came from the lobby to just inside the restaurant. He could see and hear where things were going from the front desk, so he called the HOS headquarters just a few blocks away. Within minutes of being called, a contingent of HOS soldiers donning MP arm patches showed up and diplomatically extracted all the soldiers from the restaurant.

I'm certain the oblivious journalists never knew how close they came to being killed that night.

For the moment I was still stuck in a sort of limbo while I waited for word about getting to Merčep's group. So, I continued trying to at least contribute what I could by influencing the journalists while posing as a journalist using my press credentials. But as weeks dragged by, it was getting more and more frustrating to wait for someone who may never show up. Davor Butković Žu, who was still acting as a go-between, was appearing less dependable than I had originally believed. I began to question myself. Maybe it a mistake not to have gone with Pero, Božo and Žuka to Split when I had the chance? But since Ante Pranić was still in Zagreb working out of the HOS building, I decided to follow his example and join Paraga's forces.

Dobroslav Paraga

Dobroslav Paraga is a former political prisoner who had been jailed by the Yugoslav regime for four years, beginning in 1980, in two of Yugoslavia's most infamous prisons for political prisoners: Lepoglava and Goli Otok. The international human rights group Amnesty International also adopted him as a "Prisoner of Conscience" on two occasions. He was released in 1988 from another shorter prison sentence of six months. The Yugoslav government initially refused to let him leave the country, but with the help of the German government he was allowed to travel to the West where he met with politicians and journalists regarding the many human rights violations of Communist Yugoslavia.

I met Paraga for the first time in May 1989 in Mississauga, a suburb of Toronto that has a large Croatian population. Pero, Marko and I drove from Detroit to Toronto to take part in a demonstration against Yugoslavia and demand the release of Slovenian journalist Janez Janša from one of Yugoslavia's prisons. Janša worked for the Slovenian newspaper *Mladina*. It was at the private home of political activist Dr. Josip

Gamulin that I had the pleasure of being introduced to Dobroslav Paraga, along with two journalists from *Mladina*. One of the journalists would later be killed while covering the war in Sarajevo for his newspaper. Paraga's whereabouts were always a mystery during this part of his life and rumors were always flying around regarding what happened to him after he was given permission to leave Yugoslavia. Rumors like these were common in the Croatian diaspora where there is no shortage of "experts," who all had their own theories. Given all the rumors, I recall being surprised to see him stroll out from a room in the back of the house and into the living room where we were sitting.

On our first encounter Paraga struck me as being an introvert. He was pleasant and polite with an air of old-school civility in his demeanor. It surprised me, for some reason, that he was taller than I expected – about 6' 2". His round face and thick black hair gave him the appearance of being heavier than he probably was. Paraga was well known to all patriotic Croats in diaspora and was considered a real Croatian hero for the personal sacrifices that he endured while standing up against the Yugoslav regime. On this particular day he, no doubt, was being cautious with his new acquaintances from the Croatian diaspora. It was pretty common knowledge that UDBA had infiltrated many communities and being careful was a healthy policy given the circumstances.

Our paths would cross a few times during that period as he was travelling around Europe and North America speaking to various Western politicians. His political tour included Washington D.C., where he not only informed American Senators and Congressmen about Yugoslav brutality, but lobbied them to change their positions on American-Yugoslav relations.

In May 1991 we met again, this time in Zagreb, when I was there for the release of my film *The Bleiburg Tragedy*. I was also in Croatia for the historical referendum that would finally give Croats the opportunity to vote for or against freedom from Yugoslav domination. We had talked about the Bleiburg film in our first meeting in Mississauga two years previously when I was still gathering material for final production, so Paraga was very interested in seeing the completed film in May 1991. We made arrangements to meet under the clock in Kvaternik Square in Zagreb where he picked me up and drove me to his family's house nearby. It seemed like his entire family was there. They were very courteous and hospitable towards me. We watched the documentary on their family television set. Paraga would make comments when he recognized one of the witnesses, like our mutual friend Ante Pranić. He also found it remarkable that I had former Officers from the British 8th Army recall the murders of Croats by Tito's Partisans on film.

After the five of us arrived in Zagreb in October 1991, I continued to keep in contact with Paraga. The other three didn't seem as interested in seeing Paraga, but Ante and I would often stop by his office – even before he officially volunteered to join Paraga's HOS forces. Paraga had completely occupied the Starčević Building (*Starčevićev Dom)* just across from the main train station in Zagreb. The building was named after the founder of Croatian Nationalism and the original Party of Rights (*Stranka Prava*). The building was on a prime location with Paraga's third floor corner office overlooking the King Tomislav Park and the first Croatian king's statue. By the time I arrived in his offices in October 1991 he had advanced from being the leader of the Croatian Party of Rights to also being the leader of HOS.

On a typical day, armed HOS soldiers would be stationed throughout the building's entrances and stairways. Normally, two guards would be checking identification cards. Another guard would be posted at the end of the first-floor hallway next to the staircase just off the entrance. The visitor would meet armed soldiers at each of the floor's landings before reaching Paraga's office on the third floor. There were also armed soldiers guarding the entrance to his office. At first, Ante and I would have to trudge through the gauntlet of armed soldiers in order to see Paraga. Later, after Ante joined his forces, I became such a frequent visitor that his guards already recognized me, and we greeted each other as I walked up the stairs leading to his office.

When, therefore, I finally decided to join HOS forces, I was certain that there would be no problem getting Paraga's authorization. It was my hope that Paraga would assign me to a small close-knit group of British volunteers who were all professional soldiers and very well trained within their combat specialties by the British Army. We got to know each other fairly well over an occasional beer in the bars close to HOS headquarters. On one occasion another American of Croatian descent from Chicago named Robert, who was also a HOS volunteer, joined us. Some might refer to the Brits as mercenaries, because they did receive some small stipend for helping to train the HOS forces, who like all Croatian soldiers in the autumn of 1991 were without training. It was my understanding that they were all former members of British Royal Marines, or Special Air Service who had come to Croatia after viewing the carnage perpetrated by the Serbs on the Croatian civilians. They appeared honest when they admitted that they just could not stand by and watch the bloody scenes unfold daily on British television. They said they were compelled to take sides with the Croats and offer their military expertise. Among the group of about five volunteers were snipers and specialists in explosives and booby traps. I spoke with them about my desire to join their small group. They all agreed provided Paraga also gave his blessing.

I believe it was November 21, 1991 when I wound my way up the staircase to speak with Paraga and get the necessary authorization to join HOS forces. Our meeting was very friendly as usual. After some pleasantries, I broached the subject: Paraga believed that since I spoke some Croatian, I would be an asset to the British fighters. He also did not need to worry about my loyalties since he knew that I had been in the Croatian liberation movement for many years prior to the start of the war. After getting Paraga's approval to join HOS and the small group of

Brits it was agreed that I would come to HOS headquarters the
next day with my gear ready to go to the front. I still had all the
gear that I had with me when I was arrested in Germany – minus
my weapons – but I was not worried about that because I knew
that HOS had plenty of AK-47s, SK Chinese rifles, grenades and
rocket propelled grenades (RPGs). I was already in the habit of
carrying grenades whenever I travelled to areas of Croatia that
were closer to the front, like Karlovac, Sisak and Osijek. I should
have been suspicious, however, when shortly before going to see
Paraga for authorization, the location where he stored some of
his arms and ammunition was raided by the Croatian
government's special police. In those days - before the more
modern mall was built there - there was a dirty, dark tunnel
leading under the Starčević Park to Zagreb's main train station.
There were small dingy restaurants and bars in the tunnel that
were often frequented by the same type of people that hung
around train stations in other big cities at night. In the storage
room behind one of those bars was one of the places that HOS
used to keep their arms and ammunition. It was that location that
was raided by the police.

I spent the night before reporting for my first day in
HOS packing my rucksack the way I did just one month before
when I anticipated going to Pakrac with Merčep's forces.
Dressed in my uniform, I carried the rucksack to HOS
headquarters early in the morning, but something was wrong.
There was an unusual number of HOS soldiers milling around
outside the building on the sidewalk as well as inside the
building's hallway. Among the soldiers standing in the doorway
were a couple of the British volunteers.

"What's going on?" I asked. "You didn't hear? They
arrested Paraga this morning as he was driving to the
headquarters." I stood there in disbelief. "Who arrested him?" I
asked. "Tuđman's Special Forces arrested him and charged him
with something. We're not quite sure yet what they charged him
with." There I stood in the hallway with my bags, ready to
finally do what I originally came to Croatia to do, just to learn

that once again something was preventing me. I explained to the Brits that I was just here yesterday and Paraga gave his approval for me to join their small group. "I'm here with my bags now and ready to go!" "I'm sorry," the Brit replied, "But we can't take you until we hear directly from Mr. Paraga." "Didn't he tell you yesterday after I left his office?" "No, he didn't tell us anything," was their response. Completely deflated for the second time, I cursed as I trudged back to the Hotel Astoria with my bags. I would later learn that the Croatian government had charged him with "high treason." The government would ultimately drop the charges.

It never occurred to me that I would face so many obstacles when we first began to talk about volunteering for Croatia's Homeland War. First the Germans had taken my weapons; then Pika got arrested and our hopes of joining Merčep's unit were extinguished; now the very morning I had showed up at HOS headquarters Paraga got arrested. The feeling of control was slipping away through my fingers. But the experience helped me learn important lessons that would help me a great deal while working in Croatia over the next few years.

The first lesson was that to be successful in Croatia, one should rely as little as possible on others to assist you. In most cases the assistance will come only if it is mutually beneficial to those giving assistance.

The second lesson was that I worked best alone: I could deal with failing because of my own miscalculations and even blunders, but I hated to be delayed in reaching my goals due to other people's mistakes or worse: their passive resistance.

The decision on what to do next was made easier by the fact that I accidentally stumbled upon something that I was good at when I began working deceptively as a "journalist" among journalists. If I couldn't take part in the war with a weapon in my hand, then I could at least continue to take part in this phase of the war by continuing to influence what journalists would write about Croatia's war. So, I continued to speak with journalists trying to redirect them away from their preconceived notions and the talking points that they all seemed to absorb from each other. I made it my business to mingle with them when I travelled to various cities in Croatia to document the targeting of civilians by Serb forces.

The Yugoslav news agency TANJUG and its lobbying groups (like Serb-Net) consistently portrayed their war against Croatia as a "civil war," "ethnic war," or as an "age-old ethnic conflict." So, I played the role of evangelist/journalist. In the daytime I travelled throughout Croatia photographing the effects of Serbia's war of aggression. In the evening I gathered together with my fellow journalists preaching the word of Croatian freedom, independence and self-determination, while pointing out the evils of Communism, Serbian oppression and Serbian ethnic cleansing. I simply posed the question: as long as all the blood was being shed solely within the borders of Croatia, could the war honestly be referred to as a civil war or ethnic conflict? It was genocide and should be called that! Unfortunately, it was not until the subsequent wars against Bosnia-Herzegovina and Kosovo that journalists and diplomats finally began denouncing the Serbian practice of ethnic cleansing as genocide.

By mid-December of 1991, Croatia's fledgling military managed to maintain control over seventy-five percent of its territory. But, unfortunately, the Croats in the remaining twenty-five percent of the country lost their homes and became refugees. My own family from Petrinja was forced to live in the neighboring town of Sisak for the next four years. In an attempt to buy time and acquire more weapons, President Tuđman brokered a cease-fire agreement between Yugoslavia and Croatia that appeared to be holding. Many of the volunteer soldiers returned to their homes for the next four years in hopes of eventually retaking Croatia's lost territory. The news media's interest in the Croatian war also subsided and Western journalists were reassigned to Bosnia-Herzegovina, in particular Sarajevo, for the next four years. I decided it was time to go home. If my anti-climactic departure in December 1991 left me with the feeling of having contributed little during this phase of Croatia's Homeland War, I hoped to be able to do more in the coming years. Pero, Marko and Božo also saw the cease-fire as their opportunity to return home. Ante Pranić would remain in Croatia until his death in 1996.

The plan was to resume my normal life in America while continuing to work for Croatia from there. But much to my surprise, my arrest in Germany had not simply gone away in October of 1991. U.S. Federal Agents would interrupt my plans for a quiet, normal life with an early morning raid on my home shortly after my return to America.

*An altercation with JNA officers outside JNA Headquarters,
Zagreb*

Dobroslav Paraga 2nd from right

Preparing for a trip to Osijek, 1991

Raid on HSP by Croatian Special Police

Inside JNA HQ hours after their evacuation from Croatia

City of Karlovac under mortar attack

8

Federal Agents, Open Up!

THE FIRST INDICATION that life had changed drastically was when I returned to my place of employment with the local utility company in Detroit. By that time, I had been employed by the Detroit Edison Company for over fifteen years. My supervisors and union officers confided in me that while I was gone Federal Agents had interviewed them regarding my activities prior to my departure for Croatia.

In spite of being sworn to secrecy by the Federal Agents, some of them told me that the agents were interested in profiling me. What type of employee was I? How long was I employed? They were also interested in any "unusual activity" that they may have observed. But they were especially interested in whether I had been seen bringing any items onto the property and what part of the company facilities I had access to. It was evident to me that they were under the impression that I was smuggling items destined for Croatia and that I was storing them somewhere on company property to avoid having them in my home should agents obtain a search warrant. Clearly, it was their impression that I had more items in my possession besides those found in my luggage at the Frankfurt Airport. That belief by the Federal Agents continued for many years and is corroborated by an incident I will describe shortly.

For now, however, I was trying to get back to some normalcy in my life. That attempt included trying to get articles published and doing radio interviews in Detroit about the war in Croatia.

Then on May 1, 1992, while I was shaving at six o'clock in the morning, I heard pounding on the door to the apartment I was leasing. "Federal Agents, open up!" The pounding continued as I wiped the shaving cream from my face, wondering if I was hearing correctly. Were they really yelling "Federal Agents!"? I went to open the door. I recall being embarrassed and angry that they were going to wake up all my neighbors. A middle-aged man with grey hair and a grey mustache was at the door when I opened it. What seemed like a whole hallway full of men with suits and windbreaker jackets were standing behind him. "Are you Michael Palaich?" he asked. "Yes." "We are Federal Agents. May we come in?" I asked, "Have you got a warrant?" With that he produced one, holding it up nervously in his right hand. The agent, who I later learned, was Agent John Cange with the U.S. Customs Department. Agent Cange was so nervous his hand was noticeably shaking as he held up the warrant in front of my face. Being overly cocky I patted his hand like you would a small child's head and told him, "Take it easy. Come on in if you've got a warrant." "Have you got any long guns?" he asked. "No, just a forty-five pistol that I have a permit for." He directed me to show him where the pistol was. One of the agents took it outside while the other agents began searching various parts of the apartment. There was also a uniformed police officer present and sitting on my couch who was with the Sterling Heights Police Department. This didn't surprise me, because I was aware that federal agents would often have a police officer from the local municipality escort them to the location where the warrant was being served, in this case, the City of Sterling Heights, Michigan.

There was no point in getting aggressive or argumentative with the agents. I believed they were simply doing their jobs. They did their job and I did my job, I always thought. "You guys want some coffee?" I asked. To my surprise two of the agents sitting around the dining room table said, "Sure, I'll take a coffee." Agent Cange, the lead agent, refused. With the coffee poured for the two agents and myself, I was directed to sit at the dining room table. As the four of us sat at the table, other agents were in other parts of the home going through drawers, closets, cabinets, dressers, boxes, photos and documents. One agent, who was their information technology man, was going through my computer looking for evidence.

"What did you take to Germany?" Agent Cange asked. "Whatever I declared, is what I took," I responded. "What was that?" he asked again. "Exactly what I declared." As he asked me for the third time what I took to Germany, I just happened to look at the police officer still sitting on the couch. I was surprised to see him shaking his head back and forth slightly in a subtle sign of disgust. "I think it's time to call my lawyer," I stated. "You're not under arrest. I just want to ask you a few questions." Agent Cange said. "You mean I'm not under arrest yet." I answered sarcastically. "Well, if you think you need a lawyer, I can't stop you." With that said, I got up and dialed the phone hanging on the wall only steps away.

My brother-in-law was a police officer for the City of Oak Park, Michigan, and I thought if anyone knew a good federal defense attorney it would be him. Since it was still early in the morning, I found Jim still at home. "Hey Jim, there are some federal agents here with a search warrant and I need a good defense attorney. Do you know one?" Thinking quickly, Jim gave me the phone number for one of the best attorneys in the Detroit area named Richard Lustig. Richard Lustig was not only an excellent attorney, but also a very expensive one, specializing in high-profile cases that often involved big-time drug cases. I don't remember if I called Lustig at home or in his office, but I was very fortunate that he picked up the phone. After explaining that Jim referred me, Lustig immediately agreed to represent me and take me on as his client. He told me to come into his office later that day. Before hanging up, however, Lustig said he wanted to speak to the lead agent in the search. "My lawyer wants to talk to you," I said passing the phone to Cange.

"Yes, sir." I heard Agent Cange say. "Hello. Yes. Agent John Cange with the U.S. Customs Department. Yes sir. I understand. Your lawyer wants to talk to you," Cange said as he passed the phone back to me. "Listen. I told the agent not to ask you any more questions," Lustig said. "You are not to say a single word to him, you understand? I want you to come in and see me this afternoon." After I hung up the phone, I heard what was music to my ears. One of several agents present asked Cange: "What's the name of the lawyer?" Cange answered, "Richard Lustig." The other agent dropped his head to his chest and sighed with an almost imperceptible, "Oh, shit!" That confirmed for me that my brother-in-law couldn't have chosen better when he referred me to Richard Lustig.

Agent Cange continued to ask me questions that morning in spite of having just promised Lustig that he wouldn't. On one occasion an agent came out to the dining table where we were sitting with a photo in his hand. It was a photo of me sitting on a bed with a grenade in each hand. "Are these real?" Cange asked coyly with a grin on his face. I responded by lifting and extending my chin indicating something like, "That's for you to find out". I didn't want to tell him that they were real grenades that I used to carry in my pockets while travelling around Croatia. In those early years of the war the front lines were constantly changing. My biggest fear was being captured because a bus driver took the wrong turn, or a train conductor wasn't notified of a more recent route change. My goal was never to be caught alive, because I knew that the Serbian Chetniks often tortured their victims before killing them. I was determined not to be one of those victims and I saw the grenades as a way of solving that dilemma for me: I planned on using them to blow up my captors and myself in case I was captured. I also had access to AK-47 rifles while in Croatia, but I chose to travel with grenades in my pocket because they were more discreet.

The agents continued going through all my belongings and furniture for the next four to five hours. They would occasionally walk outside with a bag or a box containing some personal belongings that they thought was valuable as evidence, such as photos, documents or a diary. When they were finally finished, Agent Cange returned the registered 1911 45-caliber pistol that he had previously taken out of the apartment. I wasn't surprised, because I had no doubt that it would show up clean and registered in my name. When they left, I discovered how thorough they had been in their search. They even removed the backs of my dressers and the paper from behind dresser mirrors during the search. Apparently, they thought I was hiding documents or money as well as weapons.

It may seem strange that I never took offense at anything the agents did. Whether it was on the day they raided my home, during all the previous interrogations accusing me of bombing buildings, or when an agent of the FBI said one day that he was going to see my name on the "Ten Most Wanted List." I continued to hold the view that they were simply doing their job. In fact, I respected them for their professionalism – most of the time. They always spoke to me in a respectful manner, so I offered them the same respect in return.

Richard Lustig

That afternoon I went to see attorney Richard Lustig at his offices in downtown Birmingham. I had no way of knowing what a high-priced attorney Lustig was. Lustig was continuously busy in spite of his high fees, because he was worth it. People he represented were more than willing to pay the legal fees he charged. He generally handled federal offenses where trials could last for years and his success rate was excellent.

Lustig was in his late forties when he accepted me as a client. He was known for his long hair, beard and Armani suits. He personified the image of a very successful big city defense attorney. He was sitting at his desk as I entered his office that afternoon of May 2, 1992. I was directed to sit down and tell him about myself, all the particulars of the case and what evidence the government had against me. He also wanted to know about my arrest in Germany. He took notes throughout our meeting and then he spoke.

He knew without me saying anything that I didn't have the kind of money that most of his clients had. He knew that I could neither pay the retainer, nor his usual fees. "I'm going to take your case pro bono. Just pay me what you can. Maybe nothing will come of it," he said in closing. Years later he would explain his reasons for taking my case pro bono.

Within just weeks of my home being raided by the agents, friends called me. "They have a news story about you on television," they said. "Did you see it?" I had not seen it, but was able to catch it being played again on the 11 o'clock news program. The story included interviews with local gun dealers, photos of weapons similar to the type the Germans said they confiscated from me, film footage shot with night-vision lenses and dramatic war footage. A television news reporter named Vince Wade brought the story.

The next day I called Lustig's office notifying him of the news story. "Don't worry about it," was Lustig's response. "They're only beating the bushes trying to get you to do something. They want to make you nervous. They want to see whom you call and what you do in response to the publicity. Vince Wade's wife works for the F.B.I. and they often feed him information for his reports." Well, that put things in a whole different light and confirmed my suspicions that they released information about the case to the reporter for a reason. Lustig didn't have to tell me not to start phoning people: I instinctively resisted calling other people involved in my case believing my phones were tapped. At the very least, I believed the agents would track my phone records, which I later discovered they did.

Before hanging up, Lustig cautioned me not to do anything stupid. I wasn't quite sure what he meant by that and I didn't press him. He closed by saying that he had a local award-winning reporter for WJR Radio in Detroit, named Rod Hansen, do freelance investigating for some of his cases. "I'll see what he can find out about your case from his sources in government." Rod Hansen would do much of the investigative work in my case which Lustig needed for trial preparation.

Over the course of the next five years I was constantly getting reports from people that I knew saying Federal Agents had just come to their homes or places of work to ask about me. The agents seemed to spare no expense. They were convinced, it seemed, that I was part of some sort of major international arms trafficking operation to Croatian forces.

Sometimes, I would catch men dressed as homeless people get out of vans and proceed to go through the garbage dumpsters behind my apartment complex. This would not be out of place if I lived in the city, but I lived in a fairly middle-class neighborhood in the suburbs where it was not common to see homeless people. I would approach them and ask them what they were searching for. "I'm just looking for food, man," was their response. The problem was that they got out of a van with State of Arizona license plates. "Did you come all the way from Arizona to go through my garbage dumpster?" I asked sarcastically. The not-so-closely held secret was that U.S. Federal Agents in Detroit loved to use undercover cars with Arizona license plates during the 1990s. On any given day a person could drive down Lafayette Boulevard and observe a whole line of illegally parked cars in front of the U.S. Federal Court House where many federal government agencies had offices. All the cars, without exception, would have Arizona license plates. I never discovered why they preferred Arizona license plates. I only theorized that it was for the same reason that Arizona was a preferred state for relocating people who were in the federal government's Witness Protection Program.

Often times they would follow me throughout the day establishing my route. On one occasion I noticed that agents were following me in an unmarked car as I was driving down Fort Street in my company vehicle. I made a right turn down McKinstry street just outside of downtown Detroit and pulled into a large four-story industrial complex that had long since been abandoned. I drove into a large open courtyard area surrounded on four sides by the walls. Ten minutes later I left the complex and continued east on Fort Street for approximately twenty minutes before turning around and returning to the abandoned building that I just left. When I passed the vacant building, I saw many unmarked cars blocking both ends of the side street that I originally drove down just forty minutes before. They also blocked the entrance to the abandoned building. One of the questions posed to my coworkers and supervisors was, "Have you noticed Palaich unloading or storing boxes on company property?" Clearly, they thought I was shipping military equipment to Croatian forces, and that I had unwittingly led them to the building where I was storing the equipment. They were wrong, but the experience did confirm for me that they were serious about getting further proof to finally indict me.

That intense level of surveillance continued for almost five years. The Statute of Limitations for that particular crime was five years. In October of 1996, only eleven days short of five years, the federal prosecutor would eventually be able to get a Grand Jury to indict me. That eventful day, however, was still a few years away, which meant I was still free to leave and travel back and forth to Croatia.

The tremendous pressure that comes from being under intense investigation for all those years can take a toll on one's nerves. However, the stubbornness that had become part of my character prevented me from submitting to the stress. I refused to allow my legal problems to hinder my activities and continued to play my role (as small as it was) in helping Croatia realize its independence.

Federal Agents, Open Up!

Search Warrant,

9

City under Siege

I CONTINUED TRAVELING frequently between Croatia and the United States following the "cease-fire" between Croatian forces and the JNA in December of 1991. After the federal agents conducted the search of my home in May 1992, my work in the area of pro-Croatia propaganda resumed with even more intensity than before the war. This work included reminding news media outlets and American politicians that Serbs (through the Yugoslav army) still unlawfully held twenty-five percent of Croatian territory. Furthermore, it also seemed important to develop closer relationships with Bosnian Muslims as well as other Muslim groups living in the state of Michigan. Following the Croatian-JNA cease-fire, the United Nations simply allowed the Yugoslav army to transport large amounts of their war-making machinery across the border and into Bosnia-Herzegovina where the JNA would be free to focus on creating new victims. When the Serbian-led JNA attacked Croatia, it was under the pretense of protecting the Serbian minority population from "Croatian extremists," or so-called "Ustaše." Once they left Croatia and began to focus on Bosnia-Herzegovina, they justified their bloodletting as a campaign to defend Europe against the spread of Islam. It was clear to any observer that much more blood would be shed – this time in Bosnia-Herzegovina. Because Bosnia-Herzegovina was three-fifths Muslim and since Michigan had one of the largest Muslim populations outside of the Middle East, we thought it was beneficial to make contact with the more general Muslim community living in the tri-county area of Michigan.

One endeavor that had long-lasting positive consequences on several levels was a symposium on Bosnia-Herzegovina I chaired and organized with the help of some local Croats from the Detroit area. Speaking at the symposium was Muhamed Sacirbey (*Šaćirbegović*), Bosnia-Herzegovina's Ambassador to the United Nations; George Kenney, Head of the Yugoslav Desk for the U.S. State Department; Mario Nobilo, Croatia's U.N. Ambassador; my good friend Dr. Ante Čuvalo, Professor of History; and Ivan Mišić, Bosnia-Herzegovina's Deputy Ambassador to the U.N. The moderator for the event was a very popular Detroit area talk show host from WXYT Radio by the name of David Newman with whom I had become well acquainted. With the exception of Ambassador Nobilo, all the people on the symposium's panel proved to be of great assistance to me over the next few years. Nobilo never refused to help; I just never contacted him with a request to help with any project.

In 1992 I began to work for Newman as a correspondent for WXYT radio whenever I traveled to Croatia. Newman was supportive of both Croatia and Bosnia-Herzegovina and viewed the murdering of civilians by Serb forces and the Yugoslav Army as barbaric and criminal. It would be my job, as defined by Newman, to call into his talk show from Croatia and report what I saw and experienced from the ground, inside the country.

It was during one of those trips to Croatia in late February of 1993 that I decided to try and find a way to get into Sarajevo. It was clear from the start that this would not be easy since the city had been surrounded by the Serbs and already under siege for months.

My wife, Sandra, would probably say that I have a natural ability to maneuver my way around obstacles and find solutions to challenges. This concept is so deeply ingrained in Croatians, who over the centuries have perfected the art in order to survive various hostile dominations, that there is even a name for it in Croatian: *snađi se*. I wondered if this ability to overcome obstacles was a genetic trait inherited from my risk-taking grandfather.

The siege of Sarajevo began on April 5, 1992 and ended on February 29, 1996. During those four years the people endured incredible suffering, fear, hunger, rapes, murders, depravity, terror and torture at the hands of the perpetrators of the diabolic siege. By contrast, my encounters with the civilians of Sarajevo during the war has left me with an enduring hope for civilization in general. It was amazing to witness how the people of that city coped with life under siege by maintaining their civility, hospitality, strength, tenacity, bravery and kindness despite the horrors they were subjected to.

With the exception of a military tunnel dug underneath Sarajevo's airport several months into the war, the only people that could freely exit and enter the city during the siege were United Nations personnel, foreign government officials, journalists and humanitarian aid workers accredited through the United Nations. Until the summer of 1993 (when the U.N. took control of the airport) even these officials would only be allowed into Sarajevo if the Serb paramilitary and Yugoslav Army authorized it. Initially, the Serbs controlled the perimeter of Sarajevo as well as air traffic in and out of Sarajevo's bombed-out airport. This usually meant that the same Serbian forces that created the siege, were demanding a portion from every United Nations' shipment of food, gas, oil and medicine for themselves.

If the ransom was not paid, nothing would get to the suffering people of Sarajevo.

In preparation for my trip to Bosnia-Herzegovina, I traveled to New York City to meet with the Bosnian Ambassador to the United Nations Muhamed Sacirbey and the Deputy Ambassador Ivan Mišić. I drove to New York with a Bosnian friend from Detroit who was very active politically by the name of Nino Crnovršanin. He was a personal friend to both men. I explained that I would be taking video equipment with me into Sarajevo and that letters of introduction from them would be very helpful in fulfilling my objective to document the Serbian aggression against their country on film. Deputy Ambassador Mišić was kind enough to write a very complimentary letter asking all Bosnian government officials to assist me in any way that they could during my time in Bosnia-Herzegovina. That letter was essential in opening every door I knocked on for help. It read in part:

> *"We are asking the Republic of Bosnia and Herzegovina and the Republic of Croatia, to please assist Mr. Palaic in any way necessary, and to make his stay in both Republics as easy as possible, so as to allow him to complete his work."*

Nino was also very helpful in providing contacts inside Sarajevo. When word spread within Detroit's Bosnian community that I would be travelling to Sarajevo, many people with family members there approached me with requests to take money, food, medicine, vitamins and even chocolate bars to their loved ones if I was able to find a way to enter.

Believing I could somehow find a way to enter Sarajevo by land I made my way by bus down to Split, Croatia's second largest city on the coast, and eventually across the Bosnia-Herzegovina border to a town called Livno. This was in itself a little tricky, because the Maslenica bridge connecting mainland Croatia with its coast had been destroyed by the JNA. This required all cars and buses traveling to the coast to take a ferry to the island of Pag until a temporary pontoon bridge was built in Maslenica in July.

It wasn't just a coincidence, however, that I was going to Livno. I had heard that the former Argentine soldier Rodolfo Barrios Saavedra (a.k.a. Žuka), with whom I shared an apartment just over a year ago, was the new commander of Croatian military operations in Livno. Barrios had relieved then-Colonel Ante Gotovina who had just successfully led Operation Maslenica to liberate Northern Dalmatia and Lika from JNA control. Livno is situated just west of Sarajevo and East of Split and it seemed like a good steppingstone to enter deeper into Bosnia. Since I had known Žuka from the first day he arrived in Croatia, it seemed like the perfect place to go.

It was a very cold February afternoon when I arrived at Livno's military headquarters asking for Barrios, since I didn't know if they knew him by the name Žuka. One of the men on guard duty directed me to wait for him outside. I was aware that the Serbs had a sizeable bounty on his head, so it didn't surprise me when I was forced to wait for over a half hour in the cold at the back entrance. It was my gut feeling that I was being observed as I waited so Barrios could figure out who I was and why I asked for him by name.

Finally, one of his men approached and led me downstairs to what looked like a situation room. I was impressed with the level of professionalism that I observed in the room full of Croatian soldiers. The room was complete with a very large map covered with a tarp. I assumed the covered map was because of the stranger that was entering to speak with Barrios. That type of care to small details impressed me, especially because such attention to security wasn't always practiced in Croatia in those early days. I greeted Barrios in Spanish and reminded him that we both shared an apartment with our mutual friend Mario in Zagreb several months previously. Although Barrios spoke English well, I spoke in Spanish, because I knew the Croats around him would understand English and I wasn't sure if he wanted his people to know under what circumstances we met each other. It took a few seconds for him to remember and then his demeanor quickly changed from cold and cautious to friendly.

We spent the next couple of hours having lunch of Wiener schnitzel and beer at the nearby restaurant while I explained my plans to get into Sarajevo. He was a little shocked that I was trying to get into the city that so many were hoping to flee from. Barrios explained that Livno was right on the frontlines of the new war being waged by JNA forces in Bosnia-Herzegovina. He and his men had had several serious encounters just recently and his orders were to keep and defend all the territory under his command due to its strategic importance. He continued to say that he couldn't offer any assistance or manpower due to the present military situation and his orders. It was clear that Barrios was not hopeful of my chances of reaching Sarajevo. He suggested I find another way to enter the city. I thanked him for his honesty and then he told one of his soldiers to drive me over the snow-covered roads and back to Split. Three hours later I was back on Croatian territory drinking a coffee in the lobby of the Hotel Split not knowing what my next move would be.

The next morning, I observed something strange and unnerving as I was sitting in the lobby watching people come and go. There were small groups of bearded Middle Eastern looking men congregating in distant areas of the lobby. They were clearly trying their best to keep a low profile as they isolated themselves away from the places that most people flocked to – the bar. Was it possible that nobody else questioned why these young bearded Middle Easterners were in Split, a city with an international airport just a short distance from Muslim-dominated Bosnia-Herzegovina? The pieces began to fall into place as I continued to watch, however. Most of the military-age Croatian men in the hotel's lobby were in military camouflage uniforms except for me, the Middle Easterners and one other man who gave me every impression of being Bosnian, by his physical appearance and his demeanor. The Bosnian-looking man was very thin, and he seemed out of place in his oversized dirty clothes as he moved from table to table talking with the Middle Easterners. He also had the same look in his eyes as the young Croatian men I had observed months ago coming back from the frontlines at the beginning of Croatia's Homeland War.

After observing the activity that morning in the lobby, I came to theorize that the man was a Bosnian soldier who was in civilian clothes to maintain a low profile. Furthermore, the Bosnians were using Hotel Split as the pick-up point for the Middle Easterners, who were, in fact, Mujahedin fighters that were volunteering to fight on behalf of the Muslims in Bosnia as jihadists. As far-fetched as this may have seemed in February 1993, today we know that hundreds of Mujahedin did come to Bosnia to volunteer as foreign fighters. From American intelligence sources we also know that at least one hundred Mujahedin remained in Bosnia after the war; and today they enjoy Bosnian citizenship.

Going up to my room, I retrieved the letter that Deputy Ambassador Ivan Mišić had given me weeks before. The letter would serve as an icebreaker to introduce myself and at the same time it would allow me to ask the Bosnian to transport me into areas controlled by Bosnian forces. It should be remembered that Al-Qaeda was only created in 1988. What I didn't know, of course, was that Al-Qaeda would execute their first attack on New York City's Twin Towers just days later on February 26, 1993. Had I known what Al-Qaeda was capable of and that the very men that day in the lobby may have been Mujahedin fighters with Al-Qaeda, I would never have attempted to accompany them to Bosnia. But I had an unhealthy dose of ignorance, arrogance and naïveté; and so, I did.

Returning to the lobby with the letter in hand, I approached the Bosnian with a greeting and a handshake. His eyes revealed surprise and mistrust as I introduced myself. I could see him thinking, "Who is this? Does he know? Why is he greeting me? Are there others around me who know what I'm doing?" He had the look that police officers must witness when suspects are suddenly surprised with those magic words, "You're under arrest." But I was there to simply ask for a ride into Bosnia so I could eventually make my way into Sarajevo. His eyes grew wider as I spoke to him in my flawed Croatian revealing my American accent. Now, I could see, he really wanted to know what this American knew about his plans to transport his new Mujahedin fighters into Bosnia.

"Can I buy you something to drink," I asked. "No, I don't drink," was his response. "OK, he doesn't drink alcohol, maybe a practicing Muslim," I thought. "Or, he doesn't want the Middle Eastern guys to see him drink." I theorized. My experience with the Muslims of Bosnia was that the vast majority were secular Muslims and they all drank alcohol. "A coffee then," I persisted. The Bosnian was looking around nervously as we walked closer to the bar area where we took a seat in a couple of comfortable chairs next to a coffee table. As we waited for the waiter to bring our coffees, I handed him the letter typed on the letterhead of the Bosnia-Herzegovina Embassy. He began to relax as he read it and suddenly dropped his defenses. He understood that he wasn't in danger of being arrested. But he also became aware that he had been observed. He must have wondered who else was watching his activities.

As for me...I was too ignorant at the time to understand the personal risk of riding in a vehicle with Mujahedin fighters. The tension between Bosnian Muslims and Croatians fighting in areas controlled by the Croatian Defense Council (HVO) in Bosnia-Herzegovina had increased drastically in recent months. This tension, I would only later learn, was due in part to the murdering of some Croatian civilians by Mujahedin fighters. Clearly the Mujahedin did not view Croatians as allies against a common enemy, as the Bosnian Muslims did early in the war. The Mujahedin were jihadists that viewed the Croats as Christians and, therefore, infidels. The Croats and the Bosnians may have been neighbors at one time in the former Yugoslavia, and they may have been fighting a common war for freedom from a common aggressor, but the Mujahedin were there to kill Christian "infidels"- who were often civilians - in the name of Allah. This was just another fact that I was ignorant of as I drank coffee with the Bosnian and stupidly attempted to accompany him and a truck full of Mujahedin going to Bosnia.

Finally letting his guard down the Bosnian responded: "You see how many guys I am taking with me. I'm sorry, but I do not even have room for one more person in our truck. We are leaving today, and it is completely full." Nothing I could say further could get him to bend from that position. We made some further small talk about how the war was going before we said goodbye and went our separate ways. If I was ignorant regarding the danger of travelling with the Mujahedin, I was at least smart enough to realize that I had placed myself in some danger by revealing to them that I knew their plans. More caution would be required on my part until they actually left the hotel. Today I believe the only thing that prevented me from having a problem with the Bosnian or the Mujahedin he was smuggling, was the letter from Deputy Ambassador Mišić that confirmed to them that I was on their side. Later, once I did get into Sarajevo, my naïveté would be replaced with cynicism when I discovered that Croatians and the people of Bosnia-Hercegovina were fighting the JNA for very different reasons. But for the time being I believed in the ancient proverb: the enemy of my enemy is my friend.

Croatia's Ministry of Information had changed its name to the Croatian Information Center (CIC) some time in 1992. This name change was probably designed so it would sound more Western in tone and less like a department in the former Communist government. The CIC had a small office on the third floor of the Hotel Split and feeling disheartened over failing in my last two attempts to get into Sarajevo, I stumbled in to talk to Dado Lozančić, a volunteer working in the CIC office. Dado was a second-generation Croatian from the diaspora and was sitting behind the desk when I entered. He had come to Croatia during the Homeland War to offer his assistance by working in the CIC.

I remember that I came into the office wearing a green T-shirt and camouflage military pants because my civilian clothes were dirty. I showed him my press pass, but not knowing who I was, or why I was there, he advised me not to wear camouflage pants, because I may be confused with the military. I chose not to respond to his comment. During some casual banter I mentioned that I was intent on getting into Sarajevo, but had failed on two occasions to find a way in. He looked at me calmly and said, "Why don't you catch a U.N. flight? They leave every day." I thought he was joking at first. "What? Just fly into Sarajevo?" I asked disbelievingly. "Yeah, they fly in C-130 planes every day into Sarajevo. Sometimes they drop humanitarian supplies into Bosnian territory by parachute. All you need are U.N. press credentials." He went on to explain further: "Just have your editor fax over a request for credentials to the U.N. Press Office. Give them a photo for identification, and they'll give you a press pass. With that pass you can simply board the plane that departs Split daily for Sarajevo. The only thing that you will need that you probably don't have is a bulletproof vest. They require all journalist to have one. Do you have one?" I explained that I still had the vest that I brought with me initially in October 1991. "Then you're all set." It was unbelievable! Here I was trying to get into the city using a dangerous land route through the mountains and in the meantime accidently discovered that it was possible to simply fly into Sarajevo at the U.N.'s expense.

Armed with this new, incredible information, I contacted Patrick Sheehan, the producer for David Newman at WXYT Radio back in Detroit. Since I was acting as a consultant on the war in Croatia and Bosnia-Herzegovina for WXYT he was happy to fax over a letter to the United Nations Press Office in Croatia asking them to issue press credentials to me. I simply couldn't believe that it was that easy.

As I walked across the tarmac of the Split airport in the direction of the C-130 cargo plane departing for Sarajevo, I held my new United Nations identification card in hand and remembered how Petar Ivčec had used press credentials to impose himself on a press conference years earlier with President Ronald Reagan. I filed the information away to be used later upon my return to America when I would create a fake press agency ambitiously named Pan-National News Agency. For now, however, the plane I was boarding was destined for a city under siege that some described as a living hell.

City under Siege

Republic of Bosnia and Herzegovina
Permanent Mission to the United Nations
New York

February 12, 1993

Dear Sirs:

Mr. Michael Palaic, an American journalist and television producer, will be filming a documentary on the Serbian aggression in the Republics of Bosnia and Herzegovina and Croatia.

During the preparation of the film, Mr. Palaic will update an American radio station on both the military and political situation.

We are asking the Republic of Bosnia and Herzegovina and the Republic of Croatia, to please assist Mr. Palaic in any way necessary, and to make his stay in both Republics as easy as possible, so as to allow him to complete his work.

Thank you,

Ivan Z. Misic
Ivan Z. Misic
Ambassador
Deputy Permanent Representative

P.O. Box 1896 • New York, NY 10163 • Phone (212) 867-6743 • Fax (212) 867-5416

Embassy letter requesting cooperation

Author with Commander Rudolfo Barrios Saavedra (a.k.a. Žuka) in Livno, BiH, 1993

U.N. press credentials for fictitious Pan-National News Agency

10

Welcome to Sarajevo!

AS THE C-130 WAS taxing for takeoff one of the guys from the French Air Force (the plane and pilots were French) informed me that prior to landing in Sarajevo we would have to drop off a good portion of the plane's cargo that was stacked on rolling pallets in the center of the plane. Our takeoff was relatively routine and about twenty minutes into the flight the back ramp of the massive plane opened and was lowered like a giant metal tongue. The pallets of humanitarian goods were on wheels and one-by-one the cargo began rolling towards the back of the plane where it eventually rolled right off the ramp and out into the sky below. I was fascinated with how quickly it was done. The weight of the moving goods transferred vibrations to the soles of my feet as the plane spewed out its precious cargo to the ground below. One of the crewmen who had just pushed the rolling bundles off the back of the plane disconnected his safety line and informed me that we would soon be making our descent for landing in Sarajevo. He advised me that it would be a good idea to take off my bulletproof vest that the U.N. required journalists to wear and sit on it rather than wear it. The thought was that a Serb bullet fired at the plane could penetrate the bottom of the plane's fuselage and, therefore, sitting on the vest would be more effective than wearing it. As if that wasn't enough, he warned me that it would be a very steep descent, because the Serb forces below would often shoot at planes approaching the airport's runway. A steep descent would offer the Serb forces a smaller target over a shorter period of time. The airman was right: it was the steepest descent that I had ever experienced. I had the uncanny sensation that the plane was in a free-falling nose-dive. It was unsettling due to the immense size of the plane, but the landing went fine and as far as I know we did not take any direct fire that day.

After more than twenty-five years I can still vividly recall the feeling of disorientation associated with experiencing the sudden and dramatic difference between the relative peace of the Croatian city of Split in February of 1993, which I had just left, and my first experience of Sarajevo under siege. It took me a while to come to grips with the fact that only forty-five minutes ago I was drinking a beer in Split's airport lounge, and now, as I walked off the ramp of the C-130 plane, I was looking at the bombed-out airport and the plumes of smoke from exploding mortars in the distance. There wasn't a single window left intact in what was left of the airport. Sandbags were piled high and spread sporadically around the empty terminal building. Soldiers driving forklifts quickly scurried between the building and the airplane parked on the tarmac: they were removing what was left of the C-130's cargo quickly, because U.N. personnel at the airport also came under sniper fire at times.

The first stop was a small office where a U.N. officer standing behind a counter checked my passport and credentials. "Do you want me to stamp your passport?" he asked. Assuming it was some official stamp, I replied, "Yes." Later when I looked closer at the passport, I could see the humorous red stamp he had used which read: "MAYBE AIRLINES."

He directed me to a spot just off the edge of the tarmac to wait. There was a three-sided wall of sandbags stacked about shoulder high meant to offer protection in case of mortar or sniper fire. Someone, in an attempt to be humorous, had placed a sign outside the sandbags that read in English "Taxi." In addition to providing general protection, this is where the white UNPROFOR armored personnel carriers (APCs) would pick up recent arrivals and transport them across hostile Serb-occupied territory to another U.N. building situated between the airport and the city. The building was about three kilometers outside Sarajevo and served as offices for the U.N. and as a transfer station for U.N. soldiers, journalists and humanitarian aid workers.

Crossing the area controlled by Serbian forces could still be potentially dangerous, in spite of the thick armor plating of the APC. Just one month before I arrived, the Deputy Prime Minister for Bosnia-Herzegovina, Hakija Turajlić, was in a similar APC bearing the blue U.N. insignia just 500 meters from the airport exit when the vehicle was stopped by two tanks and a contingent of about forty Serbian soldiers. The three French U.N. soldiers escorting the government official were ordered to hand over Turajlić. After a stand-off of almost two hours, one of the Serbian soldiers simply raised his rifle and began shooting into the back door of the APC. The shots instantly killed Turajlić; the Serb gunmen fled the scene and the French soldiers remained frozen in place unable to return fire. Such was the "courage" of the U.N. Protective Forces that would be on display again in July 1995 when the Serbs under General Mladić massacred eight thousand Bosnian men and boys in Srebrenica - all under the watchful eye of Dutch UNPROFOR soldiers.

In fact, there was no area of Sarajevo that was not extremely dangerous in February of 1993. No matter where a person went, they were exposed to sniper fire, mortar rounds or both. The risk of being killed was not limited to adults. Children playing or carrying water by sled through the snow-covered streets were also targets.

The Sarajevans developed a particular running technique whenever they were forced to sprint across a particularly dangerous intersection. Their shoulders would rise as their heads retracted downward. Men and women alike would sprint hunched over across the street with bent knees and making short strides. The strategy was to become a smaller target for the snipers, but, unfortunately, that also made them a much slower-moving target. Residents developed favorite routes that were thought to be safer than others when traversing from one part of town to the other. Some thought there were times of the day when it was safer. Mornings were preferred by some who theorized that the Serb snipers would still be sleeping off their hangovers from a late night of drinking and would, therefore, be less likely to shoot at the civilians below. If they did try to shoot, the hope was that they would be less accurate early in the morning.

One quickly learned that the best way to avoid sniper fire was to avoid streets that offered a view of one of the surrounding mountains, where the Serbian snipers cowardly positioned their sniper rifles. Various people gave valuable advice on how to travel through the city: they would say that if you couldn't see the mountain, then the snipers couldn't see you through their riflescopes. Crossing intersections and bridges, however, made it impossible to avoid some sniper fire. So-called "soldiers" in the mountains firing on the civilians below killed many people in this way.

Avoiding views of the mountain was a practice that I personally followed once I made it to the city. Intersections were, however, a major problem: some were so wide that no matter how fast of a runner one was, even an unskilled sniper could hit his civilian target. It was across these intersections that large steel plates were erected jutting out from each side of the intersection. The intersections were so wide, however, that the protective plates did not meet in the middle of the street. This resulted in a large gap that people still had to sprint past. The protective plates saved many lives - mine included on at least one memorable occasion - but unfortunately the older and slower people were not always so fortunate. The interesting thing was that when the steel plate saved your life, you knew it. The sniper bullet makes a very distinct sound when it hits a steel plate. In fact, the pinging sound of a bullet hitting steel as you run past actually signals which part of your body the bullet would have hit had the cowardly sniper hit his mark. On one occasion that distinct pinging rang out right next to my right ear just a fraction of a second after I successfully stepped within the protection of the steel plate.

Back at the airport, however, I knew that the airport itself and the surrounding territory were under the complete control of Serbian forces, so I decided to wait outside in the safety of the sandbags at the APC "taxi stand" rather than seek the shelter and warmth of a small nearby building. Remaining in a spot that was observed by U.N. personnel seemed like the wisest option. It was a bone-chilling day in February, so after waiting in the freezing cold for over a half hour, my need to find warmth overcame my desire for safety. Against my better judgment, I moved in the direction of a small makeshift building standing just off the runway in search of warmth.

As I entered, I saw that the small building was being used as a temporary office by Serb forces. Glancing around, I saw that all soldiers had the emblem of the so-called "Serbian Krajina" on their shoulders. It was easy to see that I was the only non-Serbian in the building. "Oh, crap," I thought to myself. "Why did I have to come in here?" I didn't see a single U.N. soldier or official. But it was too late to turn around and exit the building without arousing suspicion. I remained close to the door where there was a heater on the wall. Standing in front of the heater, I took my gloves off and began a theatrical show of warming my hands in an attempt to let them know that I was just there in search of warmth. One Serbian officer came from around the counter to speak to me as he continued eating a banana. I would later learn that the citizens being held under siege hadn't seen a banana or any other fruit in many months. He was wearing a traditional military cap worn by Serbian forces called a *šajkača*. "Where are you from?" he asked. He spoke American English so well that I quickly concluded that he had spent many years in America at some point in his life. "America." I answered. He took the I.D. badge clipped to my coat between his thumb and forefinger. Looking at my UNPROFOR press pass he asked, "Palaich, what kind of name is that?" Here I was, face-to-face with this Serbian officer who had total control over the area I found myself in, and I was completely isolated from any UNPROFOR personnel. "Why didn't I just stay outside in the cold wind?" I thought to myself.

I immediately realized the seriousness of the situation and my mind temporarily froze: I knew the dangers of being questioned by a Serbian officer on his turf, and because I had many times in the past been in difficult situations, I was able to recognize the early warning signs of the body's natural reaction to fight-or-flight situations. By the time I found myself face-to-face with this enemy in Sarajevo's airport in February 1993, I had already been involved in the Croatian independence movement close to fifteen years. One might view that period as on-the-job training for what was to come later during the War for Croatian Independence. During that training period I had smuggled everything from revolutionary audio and video tapes to weapons destined for Croatia. The fear one feels when being questioned by Customs Agents as you're smuggling weapons across international borders is real. During my early political life, F.B.I. Agents questioned me many times asking why I had committed some crime that they were investigating and which they thought I had knowledge of. That kind of abrupt question always came out of the blue and followed some pleasant conversation that was intended to lower a person's defenses and catch them by surprise. By the time the war in Bosnia-Herzegovina started I also had the experience of being interrogated by German Federal Agents following my arrest in

Germany and by the U.S. Federal Agents who had executed the search of my home the year before.

This was different, however. This time I was in the middle of a war zone controlled by the enemy, being questioned by an officer of that enemy's army. This time the Serbian officer standing before me had the power to take my life if he wanted to. There were no rules in this war – not with this enemy. So, trying very hard to appear nonchalant, I responded to the question of my nationality by saying: "I'm not sure actually, you know how we Americans are, we're all mixed up with different nationalities...Poles, Germans, Irish, Czechs." I was thankful that my grandfather had changed the spelling of our family name from Palaić to Palaich when he came to America. The H was often added to the end of such a name at the beginning of the twentieth century in America so that Americans would be more likely to pronounce it correctly. The name change was just subtle enough to put some doubt into the mind of my Serbian questioner. I'm not sure if he believed me, but while he was pondering my response, the phone on the desk behind the counter rang. As he went back around the counter to answer it, I moved closer to the entrance and quickly left the shelter relieved that no future conversations with the Serb would be necessary. A white APC arrived for my pick-up within ten minutes. I threw my bag into the back of the APC, stepped up and crouched through the small opening to grab a bench seat along the side of the vehicle. The only other person in the APC on this occasion was a large, muscular bald-headed man with a French passport who was travelling with Humanitarian Aid Worker documents. He also spoke Bosnian and was a caricature of someone you would expect to see in an action movie about The French Foreign Legion. It was clear to me that he was a volunteer who had returned home to help his people in some sort of military capacity – perhaps training.

When we arrived at the U.N. transfer building, we bailed out of the small armor-plated hatch door and went our separate ways. The transfer station was about three kilometers from the city, if I remember correctly. That meant eventually begging for a ride from one of the very rare drivers still brave enough to dash down the dangerous streets of Sarajevo. We were the only car on the snowy streets that day. He dropped me off just outside the city's center. The amount of utter devastation inflicted on this once-beautiful old city with one foot in the Austro-Hungarian and the other in the Byzantine Empire was heartbreaking: bombed-out crumbling buildings, blackened shells of burned-out cars, buses and kiosks, and almost no sign of life in the streets.

Not knowing the city, I don't recall where I was dropped off to this day. What I do remember was being weighed down with two full duffle bags and being greeted immediately by sniper fire. The bags were filled mostly with items that Bosnian friends and others asked me to take to their respective family members living in Sarajevo. Running under sniper fire is dangerous in itself, I learned, but being weighed down with duffle bags made it near-suicidal. I was torn between dropping the bags, whose contents meant so much to the recipients, and taking my chances with the load I was carrying in hope that the Serbs shooting at me were just bad shots. Welcome to Sarajevo!

It was not the first time I experienced the dangers of sniper fire. Serbian snipers had also been common in Osijek when I was there in 1991, or in Karlovac if one meandered close to the Drava and Korana rivers that served as the geographical borders between Serb-occupied zones and Croatian-controlled areas. But Sarajevo was a completely different situation: at times, and depending on where you were in the city, sniper fire in Sarajevo could be so intense that it appeared as if the sky was raining bullets.

Another interesting dilemma I had while dodging sniper fire in Sarajevo was this: should a person run in a straight line or zigzag while being fired on? On many occasions while running in a straight line, a bullet would wiz past my head by what seemed like centimeters. The bullets were so close, in fact, that I can still remember the sound they made as they travelled past my head. Some sounded as if they were tumbling in mid-air.

Running in a straight line would logically seem to give the snipers an easier target; but since the bullets were passing by my head so closely, I wondered if they would have hit me if I had been running in a zigzag pattern instead? I didn't remember much from my geometry classes in school, but I knew the shortest distance between two points was a straight line. I finally decided that the best way to seek cover was by the shortest route and, therefore, opted for the straight-line approach. I also chose not to use the duck-and-crouch method employed by so many Sarajevans. My goal was to get across the street as fast as possible: zigzagging and crouching would just slow me down.

This method seemed to serve me well, until one day just outside of the Holiday Inn Hotel. There was a rather large open field there, which must have been grass-covered prior to the war. At the time, however, it was overgrown with weeds, and the overgrowth hid the fact that the field was pockmarked with small craters left by the exploded mortars. Running as fast as I could in a straight line for the protection of the buildings in the distance, I stepped into one of those mortar holes and partially tore the meniscus in my right knee. It was an injury that would leave me hobbled for the rest of my time in Sarajevo and eventually require two surgeries in subsequent years. The knee pain continues to serve as a thankful reminder of the only injury I acquired during the wars in Croatia and Bosnia-Herzegovina.

My Detroit friend Nino Crnovršanin was kind enough to give me the name and address of his cousin Nidžara Šarenkapa, who lived in Sarajevo with her elderly parents. Nino gave me a letter of introduction for the family asking them to give me a place to stay while I was in Sarajevo. Thankfully, the family agreed. I will never forget the generous hospitality that this devout Muslim family showed to this unannounced stranger who appeared at their doorstep one day out of nowhere.

When I materialized at this Muslim family's door in the middle of the siege, there was, of course, very little food, other than what they could bargain for with their neighbors. In order to get the water they needed for drinking, washing themselves and their clothes, and flushing their toilets, they had to walk three kilometers or more under sniper fire. Children's sleighs would often be used to carry the heavy jugs over snow-covered streets. In the summer, if they were lucky enough to have them, people used small wagons to transport the water. Often times, however, individuals would have to traverse the dangerous route from home to the central watering station on foot, carrying the jugs by hand. Not only were the roads leading to and from the watering locations dangerous because of sniper attacks, but the locations themselves came under sniper and mortar fire by Serbian aggressors who fired on civilians standing in line for their chance to get some water for their families. The image of elderly men, women and children coming under sniper fire will forever be etched into my memory. Sadly, many of them became victims because they could not run fast enough to reach safety. They were killed and left to lay in the intersection - sometimes for days - until their corpses could be removed safely.

The tenacity of one such old woman was on display one unusually sunny day as she attempted to cross what was left of one of the bridges across the Miljacka River carrying a jug of water in each hand. All that remained of the bridge were the steel support beams on which the old lady was balancing herself with one water jug in each hand as if she was part of some sort of dangerous circus act. The bridge's concrete had long since been blown away by Serbian mortars and now the running water of the river could be seen flowing below. As the sniper's bullets were whizzing past her from behind and ricocheting off the beams, she began to curse their mothers defiantly over her shoulder. Of course, the snipers, who were probably shooting at her from over 1,000 meters away, didn't hear a single word of her profanity-laced invectives, but the incident provided insight into the tenacity and resolve of the population. The old lady had just walked a couple of kilometers to retrieve water for her family and no cowardly sniper was going to make her drop the precious cargo destined for her family – even if it meant risking her life.

On another occasion I witnessed a profound example of bravery that demonstrated the better side of human nature, while at the same time forcing me to face my own personal character flaws. While crossing a park, a group of civilians and I came under sniper fire once again. A man of about forty-five and I ran for the protection of a nearby doorway. As we huddled inside as deep as we could to avoid being shot, we turned to face the street that we had just crossed. We both witnessed a slow-moving old lady that was pulling a sled with several plastic jugs of water. As she attempted to pull the sled across the street and head for the safety of the building's doorway, the steel rails of the sled got stuck on a bare section of cement that was showing through on the snow-covered street. She pulled on the sleigh's rope again, but the sled was too heavy due to the weight of her precious cargo. We began to yell at her, *"Pusti to! Pusti to!"* (Leave it! Leave it!), but she simply refused to drop the rope. She seemed oblivious to the many bullets whizzing all around her and ricocheting off the sidewalk and the wall of the building we were hiding behind. Nothing we said could make her drop the rope and join us in the safety of the doorway.

At that distressing moment, I was forced to come face-to-face with my own cowardice. Yes, I could have stepped away from the doorway and quickly grabbed the rope from the old lady. I could have pulled the sleigh over the exposed portion of cement. She was only ten or fifteen feet away from me. The thought actually crossed my mind for one second until the more rational side of me overruled the idea as foolish. "If she places more importance on water than her own life, then that's her problem," I thought to myself. "Why should I put myself at risk for her water?" Thankfully, the stranger at my side had no such thoughts of self-preservation. Seeing that there was no way the woman would let go of the rope, and with sniper fire all around, he selflessly ran out to the woman, grabbed the rope and pulled both her and her precious water to safety. I learned that day that even during the most brutal of wars, examples of human kindness, bravery and civility could still be witnessed.

The need for water cannot be overemphasized when talking about a city under siege. Until I experienced this personally, I had no idea just how much water a family needs and uses for all types of daily activity. Anyone living with unlimited amounts of water available by simply turning on the faucet in their home is bound to take water for granted. The people of Sarajevo also took their water supply for granted prior to the siege as they watched the nightly news programs showing the devastation inflicted on their neighbors living in Croatia. Most believed at the time that war would never come to them.

The last thing that Nidžara and her family needed, or wanted, under those circumstances was an additional person to feed and with whom to share their precious water. But they never failed to graciously offer their uninvited guest something to eat and drink. Knowing how precious each drop of water was, I felt compelled to use it as efficiently as possible. This required first washing with a single cup of water, then brushing one's teeth with that same cup of water and, finally, rinsing the toilet with what water was left over. In spite of begging Nidžara and her family to let me make the almost daily trek to the watering station to replenish their reserve, they always refused my help. Their desire to show hospitality, while at the same time protecting me, was greater than their fear of making the dangerous trek themselves. Nidžara's elderly father would continue to lug his five-liter water jugs through the dangerous thoroughfares of the city under siege for three more years.

I was dumbfounded to learn that Nidžara could have left the living hell in which she found herself at any time. She had lived in Australia prior to the war and was married to an Australian citizen. She was herself an Australian citizen. Because of the loyalty she felt toward her aging parents, however, she courageously chose to remain in Sarajevo rather than leave her mother and father to fend for themselves.

As if the shortage of water and food wasn't bad enough, one quickly realized there was also a shortage of wood. The old city's streets and parks that were full of trees prior to the war were almost all bare by the time I arrived that winter in 1993. It wasn't uncommon to see people in desperate need to provide heat for their families searching through the parks with a saw or axe in their hands looking for remnants of trees once in abundance. Most of the trees had already been scavenged, so this meant chopping up the few centimeters of remaining tree stumps left protruding out of the snow-covered ground. Walking down some of the narrower streets of the city one could also hear the sound of wood scavengers tearing up parquet wood floors from homes that had long ago been abandoned. This wood flooring would be used for heating or traded for other goods like food. Scavenging for wood in the winter became as important as searching for water and food. Humans can become very creative when it comes to surviving, and the people of Sarajevo perfected the art of survival during the siege.

Many of the people living in the center of Sarajevo lived (or should I say survived) in modern high-rise apartment buildings before and during the siege. As in other big cities, the modern apartments in Sarajevo did not have fireplaces and wood-burning stoves. Some enterprising men with access to welders and pieces of steel discovered that they could fill a demand for wood burning stoves among residents of high-rise apartments who no longer had central heating. Most apartment dwellers acquired these small handcrafted stoves that they would place in the living room with a horizontal stove pipe extending through the middle of an outside wall where a painting had once hung. It was very common to observe smoke billowing out of many such stove pipes that protruded through the façade of apartment buildings, which resembled a gray-faced adolescent pockmarked with some kind of grotesque acne.

The Bakalović family was one family that had incorporated this old yet creative heating method in their modern apartment building when Nidžara introduced me to them in the winter of 1993.

Hasan Bakalović was a federal judge who lived in the apartment with his wife, Mira, and daughter Sejla. His son, Nino, was lucky enough to have moved to America as a foreign exchange student before the siege began. It was difficult for me to believe that the family could be living in such terrible conditions of deprivation and yet be so warm and welcoming to a stranger from America that had unexpectedly dropped into their lives. On that particular first encounter it was a very cold day in February. As I said, firewood was in both short supply and high demand, but that did not prevent Hasan from generously making a fire with the treasured pieces of wood in honor of his new American visitor. And as if that wasn't hospitable enough, he insisted I take his chair positioned closest to the stove. Eventually, when wood from parquet floors ran out and things got really desperate, Hasan and Mira were forced to burn the precious books from the family library for heat. That must have been particularly distressing for this highly educated couple.

My first official stop after arriving in Sarajevo that winter was an office of the Bosnian Army located in the basement of the bombed-out Executive Council Building, commonly referred to as the Parliament building. The high-rise twin-towered building was one of the first Serbian targets at the beginning of the siege. Several of the floors above had been bombed and engulfed in flames. The result was that the building was completely uninhabitable, except for the basement which was used by the military. A Bosnian soldier standing guard outside escorted me through the maze of passages dripping with water from the snowy floors above. The experience was like walking through some kind of Mad Max movie. We traversed through puddles of water, falling concrete and loose water pipes dangling from the ceilings above the passageways. Finally, I was met by a couple of soldiers and one sitting at a desk in the hallway. I presented the letter from Deputy Ambassador Mišić, which he read prior to typing my information on an invaluable Bosnian Army Press Pass. The press credentials proved instrumental in getting an exclusive interview with a captured Serbian War Criminal named Borislav Herak. Herak had just pleaded guilty to committing war crimes against Bosnian civilians. When I interviewed him, he was awaiting sentencing and asking to be executed.

In search of water in a city under siege

Serbian checkpoint outside Sarajevo

Author with Bosnian soldiers in Sarajevo 1993

Welcome to Sarajevo!

Author waiting at U.N. transfer station outside Sarajevo

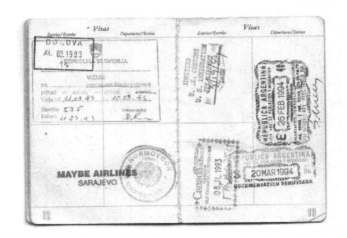

Author's passport stamp from U.N. (bottom left)

11

Looking in the Eyes of a War Criminal

THE STORY OF BORISLAV Herak first came to my attention via Gordana Knezević and Kemal Kurspahić, two of the brave editors for a Bosnian newspaper called *Oslobođenje*. *Oslobođenje* was operating out of a small office in the heart of Sarajevo after its original building was bombed by Serbian/Yugoslav Army artillery at the beginning of the siege. It was a shock for me to be greeted by a picture of Tito hanging prominently on the wall of *Oslobođenje*'s office as I entered. For most Croats, Tito had become the symbol of Yugoslav oppression. Before the dissolution of Yugoslavia, Tito's picture could also be found hanging on every government office wall and even on the walls of shops in Croatia. Removing Tito's picture, however, was one of the first acts of Croatian defiance, even before Croatians officially declared independence from Yugoslavia in May 1991. Nobody in Croatia during the

Homeland War would have even thought about publicly displaying Tito's image like the Bosnians were fond of doing. One personal friend of mine in Croatia ordered a shopkeeper to remove Tito's picture from his wall and hand it over to him just to make sure it didn't reappear after he left the store. It was disconcerting to see Tito's picture hanging in the offices of a major Bosnian newspaper in a city under siege.

This was my first glimpse into the differences that existed between Croatians and Bosnians regarding the war they were in with the JNA. Both Bosnia and Croatia had a common enemy in the JNA and both countries had a bloody war of aggression thrust upon them after declaring independence from Yugoslavia. However, Croatia had a long history of fighting for independence from the various oppressors that had dominated them historically. Communist Yugoslavia was just the most recent regime in a long list of occupiers. It was both disheartening and significant to discover that Bosnians Muslims had a much different view of Tito and Yugoslavia.

According to George Kenney, the former Head of the Yugoslav Desk for the U.S. State Department, Bosnia was reluctant to declare independence from Yugoslavia. I interviewed Kenney, who had just resigned in protest over the U.S. policy toward Bosnia-Herzegovina, in September 1992 in the offices of the Woodrow Wilson Institute for Peace in Washington, D.C. According to Kenney, the U.N. pressured Bosnia-Herzegovina to declare independence before the summer of 1992, or they would lose any chance of U.N. recognition. Bosnia-Herzegovina's president, Alija Izetbegović, ultimately succumbed (reluctantly) to the pressure, held a referendum and declared independence from Yugoslavia on March 3, 1992. The JNA and Serbian paramilitary began bombing the city of Sarajevo on April 6, 1992.

Trying not to focus on the picture of Tito hanging on the wall, I listened as Knezević informed me that there was a Serbian soldier that had been captured by Bosnian forces when he accidentally crossed the front lines with another JNA soldier.

His name was Borislav Herak, and he was captured in the suburb of Sarajevo called Vogošća with Sretko Damjanović. Both soldiers were operating in the so-called "Serbian Krajina" region of Bosnia-Herzegovina. Knezević further explained that Herak had already pleaded guilty to war crimes, but that she could arrange for me to interview him in the Bosnian military headquarters where he was being held until his sentencing. Of course, I jumped at the opportunity and rushed to the headquarters with my video camera. A translator supplied by *Oslobođenje* accompanied me.

To get to the Viktor Bubanj military barracks required getting access to one of the few cars operating during the war. Few people were able to acquire the very precious gasoline during the siege. Even if they managed to get their hands on it, the snipers made driving through the streets very dangerous. Therefore, with the exception of debris and bombed-out vehicles left from previous attacks, the streets were void of vehicles and people. The driver informed me that it would be necessary to take the Maršal Tito Boulevard, the main artery that the locals had ominously come to refer to as "Sniper Alley".

Based on the way he drove, it was obvious that the driver expected to be fired on at any moment. Dodging bombed-out cars and other debris, we drove at neck-break speeds and at times it felt as though the car was swerving so quickly that only two tires were in contact with the pavement as we sped to our destination.

We were escorted to a large office within the headquarters and were directed to take a seat at one side of a rectangular table. We were informed that Herak would be brought to us from his cell momentarily. The translator and I passed the time talking as I tried not to be distracted by yet another picture of Tito placed prominently on the wall facing me. Within ten minutes the office door opened, and I got my first glance of the convicted war criminal Borislav Herak.

Herak was a lanky young man of twenty-two born on January 18, 1971. His black hair was cut awkwardly short at uneven lengths. I imagined that someone without barbering skills had just arbitrarily used shears to chop away his excess hair. The result gave this already gaunt young man the appearance of a younger and skinnier version of Frankenstein's monster. His face had large pores and an ashen complexion. To add to this image, his shoes were missing shoelaces and were obviously too big for his feet. As he shuffled to the chair across from me, I saw that his coat was at least two sizes too small.

It was clear to me even before he entered the room that I may have trouble with my own emotions during the interview. I was prepared, however, to do what was necessary and conceal any obvious revulsion that I may feel while questioning him. I wasn't so sure, however, about my female translator. She confided in me prior to the interview that she personally had family members that were killed by Serbian irregulars during the war. I knew that we would be discussing his role in the murders and rapes of young Bosnian women and I was concerned that she may break down at some point as Herak recalled details of his crimes. Both of us introduced ourselves making sure that we did not shake his hand. Maintaining an air of professional detachment was one thing, but shaking the hand of an admitted mass murderer and rapist was unthinkable.

The interview began by establishing the standard facts: name, age, place of birth and where he grew up. Herak was a Serb born in Sarajevo. He was born and lived his entire life in Sarajevo. He explained that he had many Muslim and Croatian friends while growing up. It was impossible to spend one's entire life growing up in multi-cultural Sarajevo during Yugoslavia without having friends and schoolmates, and even family members, from the other ethnic groups. That all changed in 1992, when the JNA was forced out of Croatia as a result of negotiations between Croatia and Yugoslavia. The JNA forces evacuated from much of Croatia, taking with them the military equipment they would need to continue their quest to occupy yet another neighbor's land and incorporate it into a "Greater Serbia."

Herak explained that prior to the siege of Sarajevo, the Serbs living in that historical city were encouraged to evacuate the city for the area that Serbs to this day refer to as "Serbian Krajina." Herak stated matter-of-factly that the Serbs choosing to remain behind in Sarajevo would be viewed as the enemy and would be treated as such by both Serbian paramilitary forces and the JNA. Herak stated that for this reason he deserted Sarajevo with the other Serbs for the neighboring hills prior to the siege.

This was not the first time that Sarajevo would experience this extreme form of Serbian nationalism. The assassination of Archduke Franz Ferdinand, less than eighty years previously, had sparked the outbreak of WWI. On June 28, 1914 delusional members of a Serbian nationalist group operating in Sarajevo, The Black Hand, assassinated Ferdinand in hopes of unifying Bosnia with Greater Serbia. The war of aggression perpetrated against Croatia and Bosnia-Herzegovina in the 1990s was rooted in the same fantasy of Greater Serbia that led to the assassination of Archduke Ferdinand. Borislav Herak was a minor pawn in the same doomed idea. Unlike Gavrilo Princip, who murdered a head of state, Herak and his Serbian comrades would try to realize their objective by murdering men, women and children who had been former neighbors.

Herak admitted to getting his murderous start in May of 1992 when he succumbed to his cousin's pleadings to leave Sarajevo for the village of Ilijaš, a suburb of Sarajevo. It was in Ilijaš that he joined the Serbian irregular forces and received a salary and a house formerly belonging to a Muslim family. The initial training that he received for his future job of "cleansing" (a term synonymous with genocide and ethnic cleansing) was to slit the throats of pigs. The killing of pigs was a tactic used by his superiors to desensitize the new recruits, many of whom were former city dwellers like Herak. They would eventually be ordered to murder people using similar methods.

Exploding mortars and machine gun fire continued outside as we sat in the office listening to Herak describe the first order he received after joining the Serbian paramilitary group called the Romanija Corps. That first order was to "cleanse" a village of every living non-Serb. Herak said the order came from his commander, Ratko Adžić. Herak's group of new recruits joined with other paramilitary groups like the White Eagles and Chetniks as well as platoons from the JNA barracks in Rajlovac to carry out the grisly task. Herak remembered that his order from Adžić was, "Kill everyone and burn all the houses." Herak related that he had personally taken part in the murdering of civilians that day in addition to raping any young girls that he could find. He committed the murders using his machine gun, but he recalled observing some of the Chetniks killing with knives while they sang Chetnik songs, swearing at their victims through pursed lips. Herak estimates that they slaughtered one hundred and fifty people that day in Vogošća. This number included men, women, children and even babies. After the slaughter, Herak recalls taking the bodies to the town of Reljevo where they were dumped into a mass grave.

I questioned Herak extensively on his involvement in the rape camp called "Sonja." The rape camp was situated in Vogošća – the first village that Herak had "cleansed." In 2011, Angelina Jolie directed an award-winning film called *In the Land of Blood and Honey* that depicted the Camp Sonja located in a former hotel. While the film does its best to accurately portray the suffering experienced by the poor captive women of Camp Sonja, it could not detail all the inhumane crimes committed within its walls. According to the testimony of Borislav Herak there were approximately sixty women being held captive in the rape camp at any one time. The Serbian forces of all kinds, including JNA military police, would use the women as their own personal sex objects. Herak claims that his commander ordered the entire Romanija Corps to go to the camp and rape the women claiming it would be a "morale builder." On one occasion he recalled taking women outside and shooting them in the head. On top of the nausea I felt at his recollections, what left me speechless was Herak's claim that he also saw United Nations Peacekeepers frequenting the camp.

Herak claimed that not only did the U.N. Peacekeepers take part in eating roasted lamb, courtesy of the camp's manager Miro Vuković, but that they also took part in raping the women held captive in the camp. Herak went even further to say that he personally observed U.N. General Lewis MacKenzie, who was named Chief of Staff for the United Nations Peacekeeping Forces (UNPROFOR) in 1992, leaving Camp Sonja with a young girl that he placed in an armored personnel carrier parked outside the camp.

One of Borislav Herak's defense attorneys, who I came to know while in Sarajevo, told me on several occasions that he had video footage in his possession of General MacKenzie at Camp Sonja. If the tape ever did exist, it was never released. While there is no proof that General MacKenzie personally took part in any wrongdoing during the siege of Sarajevo, in 1993 he did admit to Pulitzer Prize winner Roy Gutman, that he was on the payroll of a pro-Serbian propaganda organization SERBNET. Gutman would break the story in *Newsday* on June 23, 1993. Gutman additionally wrote that Mackenzie was under contract with SERBNET while he was giving expert testimony in front of the U.S. House Armed Services Committee in May of 1993. The congressional committee was not aware at the time of the testimony that Mackenzie had a financial arrangement with SERBNET. But an anonymous U.N. official quoted by Gutman in the article said: "We quite frankly are displeased with his lack of judgment." When asked about the perceived conflict of interest, MacKenzie stated: "My position is always one of objectivity because I don't blame only the Serbs." However, the positions taken by MacKenzie during his speaking tour were in direct conflict with the U.N. position that the Serbs were overwhelmingly responsible for the mass killings, rapes and ethnic cleansing. Although he would not say how much money he was paid by SERBNET, MacKenzie has subsequently claimed that he donated the payments to the Canadian Foundation for AIDS Research.

Herak ultimately pleaded guilty to personally murdering 32 civilians (including women and children) and raping twelve women and girls. One girl he admitted to raping and killing was only twelve years old. He reported that he shot her in the back of the head when he finished using her like an object of his sadistic pleasure.

The feeling of revulsion I felt for Herak still stays with me more than two decades later. It was difficult to sit across from this admitted war criminal as he recounted the murders and rapes he committed while he chain-smoked cigarettes that were ironically given to him by the young Bosnian woman assisting me with the translation. It took quite a bit of self-restraint to continue the interview and not jump across the table at him. When I watch the videotaped interview today, the pauses in my follow-up questions reveal just how emotionally affected I became while listening to the twenty-two-year-old recount details of his bloodthirsty rampage in the idyllic Sarajevo countryside in 1992.

On my return to America in March 1993, and before Roy Gutman published his article on General MacKenzie, I contacted Gutman by phone. We talked about the accusations against MacKenzie and the U.N. Peacekeepers. Gutman acknowledged that he had heard the same rumors. He also informed me that the U.N. had conducted an investigation into the charges of wrongdoing against UNPROFOR soldiers at Camp Sonja, but the U.N. refused to release any information regarding the findings of the investigation.

By this time, I had developed a good relationship with Muhamed Sacirbey, Bosnia's Ambassador to the U.N., so I called him regarding the accusations. Surely, I thought, the Bosnian government would be fully informed by the United Nations regarding the serious crimes being committed on Bosnian soil by UNPROFOR soldiers. It was shocking to hear his answer: "The U.N. won't release any information about the case against the UNPROFOR soldiers, the charges or the judgment - even to us." It was becoming clearer to me why the people of Bosnia-Herzegovina were beginning to hold the U.N. and UNPROFOR in such contempt.

In March of 1993, Borislav Herak and Sretko Damjanović were found guilty of genocide, war crimes against civilians and war crimes against prisoners of war. They were both sentenced to death. In his taped interview with me, Herak clearly stated that his desire was to receive the death penalty from the courts. However, the case was appealed anyway, and they were again found guilty. Then in January 1996, while awaiting his execution, Herak recanted his testimony claiming that the confession had been beaten out of him during his initial arrest and imprisonment.

Clearly, Herak had every opportunity to notify western journalists prior to his trial of any forced confession that resulted from beatings or torture. During my interview with him in February 1993 Herak answered "no" when I asked him if he had been mistreated in any way in order to get him to confess to the crimes he was charged with.

New York Times journalist John Burns received a Pulitzer Prize for his coverage of the siege of Sarajevo. Burns wrote one of the first articles about Herak's trial and published it in the N.Y. Times on November 27, 1992, just three months prior to my interview with him. Burns wrote that he repeatedly asked Herak if he had been put under pressure to talk or promised a lighter sentence or relief from harsh treatment for confessing, and Herak said that he had not. Furthermore, Burns interviewed Herak's own father, Sretko, about his son's crimes. The father told him: "I would be happier if he had simply killed me and gone to prison for it. Now, I am alive and tortured by what my boy has done to innocent people." Ironically, as is so often the case in Sarajevo, Herak's own family was a mix of ethnic groups. Sretko Herak stated that Borislav's own grandmother was a Croat and his brother-in-law was a Muslim.

In the end, Borislav Herak was never executed... His

request for a new trial was rejected, but his death sentence was commuted to twenty years in prison and he was released after serving his sentence. In the year 2000 his co-defendant's guilty verdict was overturned on appeal. Damjanović walked free. Herak will, however, be forever remembered as the first person convicted of war crimes since the end of World War II and the last person to receive the death penalty in Bosnia-Herzegovina.

Upon returning to the United States I contacted the magazine called *Soldier of Fortune*. This magazine is focused mostly on military matters and mercenaries. They had a rather large readership, but they also devoted many articles to the war against Croatia and Bosnia-Herzegovina. They published my article titled "Man or Monster: Confessions of a Serb War Criminal" in August 1993 with a picture of Herak on the cover.

The *Detroit Free Press* also published a Question-and-Answer article of my interview with Herak on March 28, 1993 just days after he was found guilty of war crimes by the Bosnian government's court. The article was titled, "Serb Soldier: The Order Was to Kill Everybody." Subsequently, my Herak article was published in several newspapers across the United States owned and operated by Gannett Co. Inc.

While working to get the Herak articles published, I also followed up on establishing a phony press agency for the purpose of accessing U.N. flights back into Sarajevo without having to rely on any of the news outlets for letters of verification. In addition to flights into the besieged city, the U.N. accreditation would also give me access to many of the U.N. facilities strewn throughout Croatia and Bosna-Herzegovina.

Creating a sole-proprietor company in America is as simple as going to the offices of the county government and paying a ten-dollar registration fee. Five minutes later the applicant walks out with a registered company name. Next came the design of a logo and letterhead in the company name. I chose the somewhat grandiose name Pan-National News Agency, because I thought it gave the perception of being both international and unrelated to Croatia. I did not want to set off any alarm bells with U.N. officials. The letterhead further ambitiously listed Pan National's foreign press bureaus in Argentina, Bosnia-Herzegovina, Canada, Croatia and the U.S – all fictitious, of course. Finally, I would need to print business cards as well as laminated identification cards that I could use for myself as well as some people in Sarajevo that I would attempt to get out of the city using the U.N. flights. These documents were all designed by a graphic artist I knew in Detroit. Just in case I wouldn't be successful in getting a U.N. identity card renewed, I also had him forge a blank U.N. press accreditation card as a backup plan.

There was no need for any "plan B," however, because on my return to Zagreb in June of 1993, I simply walked into UNPROFOR headquarters, presented a letter on Pan-National News Agency letterhead requesting accreditation, showed my fake employee identification card and walked out with a legitimate U.N. press card in my hand. Even I was amazed at how easy it was. The ease with which it was done left me wondering if anyone else had discovered this weakness in the U.N. bureaucracy.

With a stack of Pan-National News Agency identification cards and a newly-issued U.N. press pass in hand, I once again climbed into the C-130 U.N. aircraft destined for Sarajevo in June of 1993. I would issue the employee identification cards to several people I met on my previous trip to the city in hopes they could access the same U.N. flights that I did and thereby fly out of the nightmare they found themselves living in.

The airport in Sarajevo had changed slightly in the four months since I had last been there. Most notably, the Serbs no longer controlled the airport facilities directly. Unlike in February, there was no visible sign that they were even on the premises. The Serbs, however, continued to maintain checkpoints between the airport and the city, and prevented free movement of people and goods. The U.N. also seemed to have worked out all the logistical problems associated with administrating tons of food and supplies that were coming into the city through the airport every day.

On this occasion, not wanting to impose myself on Nidžara and her family's hospitality again, I accepted the Bakalović family's offer to stay in their apartment during my visit. They were again as gracious as the last time I saw them.

Since cigarettes had become an important new currency for the chain-smoking Sarajevans, I brought a few cartons of Marlboro cigarettes (an especially sought-after brand) to the family together with some other personal items. The most valuable item that I brought, however, was an identification card for Sejla Bakalović issued by Pan-National News Agency stating that she was an employee of the agency. This card together with letters written on my agency's letterhead eventually resulted in Sejla being flown out of the city – compliments of the United Nations. She lives today in Houston, Texas with her husband, Damir Rudić (also from Sarajevo) and their daughter, Tess. They remain dear friends.

The Pan-National News Agency and U.N. accreditation would continue to be of assistance over the next couple of years when I would occasionally share information I came across with Drago Sudar. Drago had lived in the diaspora and served almost twenty years in prison before returning to Croatia where he was employed as an analyst for Croatian intelligence.

Convicted Serbian war criminal Borislav Herak

12

Agents in a Storm

FOLLOWING MY LAST trip to Sarajevo in June of 1993, I joined three friends, Petar Ivčec, Tomislav Marušić and Zdenko Mrakovčić, in order to explore the possibility of creating a company that would serve as a check against the rumors of corruption in the Croatia's Ministry of Defense we were hearing about . We named the company Global Enterprises Group, Inc. The personal contacts that I would make while representing the Ministry of Defense would, ironically, also have a dramatic effect on my personal life years later. In November of 1993, however, my sole focus was: what could I do for Baka's homeland at this time in the war?

We met on several occasions to discuss what we could do as patriots. Clearly, one way was to supply anything the Ministry may need for Croatia to win Croatia's War of Independence. We knew that Croatia's Ministry of Defense would need to acquire a lot of material and equipment when the time was right for Croatia to reclaim the twenty-five percent of its land that was still under the control of the Serbian-led JNA. We were also prepared to assist by influencing American politicians and participating in the information war being waged through the American and Canadian news media. This would require meeting three objectives. First, we would have to receive authorization from the Ministry of Defense to act on their behalf and at their request. Second, we had to incorporate our company with the State of Michigan where our offices would be headquartered. Finally, we would be required under U.S. law to register as agents of the Croatian government under the Federal Agent Registration Act (FARA). Failing to register with the U.S. Justice Department would enable the Yugoslav government to petition the American Justice Department to charge us criminally under the same act.

My old friend Petar Ivčec and Tomislav Marušić had been friends for many years through their membership in the Croatian Republican Party headquartered in Buenos Aires Argentina.

Tomislav was from the small town of Široki Brijeg, the same town that the Minister of Defense, Gojko Šušak, was from. Fortunately for us, Šušak was also Tomislav's Godfather or Kum. The title Kum not only conveys the relationship of one person to another, but it becomes the lifelong title used in addressing one another. Using it denotes much more in Croatian culture than in Anglo-Saxon culture. Needless to say, their relationship went back long before either one of them immigrated to North America and it was very close. It predated the time when Dr. Franjo Tuđman asked Gojko Šušak to give up his successful business in Canada and come to Croatia to assist him in Croatia's struggle for freedom. Like Petar, Tomislav had impeccable credentials as a man devoted to the cause of freedom for Croatia. Also, like Petar, he had worked tirelessly for decades and had sacrificed both time and money at a time when it was dangerous to be involved in the Croatian independence movement.

Agents in a Storm

The last partner chosen to be in Global Enterprises Group was Zdenko Mrakovčić. He was the least known to any of us. Zdenko had already lived in Detroit for several years prior to Croatian Independence, but none of us had ever seen him at our various Croatian events over the years. This was a big red flag for us, because it often indicated the person's leanings were more pro-Yugoslav than pro-Croatian. He had moved to Detroit from New York after buying a large apartment building just outside Detroit's city center. According to Zdenko, he attempted other business ventures while living in New York. We discovered, after checking him out with our Croatian contacts in New York, that he was practically unknown to our Croatian friends there as well.

Croatians who immigrated post-WWII could be divided into three basic groups.

First, there were the immigrants who left Croatia for political reasons during the Croatian Spring of 1971, when Tito cracked down on Croatians who had demanded more autonomy from the Yugoslav federal government. They left Yugoslavia for political reasons and often times were forced to make the dangerous trek to the West without a passport. Yugoslavia would not give passports to people they viewed as a threat. Petar Ivčec, who escaped across the Yugoslav border under a train, fell under this category. People like him could never return to a Croatia that was still held captive by Yugoslavia.

Second, there was the group of émigrés that left Yugoslavia for economic reasons. Of this group there were two sub-groups: Croats who chose to be part of the larger "Croatian community" but refrained from anti-Yugoslav politics so they could return to Yugoslavia to visit family members, and those who became involved in anti-Yugoslav politics and activities and could never again return to Croatia and their families. I developed a deep respect for émigrés in this second sub-group who consciously chose a life of exile rather than remain silent.

The third group, however, would not associate with any segment of Croatia's diaspora that the Yugoslav regime might label "extremists." They didn't want to do anything that risked their ability to travel back home on vacations or return home permanently. Since the Yugoslav government considered many of the Croatian Catholic churches and organizations found in North America to be havens for extremists, those Croatian émigrés who did not want to take a chance of being labeled "extremist" or "anti-Yugoslav" simply stayed away from our churches and community completely. The Croatian Fraternal Union was the only Croatian organization that was safe for these fearful Croats to join if they wished to appear "loyal" to the Yugoslav regime but still associate with some Croats while in emigration.

We were concerned that Zdenko belonged to this last category and we questioned whether it was for this reason that our friends in New York and Detroit had not heard of him before. In spite of our concerns, he was a successful businessman and, therefore, we approached him believing that he could be an asset to our future company. In addition, Zdenko had offered to allow the use of one of his vacant apartments as offices for the Global Enterprises Group. Since we were always wary of Yugoslav spies or American intelligence agencies, we felt that it was better to set up our offices in one of Zdenko's vacant apartments than take a chance and rent office space from strangers who could be co-opted. And so, we invited Mrakovčić to join the company in spite of our misgivings.

The four of us travelled to Croatia in November 1993, in hopes of getting a meeting with Minister Šušak where we would pitch our idea to him. Tomislav was able to arrange a dinner meeting with Šušak at a restaurant on the top floor of the Hotel Intercontinental in Zagreb. Šušak's wife Đurđa was also kind enough to join us for dinner that evening. Her intelligence and beauty impressed me. The service that we received at the restaurant that evening was impressive and the way our table was fawned over gave me an insight into the addictive aspects of power. Not only were there several waiters attending to our table that night, but the manager made a point of dropping by the table to also pay his respects and pick up the check for all six of us.

Šušak was a slim and charismatic man who was very comfortable in his skin when we met him that evening in 1993. He wielded immense power within Croatia as well as outside – as I would personally learn and explain in a later chapter. At the same time, Šušak's character had not changed since leaving Herzegovina. It was clear that he had great confidence and exhibited great leadership skills. This always amazed me, since there was nothing obvious in his past to qualify him for the position he held as a Minister of Defense.

Gojko Šušak was born in Široki Brijeg on March 15, 1945, just two months before the end of WWII. His father and brother were members of Croatian forces during WWII. Like tens of thousands of other former Croatian soldiers, they were both killed by Tito's partisans following their surrender after the war. Šušak attended grade school and high school in Široki Brijeg. In 1963, he attended Teachers College in the northern Croatian city of Rijeka. He escaped Yugoslavia, first to Austria for six months, then to Canada, in 1969. Šušak worked for a restaurant chain his first four years in Canada and in 1972 went into business operating a successful pizza restaurant chain called Tops.

Šušak also became more involved in Croatian emigration matters during his life in Canada. Most notably among his accomplishments was his involvement with the Croatian Cultural Federation and the Croatian Soccer League in Canada as well as assisting in the establishment of the Croatian Studies Chair at the University of Waterloo.

When Dr. Franjo Tuđman came to North America for the first time in 1987, his first objective was to establish contact with people recognized as Croatian patriots, but who were not officially members of any anti-Yugoslav political group. Gojko Šušak and others were instrumental in helping Tuđman meet that objective. Tuđman was wise enough to know that if he hoped to ever win an election in Croatia his campaign would have to be financed with the money from the worldwide Croatian diaspora. He spent years in Tito's Lepoglava Prison as a political dissident. He was unique, because he was also a former JNA General under Josip Broz Tito prior to coming into conflict with him. The Croatian diaspora did not immediately support the former JNA general in spite of him having been jailed by Tito. Therefore, the diaspora would be a hard nut for Tuđman to crack if he didn't first get the blessing of notable Croatian leaders in the diaspora. The first Croatian patriots that Tuđman approached for support were very vocal and active Croatian critics of Yugoslavia from the region of Herzegovina. Uncompromising Croatian patriots living in Canada, like Gojko Šušak, were at the top of Tuđman's list. Šušak answered the call and wholeheartedly supported Tuđman along with other Herzegovinian leaders living in Canada. This early support for Tuđman came at a great political risk for anyone in the Croatian diaspora. With the exception of The Croatian National Resistance (OTPOR) and the Croatian Republican Party, there were very few hardline political supporters for Franjo Tuđman in those early days after his release from Lepoglava prison.

Tuđman faced vocal and boisterous outbursts at each Croatian speaking event, regardless of which country and which city he visited in 1987. Many, if not most, of those in attendance could not get past the fact that he was once a general in the Yugoslav National Army. If it wasn't for the support of the Herzegovina faction, OTPOR (whose leadership was overwhelmingly from Herzegovina) and the Croatian Republican Party, Tuđman would have returned to the former Yugoslavia empty-handed. Several of those early supporters (Gojko Šušak, Ante Beljo and Marin Sopta) would be rewarded by Tuđman with various positions when he was elected president. He first rewarded Šušak's loyalty by appointing him Minister of Emigration in the fledgling Croatian state. Šušak's leadership abilities soon became obvious, however, and he was finally appointed Minister of Defense in September of 1991.

Several topics were discussed during dinner that evening. Minister Šušak was interested in recent news about people he had known in the diaspora. Since Marušić and he had a much longer and closer relationship than any of the rest of us at the table, he sat next to Šušak. His wife Đurđa, who sat across from him at my right, was working in the offices of UNS for President Tuđman's son Miroslav. At one point, while talking about the great things that Croats from the diaspora were doing, she mentioned my film *The Bleiburg Tragedy* stating that it was on their bookshelf at home. She apparently didn't seem to realize that I was the author of the film and I didn't bother to tell her.

Mr. Šušak went on to talk about the UDBA files that the Yugoslavs had failed to destroy prior to fleeing Zagreb in December 1991. He was surprised, he said, by some of the names that he recognized from the Croatian diaspora who had worked as spies for UDBA while pretending to be Croatian patriots.

Finally, over desert and drinks we broached the subject of our business plan. We expressed in honest terms why we thought that we, as patriots, could help Croatia by registering as Foreign Agents in America. Our goal was to help the Ministry of Defense acquire any materials Croatia would need in fighting the last phase of the Homeland War to regain the remaining territory occupied by the Serbs. We explained that we could help by acting as a check-and-balance against any elements in the new government that were more interested in profits than in securing freedom for Croatia. We firmly believed that our company could limit corruption in the Ministry if Mr. Šušak had quotes from us to compare with inflated quotes by other companies who had friends in the Ministry. It was our belief that many of the quotes given to the Ministry for materials included kickbacks to corrupt individuals inside the Ministry. It was perhaps naïve to think we could eliminate most corruption, but Minister Šušak liked the idea and agreed that evening to allow us to form the corporation and register as Foreign Agents on behalf of the Ministry of Defense.

The next day Tomislav Marušić and I went to see General Krešimir Ćosić in his office to prepare the letter of authorization for Šušak's signature. Ćosić had been a strong supporter of us during this time and afterwards. Ćosić is very intelligent and I believe he recognized, early on, the importance of Marušić's relationship with Šušak and how that relationship could affect his personal advancement within the Ministry of Defense. Ćosić was very capable and would eventually be promoted to Deputy Minister of Defense.

The following day we went to Šušak's office in the Ministry of Defense Headquarters to have the letter printed on Defense Ministry letterhead and to have it signed. The new Ministry of Defense Headquarters was in the building formerly occupied by the Yugoslav Amy. Šušak was not in, but his secretary agreed to print the letter and have it signed for us. And with that, we became Agents for the Croatian Ministry of Defense, ready to register with the U.S. Department of Justice when we returned to America.

Author with President Franjo Tuđman

For Baka's Homeland

REPUBLIKA HRVATSKA
MINISTARSTVO OBRANE

Zagreb, 15th November 1993.

AUTHORIZATION

I Gojko Šušak, Minister of Defense of the Republic of Croatia, hereby authorize the individuals Tomica Marušić, Zdenko Mrakovčić, Michael Palaich and Petar Ivčec to register as foreign agents for the Croatian Ministry of Defense, with the United States Government, under the corporation name GLOBAL ENTERPRISES, INCORPORATED.

*REPUBLIC OF CROATIA
DEFENSE MINISTER*

Gojko Šušak

Authorization letter from the Croatian Minister of Defense

Ćosić would continue to help us with almost anything we asked of him and we continued to help him as well. For example, on one occasion Ćosić arranged a meeting for me while I was in Argentina with an officer working in the Argentine Ministry of Defense who was of Croatian heritage. Ćosić was extremely interested in military flight training simulators and thought that the Argentine military might be interested in selling Croatia some of their used equipment.

When General Ćosić was in America to attend a conference at the University of Michigan located 240 miles from Chicago, we took the opportunity to have an exploratory and introductory conversation with a friend of a friend from Argentina who was also a business owner with contacts in Argentine aviation businesses. Our meeting between Ćosić and the Argentine took place while we walked around the Chicago suburb of River Forest where Tomica Marušić lived. By this time, we all avoided having sensitive conversations like this in our homes. Ćosić explained to the Argentine that the Croatian Ministry might be interested in a particular type of aircraft manufactured in Argentina called the FMA-IA Pucará. The Pucará was a low-flying, turbo prop aircraft that had proved to be effective in counterinsurgency fighting against Communist guerrillas in Argentina. General Ćosić thought the plane could also be effective in the Croatian Homeland War against Serbian paramilitary units as well as against the JNA working alongside them.

Ćosić initiated another meeting while we were in Zagreb that I was very uncomfortable attending, but attended nonetheless. That meeting took place at the Črnomerec military barracks in Zagreb with two American Military Attachés. Ćosić, Marušić and I met with the American Attachés Ivan Šarac and Richard Herrick, both officers in the American military.

I knew from my own days in the military that Military Attachés were often CIA employees operating in foreign countries under the "official" cover of Military Attaché. I also knew from conversations with Drago Sudar, a friend who worked for Miroslav Tuđman in the UNS Office, that Ivan Šarac was training members of the Croatian intelligence agencies on behalf of the CIA. I was not certain that the CIA officially employed him, but the CIA did award Šarac its Exceptional Collectors Award for his work as Military Attaché while in Zagreb. It is interesting to note here that Šarac was Croatian and born in the former Yugoslavia. When younger and living in New York City he was also actively involved (or at least pretended to be) in the Croatian Liberation Movement (HOP). According to Drago Sudar, Ivan Šarac would eventually be evicted from Croatia as "persona non grata" due to his covert and unauthorized activity in Croatia.

Colonel Herrick would go on to play an instrumental role in helping Croatian forces recapture Serb-occupied territory during Croatia's Operation Flash (*Bljesak*) in May 1995 and Operation Storm (*Oluja*) in August 1995. Military Professional Resources Incorporated (MPRI), a U.S. company with headquarters in Alexandria, Virginia, also played a major role in training the Croatian military prior to the August offensive with Herrick's help. MPRI is said to be indirectly tied to the CIA.

But, on this day, the five of us were brought together by General Ćosić simply to meet. Ćosić sent a driver to our hotel to pick us up and take us to Črnomerec. Upon my introduction to the two U.S. Military Attachés, Šarac identified himself and Herrick as being former Special Forces and then asked me, "Were you Special Forces too?" "No, I was just a shmuck in the Navy," I answered. "But I am very proud of the way the Croatian military has been able to transform itself with the help of General Ćosić." I was uncomfortable with the meeting because I wasn't sure exactly who initiated it. I wondered to myself whether the Americans initiated the meeting simply to identify us. Or, did Ćosić initiate it in order to ingratiate himself with the Americans as a high-ranking Croatian officer? Either answer would have troubled me. I was certain, however, that they would file a report of our conversation upon returning to their office at the American Embassy. It was getting increasingly more difficult to remain in the shadows where I always felt more comfortable.

General Ćosić confided in us that during this same period, the Tuđman government was increasingly under pressure to give away land for peace. Apparently, the EU and America in particular wanted Croatia to relinquish all claims to the 25% of Croatian territory occupied by the Serb paramilitary and JNA forces in the interest of "peace in the region." From what we were told, the subject was constantly being broached by American diplomats in particular. This really stuck in my craw, so I had to respond.

The Croatian territory that Serbia occupied had never been within the territory of Serbia. The same could not be said, however, for the American states like Arizona, Texas, New Mexico and California that had once been within the boundaries of Mexico. I advised General Ćosić that the next time a proposition was made to sacrifice Croatian land for peace he should propose the following: "For each centimeter of American territory returned to Mexico, Croatia would sacrifice one kilometer of its territory for peace." Of course, it was a purely rhetorical argument. America would never return even a millimeter of American territory to Mexico voluntarily. It was meant to drive home a point: it is always easier to give away someone else's territory for peace rather than one's own. The occupied territory was and has always been Croatian, and therefore, should never be relinquished.

For the next two years, our company searched for every item that the Ministry asked us to purchase. We submitted countless quotes for items from uniforms and boots to communications equipment. While we were successful in getting very few contracts for those items, I believe we were successful in limiting the amount of corruption in the Ministry. Our reasonable quotes for a variety of materials made it much more difficult for war profiteers to receive the winning contract if their quotes were markedly higher than ours.

The most frustrating item we were asked to acquire were vehicles from the Hummer Corporation. We contacted the Headquarters for Hummer vehicles and we were referred to their Eastern European Headquarters. To our surprise the distributorship for Hummers in Eastern Europe had already been given to a Slovenian company. Hummer Inc. informed us that if the Croatian Ministry of Defense wished to purchase Hummer vehicles, they would be required to purchase them from the Slovenian distributor. In addition, Croatia would be required to have the vehicles serviced by service centers in Slovenia. Since the job of getting quotes largely fell on me, I again contacted Hummer Headquarters and explained that this was unacceptable. Certainly, that would be acceptable if we were buying the Hummers for private use, but I explained that the Croatian government, as a sovereign state, could not be required to purchase vehicles from the Slovenians and have them serviced by Slovenians. It was our view that the Croatian government should be able to buy them directly and have them serviced in Croatia by a Croatian service center.

At one point our office was contacted directly by a person from the Slovenian distributor for Hummer Inc. who was very angry that Croatia had the nerve to ask for its own distributorship for Hummer vehicles. He began yelling over the phone that his company had the distributorship for all of Eastern Europe and that included any future sales to Croatia. I explained that Croatia was an independent nation and as such Croatia could never agree to purchase vehicles through him, nor would we ever agree to have the Slovenian company service Croatian military grade Hummer vehicles. In spite of many communications with the company at all levels we were never able to get Hummer International to agree to direct sales with Croatia. I am not sure if Croatia ever purchased even one Hummer for the military, but I have seen many Land Rovers driven by the Croatian military over the years.

The most satisfying contract that we signed with the Ministry of Defense was in 1995 involving Motorola communication devices of various types that were successfully used during Operation Storm on August 4, 1995. The three-day operation was successful in retaking almost twenty percent of the Croatian territory that the Serbs had occupied since the beginning of their aggression. It is amazing to think that this feat was accomplished by a fledgling new state whose military arsenal initially amounted to very few light arms and virtually no heavy equipment. It was my early prediction that Croatia would take back the occupied territories within two weeks and people would openly scoff at that estimate. Everyone - including me - was astonished, therefore, when the main portion of the operation was over in three days, with the remaining mopping-up operations ending on August 4.

Very few individuals knew at the time that the U.S. government assisted in Operation Storm with surveillance, logistics and even military training by third-party military contractors like MPRI. One of the most interesting and successful elements of Operation Storm was the manner in which the Croatian military was able to move soldiers to various parts of the country that the Croatian military controlled through the use of commercial transport trucks. In an attempt to keep the enemy in the dark regarding troop movements, delivery trucks from various commercial businesses were loaded with soldiers who were transported to places that the military viewed as important and strategic to the operation. By the time Operation Storm was set to begin, most of the Croatian soldiers were already in place, adding to the surprise element of the operation and, therefore, its huge success. To our great satisfaction, thousands of the Motorola communication devices that we supplied to the Croatian forces were ultimately used in this tremendously successful and historic military operation.

Events following Operation Storm, however, brought both disillusionment and a feeling of betrayal caused by the actions of two partners of Global Enterprises Group, Inc. When we originally pitched the idea of our company to Minister Šušak, our promise was to help limit the potential for corruption within the Croatian Ministry of Defense. In 1995, however, I was shocked to learn of irregularities from within our own company. To make matters even worse, the irregular financial transactions occurred between two partners of our company and at least one member of the Ministry of Defense. It was my opinion that the irregularities were probably in violation of several U.S. laws. I prudently made copies documenting the irregular transactions that remain in my possession today.

A company with offices in Zagreb sent us a list of items that they wanted a quotation for. A quote was subsequently sent to them for the amount of $84,666.20. On September 8, 1995, Global Enterprises received a wire transfer into our account for that exact amount. A few days later we received a call from one of the partners in Croatia, Tomica Marušić, asking us to return the money, because the deal had fallen through, and they no longer needed the items that they paid for. I informed Tomica that we could and would send it back under three conditions: first, we would have to withhold a customary ten percent due to breaking our contract for the items. The first five percent would be deducted immediately. Second, the purchasing company would have to return the remaining five percent to us within two weeks. Third, we could, naturally, only return the money to the exact same bank account number in Zagreb from which the money was sent. But Marušić wanted the money sent to a third account number. I explained that this would be impossible and likely illegal. It fit my understanding of classic money laundering. I held firm, refusing to send the money to an account number that was not the same as the original one. While Pero Ivčec agreed with me, Zdenko Mrakovčić did not see a problem in sending the funds to a third party's bank account. We were at a stalemate: since there were only four partners, with four equal votes, the money should have been returned only to the original sender. Pero and I were, therefore, very surprised to learn that Mrakovčić had taken it upon himself to disregard our votes as full and equal partners and sent the wire transfer for $80,432.89 to a completely different account number with Trgovačka Banka in Zagreb on September 12, 1995. It would have been unethical, and I believe illegal, to use personal funds in this way, but it was unconscionable to put all the partners of Global Enterprises in jeopardy of violating U.S. and, probably, international banking laws. I hoped that this money laundering scheme would not be uncovered by the authorities. Looking back with hindsight, I suppose the smart thing to do would have been to report the illegality and save myself from further legal problems with the Justice Department, but I chose to remain silent and take my chances with the authorities.

On January 9, 1996, I resigned from Global Enterprises Group in protest. I walked away from the company without asking for my original investment to be returned, or for any other future compensation. I knew that I was still under investigation by the U.S. Attorney in Detroit for what they considered a "Violation of the Export Control Act" over the shipment of night-vision equipment and weapons. There was still the very real possibility of being indicted by the Justice Department and I certainly didn't need to add money laundering and banking violations to any future federal indictment. I felt betrayed that Mrakovčić and Marušić had taken it upon themselves to put all the partners in legal jeopardy. Apparently, Pero Ivčec felt the same way, because he submitted his resignation in a letter dated April 10, 1996.

Subsequent to this disagreement, we had one final meeting in our offices in Detroit. The blood between us was so bad that to this day the other partners do not know that I had a 45-caliber pistol tucked away in my waistband. I thank God that the meeting, although tumultuous, was not violent. After my resignation, I broke off all contact with Marušić and Mrakovčić. I never saw them again.

Pero Ivčec, however, would continue to be one of the few friends that I would keep in contact with over the following years. He was also one of the few friends who remained loyal after I was finally indicted by the U.S. Government in 1996 following the federal investigation that had loomed over my head for five years.

13

Specter of Prison

THE PHONE RANG on the morning of October 12, 1996. It was Charlene, my attorney's secretary. "I'm sorry to have to tell you this," she said, "but the Grand Jury indicted you on six counts yesterday. You'll have to appear in court for arraignment on October 28." Needless to say, I was devastated. Of course, I always knew that it was a possibility. I also knew that I had been under fairly intense investigation and observation for almost five years. But, until it happens, a person always believes it could go the other way and it almost did. The first attempt to indict me failed when the Grand Jury came back saying "no indictment" to the U.S. District Attorney's attempt. But the prosecutor's office prevailed with its second Grand Jury investigation. The Grand Jury indicted me on six counts for violating the "Arms Export Control Act (22 U.S.C. §2778) as it relates to defense articles and defense services and the exercise of the President's authority to control such exports." I was required to sign the acknowledgement of the indictment which read: "I know that if I am convicted or plead guilty, I may be sentenced as follows: 10 years and/or $1,000,000.00 fine for each count." That translated to a potential sentence of sixty years in prison and six million dollars in fines.

In the case of most federal offenses there is a statute of limitations which limits the time that the government has to indict a person. In my case, the statute of limitations was five years. Knowing this, I was counting the days. With only 11 days shy of the statute of limitations running out, the U.S. Attorney Saul Green was finally successful in getting a Grand Jury to indict me.

I was ordered by the Court to appear before a U.S. Magistrate in Detroit's federal building on October 28, 1996 where my attorney, Richard Lustig, stood next to me and entered a plea of "Not Guilty" on my behalf. It was extremely fortunate that the magistrate was willing to give me an unsecured bond of $50,000.00. This meant I was allowed to remain free until my trial with the provision that I would be required to pay the bond in full if I failed to appear as required by the court. In short, I was allowed to remain free on my own recognizance. I was immediately escorted to an area next to the courtroom where jail cells operated by the U.S. Marshal Service were located. I was photographed for a "mug shot" and fingerprinted. My next destination, after being booked, was to the offices of the Pretrial Services Department. My Pretrial Services Officer, Thomas Nugent, explained the limitations and requirements that I would be expected to adhere to under my bond agreement with the government. These limitations included not being able to travel outside of the State of Michigan and a requirement to physically report to the Pretrial Services once per month. Of course, these instructions also included not traveling outside of the United States and especially to Croatia, so I was forced to surrender my passport.

Within days of my court appearance I contacted everyone in Croatia who I thought may be able to intervene on my behalf. My first two calls were made to Drago Sudar, who worked as an analyst for UNS, and Marijan Buconjić, who by this time was a Deputy Minister of Emigration. Luckily, five years previously, I had informed several people I knew who worked for the Croatian government of my arrest in Germany. One of those people, whom I'll call "Vinko," was employed by one of Croatia's agencies. I asked him at the time to secure the Croatian government's help in getting the confiscated guns, ammunition and night-vision scope destroyed while the items were still in the possession of the German police. I knew long before I was indicted that the evidence would eventually have to be sent back to America so that the government prosecutors could use it as evidence against me in court. Vinko, who I knew had contacts in other Croatian Intelligence Services, assured me that he would do everything in his power to get the Germans to destroy the weapons before they could be sent back to America.

Within days of my indictment in America, I received a call from Krešo Ćosić, the Deputy Defense Minister for Croatia at the time. Mr. Ćosić explained that he would do everything in his power to have the Croatian government intervene on my behalf. When I thanked Ćosić he responded in a way that not only comforted me, but also made me confident of his resolve. "There is no reason to thank me. It is our duty to do what we can to help you," Ćosić said.

As I mentioned earlier, Drago Sudar, now deceased, worked as an Analyst for the UNS at the time of my indictment. Drago was a long-time member of the Croatian Republican Party. He was convicted on terrorist charges on May 15, 1982 and sentenced to twenty years in federal prison by New York Federal Judge Constance Motley. Upon his release from prison Franjo Tuđman employed Drago in the Zagreb headquarters for UNS on Ulica fra Filipa Grabovca. Although he was one of the people that I called following my indictment, it was not the first time I talked to him about my legal problems in America.

In 1994, at a dinner at the well-known Zagreb restaurant Okrugljak, I discussed my legal problems with Drago and informed him that the U.S. government might indict me at any time. Having served a lengthy jail term himself, I believed Drago would be motivated to help me with my case even before I was indicted. More than anybody, Drago could understand what a lengthy prison sentence would mean for me. I was not disappointed. During our dinner at Okrugljak he promised that he would help me if I were ever indicted. When I called his private number in the UNS offices after my indictment, however, he was understandably reluctant to speak over the phone about the matter. I understood by his tone that he was leery that our phone conversation was being monitored – maybe even from within the offices of UNS. He instructed me to call my friend Vinko and tell him of my indictment. The fact that he was passing me off to Vinko didn't disappoint me, however. I had faith that even though he couldn't commit himself over the phone verbally, he would continue to pursue the issue from behind the scenes.

In an attempt to cover all my bases through my contacts, I even had a meeting with the Ambassador Sacirbey when he was in Detroit for a fund-raising event for Bosnia-Herzegovina at the Palace of Auburn Hills in August 1997. Noted guitar player Peter Frampton performed in concert with the legendary rock group Grand Funk Railroad. All the proceeds from the concert would be directed to help the victims of the ongoing war in Bosnia-Herzegovina. I knew Sacirbey fairly well as described earlier when he assisted me in getting press credentials to help me travel through Bosnia and Sarajevo during the war. My wife and I met with Sacirbey privately in the VIP section of Palace's entertainment facility where I explained my indictment and asked if he could give any assistance through his international political contacts as a U.N. Ambassador. Over dinner that evening he promised to do what he could, including talk to the U.S. Secretary of State, Madeleine Albright. She was his colleague at the U.N. prior to her promotion to U.S. Secretary of State in January 1997.

Then something very strange happened that I really didn't understand at the time: all of my subsequent attempts to reach the same individuals were fruitless. My messages were not being returned. The people whom I could easily reach before were all of a sudden silent. It felt as though I had become a leper within two weeks of my federal indictment. I was left to conclude one of two things. First, that I was too "hot" and that any official contact with me could be construed as detrimental to Croatian-American relations. Second, that they were in fact working behind the scenes as they all promised, but that they were instructed to break off contact with me in order to create an element of "plausible denial." I hoped like hell that their silence was the consequence of the second option. Whatever the reason was for breaking off communication with me, the result was that I felt completely isolated.

It wasn't until a few years later that I learned what had happened. Work was, in fact, being done behind the scenes through unofficial channels by several departments within the Croatian government throughout my whole ordeal, but I will get to that later.

If that wasn't bad enough, most of my Croatian friends in emigration abandoned me also. With the exception of Petar Ivčec and another old friend, Ante Čuvalo, it seemed that my Croatian friends had calculated that it was safer for them if they were no longer seen coming to my home or inviting me to their homes. With the exception of Ante and Pero, they even stopped calling me on the phone. I assumed that they didn't want to be photographed coming to my house or having their phone numbers registered as callers to my home on my phone records. Ironically, some of those people had been directly involved with me in smuggling items into Croatia earlier in the war. Several of those people were enlisted in taking motorboats across the Detroit River and into Canada. I could understand and justify the silence of the Croatian government officials, but I bitterly viewed the silence of so many former "good friends" as a betrayal.

This feeling of betrayal became even stronger when the Federal Prosecutor came to me shortly after my indictment with a plea deal: if I were to reveal everyone involved with me over the years and provide details of our operations, I would be guaranteed a jail term of fourteen months. If I went to trial, I could potentially go to prison for sixty years. I don't care who you are; when you are offered a plea deal of fourteen months versus sixty years it makes you think about the offer. I swallowed hard and said, "No!" I would take my chances at a trial. My answer wasn't because I was sure I would win in court. Nor was it simply because of any lingering loyalty to those former friends who had turned their backs on me. Perhaps it was just my inborn stubbornness. In any event, those former "friends" never knew that my silence saved them from being prosecuted as accomplices. At least two of the former "friends" whom I protected from being indicted were multi-millionaires. Another former "good friend" whom I also protected, inexplicably began spreading the false rumor that I was a C.I.A. agent. In those days, that allegation was almost as bad as being accused of working for UDBA. He died never knowing that I protected him from being prosecuted.

In light of all that, I was even more grateful for my friends who did not abandon me. In addition to offering moral support, Pero Ivčec contributed his own money to help me with legal fees. Ante Čuvalo's help was also invaluable when he organized a fund raiser in Chicago at St. Jerome Church. The Croatian community generously raised over six thousand dollars at a banquet in the church social hall that Fr. Jozo Grbeš graciously allowed us to use. For that I will be forever grateful to not only Ante Čuvalo, but Fr. Grbeš and the entire Croatian community of Chicago. My Sarajevo friend Sejla Bakalović flew in from Texas to offer her moral and material support.

Shortly after my arraignment in federal court, I went to the law offices of Richard Lustig. I was still very concerned about his high fees. Now that I was indicted, I wasn't sure that he would even agree to continue as my attorney. The only thing that I was certain of was that I could not afford his standard fees – even with the financial help from the Croatian community. Lustig charged most of his clients a retainer fee simply for agreeing to take their cases. In addition to his standard retainer fee of $30,000, he customarily charged $400 to $500 per hour for his legal services.

Lustig began by refreshing himself with my case and heard my reasons for being involved with the Croatian independence movement in a general sense. He patiently listened to me for almost one hour, just as he had five year before. He explained that he was a Jew. After listening to me articulate the Croatian cause and Croatia's desire for freedom, he said that he was compelled to help in any way that he could. He went on to say that he admired me for my belief in the cause of Croatian freedom. He could see similarities between Croatians and Jews. He appreciated their common desire to live in an independent state where they could experience self-determination. He went on to explain that he himself had often thought about joining the Israeli Defense Forces (IDF) fighting for a Jewish homeland in his younger days, but that he had not been committed enough to actually do it. What he said next floored me: "I'm going to take your case pro bono. You just pay me whatever you can." I'm certain that my eyes welled up with tears at that statement. I told him that I had almost no money, but that I would make every attempt to give him one thousand dollars every month. There have been several times in my life when I felt God had interceded on my behalf and this was certainly one of those times.

For two and a half years, Mr. Lustig worked tirelessly on my behalf. I paid him $1,000 per month as a sign of appreciation and respect. He filed motion after motion on my behalf: motion to dismiss, motion to suppress evidence, motion to disclose evidence, etc.

I could only continue to hope (since communication had broken off) that the Croatian government was working just as hard to help solve my legal problems on a diplomatic level. I am

231

not embarrassed to admit that I was very concerned about the prospect of spending several decades in prison. It was constantly on my mind and I couldn't help but continuously go over the case in my head. The one important fact that was in my favor was that the indictment included only the arms and night-vision scope that the Germans caught me with transporting into Frankfurt. I was never charged with smuggling additional military items to Croatia. Therefore, there were three things I tried to emphasize with my attorney: first, that I declared everything with the airlines prior to boarding my flight to Germany. Second, that the items I was being prosecuted for were for "personal use" and not "exported" as the government insisted. Third, the prosecution did not have the evidence in their possession, since the weapons and night-vision scopes were still (theoretically) under the control of the Germans. It was still uncertain at this time if the Croatian government had been successful in getting the evidence in Germany destroyed.

Fight or Flight?

The Last Days of Socrates written by Plato was required reading while I was in college. It brought me some comfort to re-read it during my legal battles. I tried to see some real-life similarities between it and my situation. In the chapter "The Apology of Socrates," Socrates was anything but apologetic in his defense against charges of "impiety and corrupting the youth" at his trial of 399 B.C. He was determined not to sacrifice his integrity in order to save his own life. Although my sentence could only result in a very lengthy prison term and not death, his behavior served as an example to me of how an honorable man should behave in court when facing prosecution. Those familiar with Socrates will also recall that he faced another dilemma as well: to flee Athens in order to save himself from trial and a certain guilty verdict, or to commit suicide by drinking poison following his sentence of death.

Being sentenced to a long prison term was certainly a possibility that I could not ignore. If the Croatian government

232

was not successful in persuading the American authorities to dismiss the case against me, or if the various motions by my attorney to get my case dismissed failed, the possibility of going to prison for many years was a terrifying reality. Many well-meaning people even advised me to flee prosecution in America and seek safety in Croatia during this period. Without going into detail, it was certainly an option that was available. But, as I read Socrates' "Apology," I found his arguments for remaining in Athens and facing his accusers compelling. Socrates argued that he had lived in Athens for many years and had reaped the benefits of living in that society and under its laws. He did not think it moral to leave the city, just because the laws had worked against him in that instance.

Socrates ended his life by drinking hemlock after his trial. I decided to stay and face my accusers in court, but one question still nagged at me: what if I am found guilty?

Another biography piqued my interest around the same time. I began reading everything I could about Bobby Sands. Robert Gerald Sands was a member of the Irish Republican Army (IRA). Sands was sentenced to fourteen years' imprisonment by the British government in September 1977 after being charged with possession of a handgun that was said to have been used in a gun battle with police following the bombing of a furniture warehouse. Bobby Sands was not opposed to serving out his sentence; he was opposed to being charged as a criminal rather than a political prisoner, an important distinction offered to IRA members in the past. As a member of the IRA he saw himself as a soldier rather than a terrorist. He wanted, therefore, to be incarcerated as a political prisoner as other IRA members had prior to March 1, 1976. Furthermore, he wanted all the other IRA prisoners serving sentences with him to be given the original designation, since Sands considered that title to be more accurate and honorable than the new designation of criminal. In order to force the British government to comply, Sands led a sixty-six-day hunger strike. Although Sands managed to win a seat in the British Parliament on the "Political Prisoner" ticket during his hunger strike, he died on May 5, 1981. Nine other IRA members also died of their hunger strikes shortly after his death.

The more I learned of Sands' case, the more I began to understand his reasoning. It became clear to me why he considered the classification of criminal rather than political prisoner dishonorable. It was also during this period that I read everything I could about hunger strikes and what effect starvation has on the human body leading up to one's death. As a result, I began to view a hunger strike as a possible option if I was ever found guilty and sentenced to prison. It was an unpleasant and prolonged death, but I concluded that it was the only honorable thing to do considering my situation.

As a practicing Catholic today, I see that this was also immoral and should not have been considered as an option. But at the time, the only thing I knew about life in prison was what I had learned from acquaintances like Marijan Buconjić, Jozo Brekalo and Vlado Dizdar who were all imprisoned for years due to their takeover of the Yugoslav Mission to the U.N. on June 14, 1977. My own cousin Victor Švehar had also spent years in prison for voluntary manslaughter. I visited Victor at Michigan's Jackson State Prison on several occasions. His incarceration had long-lasting and terrible consequences on his life and the life of his family. I knew myself well enough at that time in my life to know that I could never accept being abused in prison without retaliating. From my perspective, the worst aspect of receiving a prison sentence was being subjected to disrespect and humiliation by both fellow prisoners and prison staff. If past events from my life were any indication of how I would behave regarding perceived abuse, I would never get out of prison. Even if I survived the original prison sentence, it was clear to me that additional years would subsequently be added onto my sentence. I would deal with any act of abuse or disrespect with the only response I knew – violence.

One of the first times in my life that I was willing to seriously harm someone for what I considered an intolerable act of disrespect was when I was just twenty-one years old and working as a theatre manager in the Grand Circus Theatre in downtown Detroit. In the '70s, the City of Detroit was experiencing a severe increase in violent crime and murder. The city was known as "the murder capital of the world." There was a massive decrease in the police force due to cutbacks by then-Mayor Coleman Young. The city's mostly black population was also experiencing an increase in gang activity with the two most violent street gangs, Black Killers and Earl Flynns [sic], vying for control of the area in and around downtown. The Grand Circus Theatre had a capacity of 3,500 people. Being the only white guy among the black inner-city patrons required developing an abnormal degree of toughness. I learned to appreciate the difficulty black people experienced while living in that environment and how necessary it was to resort to violence if a person wanted to survive. In short, surviving in that world required that I become tougher than the most aggressive patron I encountered.

On one life-altering occasion, when the theatre was filled to capacity, I stepped out of my office to witness an altercation between a female patron and a security guard. The woman, who I later learned was Cathy Curry, the niece of Mayor Coleman Young and the wife of Johnny Curry, one of Detroit's biggest drug dealers, threw a container of Coca-Cola in the face of a candy counter attendant. When she refused to be evicted from the theatre, I intervened and that is when Curry spit in my face.

I am ashamed to say that after wiping her saliva from my face, I rushed toward her with the intention of killing her. I can still remember the smell of her saliva on my face today. Luckily, I was not carrying my gun on that occasion. If I had, she would have certainly been killed because I had gone completely crazy. My anger was so out-of-control that I inexplicably lost my vision in just a matter of seconds. Somewhere in the melee, the patrons who witnessed everything physically stopped me from getting my hands on the spitting woman's throat. I don't recall how much time passed, but I gradually began to regain my faculties.

It slowly occurred to me that I was being held against the wall of the lobby by several of the male patrons. Still not being able to see, I began to hear a voice: "What you gonna do to a woman, man? What you gonna do to a woman?" Some were holding my head, arms and torso, while at least one held me by my throat. My field of vison began opening up as if someone was using an editing technique in a movie. The men holding me saw that I was calming down and that I was finally able to focus my eyes on them. They released me unharmed. The first people that I saw as I regained my vision were two teenage black girls who were staring at me from about ten feet away. I heard one girl say to the other, "Man, I never saw a man get that mad before!"

As an aside, after Curry's husband was sentenced to ten years in prison for dealing drugs, Curry got involved with a young man called Rick Wershe Jr., a.k.a. White Boy Rick. Hollywood would make a movie about White Boy Rick starring Matthew McConaughey in 2018.

It was a life-changing incident. I had discovered that I was not capable of being subjected to what I considered blatant disrespect without responding violently. Clearly, a life in prison would result in a life of extreme violence for a person like me who was incapable of tolerating disrespect.

My then-fiancée Sandra, like most of us, had heard the horror stories about life in American prisons. She also knew that it simply was not possible for me to be subjected to being physically or verbally violated by anyone without retaliating. I explained to her that if sentenced to prison, I would go on a hunger strike. This was a terrifying prospect for Sandra, who by then knew me well enough to know that once I started on the hunger strike path there would be no turning back: it would end in my death. Somehow, she still agreed to marry me just months after my indictment.

As I sat at the defense table waiting for Judge Rosen to enter the courtroom for one of my many court appearances, I informed my attorney of my decision to go on a hunger strike if found guilty. Lustig, of course, had no way of knowing how unmoving I could be once my mind was made up. He simply dismissed my comment by saying, "Let's wait and see how things go."

And wait we did. We waited for two and a half years. After spending thousands of dollars on legal fees and after experiencing incredible psychological stress, Richard Lustig's office called me on March 17, 1999 with the incredible news. Saul Greene, the U.S. Attorney for the 6th Circuit Court, had inconceivably decided to dismiss all charges against me. I was no longer under indictment! Needless to say, I was ecstatic! It would be a couple of years before I would learn all the amazing details of what had transpired behind the scenes regarding my case. Croatia had won my freedom!

U.S. Department of Justice

United States Attorney
Eastern District of Michigan

211 W. Fort Street
Suite 2300
Detroit, Michigan 48226-3211
October 11, 1996

Richard Lustig, Esq.
240 Daines Street
Birmingham, MI 48009-6241

    Re: United States v. Michael Palaich
        Criminal No. 96-80844

Dear Mr. Lustig:

    An Indictment has been returned against your client by the
Grand Jury. Please have your client report to Pretrial Services
Agency, 464 Room Federal Building, Detroit, Michigan, at 10:00
a.m., October 28, 1996. The arraignment on the charges will take
place at 1:00 p.m. in the Courtroom of the Honorable Donald A.
Scheer, United States Magistrate-Judge, Federal Building, 231 W.
Lafayette, Detroit, Michigan.

    Please advise as soon as possible if you will not be
representing Mr. Palaich.

    Failure for your client to appear will result in the
issuance of a warrant for his arrest.

                Very truly yours,

                SAUL A. GREEN
                United States Attorney

                GARY M. FELDER
                Assistant United States Attorney

cc:
Pretrial Services Agency
464 Federal Building
Detroit, MI 48226

Special Agent John Cange
U.S. Customs Service
350 Patrick McNamara Building
477 Michigan Avenue

#695

Notice of indictment

238

UNITED STATES DISTRICT COURT
EASTERN DISTRICT OF MICHIGAN
SOUTHERN DIVISION

UNITED STATES OF AMERICA,

                        Plaintiff,   CRIM. NO. 96-80844

                                            HON.
    -vs-
                                            VIOLATION: 22 U.S.C. § 2778

D-1 MICHAEL PALAICH,

                        Defendant.
_____/

I N D I C T M E N T

THE GRAND JURY CHARGES:

A.

GENERAL ALLEGATIONS

1.   At all times material herein:

        (a)   The Office of Defense Trade Controls, United
States Department of State, was responsible for the
administration of Section 38 of the Arms Export Control Act (22
U.S.C. §2778), as it related to exports from the United States of
defense articles and defense services and the exercise of the
President's authority to control such exports.

        (b)   Title 22 U.S.C. §2778(b)(1)(A) stated in
pertinent part: " . . . [E]very person (other than an officer or
employee of the United States Government acting in an official
capacity) who engages in the business of . . . exporting . . .
any defense articles or defense services . . . shall register

1

Indictment

239

Author's U.S. booking photo from US Marshall Service

14

Rescued by Croatia

AFTER FIVE years of American agents investigating friends and neighbors, monitoring my phone, digging through my garbage, following my movements and two and a half years of court proceedings and thousands of dollars in legal expenses, the burden was finally going to be lifted from my shoulders. Federal Judge Gerald Rosen signed an order dismissing the six-count indictment against me on March 17, 1999.

My attorney Richard Lustig called me to give me the good news. He explained that my bond of $50,000 was also being lifted. He instructed me to report to my Pretrial Services Officer, Thomas Nugent, for a final interview. At the final interview my passport would be returned to me, allowing me to travel outside the country once again.

I always had a good relationship with Nugent, so I was not surprised by the respectful way that he treated me during my final interview. He had my paperwork and passport waiting for me when I arrived for my appointment. "I'm just curious," he said. "How did you get the case dismissed? Saul Greene [the U.S. District Attorney] never dismisses a case." I answered him honestly with a shrug, because although I suspected the Croatian government was mostly responsible, I didn't really know it with certainty. Before I left his office, he added: "You're not like most of the people that I see in here." I took that as a compliment, but I suspect he meant that, unlike most of the people he dealt with, I had a job, a home, a clean record and I maintained my dignity when speaking with him.

With my passport finally returned, my wife Sandra and I travelled to Croatia to visit her family that summer. The Croatian government had so far kept us in the dark, but now, for the first time, we would finally be able to get a clearer picture of everything that had transpired behind the scenes without our knowledge.

After arriving in Zagreb, Croatia's capital, we made an appointment to see my friend "Vinko" who still worked in the Croatian government. While we waited for Vinko in the restaurant of the Hotel Dubrovnik, I couldn't help but reflect on the past and how different things were in Croatia compared to just a few years ago during the war for independence. Even the Esplanade Hotel where my wife and I had a room brought memories of the past.

During the war the management of the Esplanade had allowed HOS soldiers who had occupied the previously vacant Starčević Dom just across the street, to use the hotel's showers to clean up. Today the Hotel Esplanade bills itself as a five-star hotel, but during the war the nightclub downstairs was a gathering spot for HOS soldiers as well as foreign strippers, war profiteers and every type of undesirable you might imagine operating in any war zone. As we walked past the Starčević Dom on our way to Hotel Dubrovnik, memories of HOS soldiers milling around outside just a few years ago flooded my mind. I recalled the shoot-out I experienced one night while standing in the park sandwiched between the Starčević Dom and Zagreb's main train station. HOS soldiers believed some men in the building to be members of Yugoslav Military Intelligence when a brief series of shots rang out. I stood behind a lamppost eating roasted chestnuts as HOS soldiers stationed outside pointed their weapons toward the building's entrance. It was in that building that the President of Stranka Prava, Dobroslav Paraga, had his third-floor office just a few years prior. Leading to the office was the stairway previously lined with rifle-carrying soldiers I encountered going to visit Paraga on so many occasions. As we walked past the now empty building, I was certain that the young lovers sitting on the benches on tree-lined park called Tomislavov Trg, just across the street, knew nothing of Stranka Prava, Dobroslav Paraga or the significance of the building. They were also unaware, I was sure, that just a few years previously, the Croatian Special Police had evicted the Stranka Party leadership and HOS soldiers from the premises. Even if the young lovers were aware of what happened in that building, it was already ancient history to them.

As I sat in the hotel's restaurant facing Jelačić Square, I recalled just a few years before observing all the refugees (primarily from Slavonia) that were given rooms at the hotel. The refugees had been fed bean soup in the restaurant for lunch every day. It was there that one could observe whole families that had been uprooted from their homes and villages by Serbian aggressors. It was heartbreaking to see generations of the same family sitting at the tables set up for them to eat their meal of bread and bean soup. Grandmothers and mothers, who just months before had lovingly prepared food for their own husbands and grandchildren in their own homes, were now left homeless and living in a hotel in the center of Zagreb with their unemployed husbands and sons, forced to rely on handouts from the government to survive. When the children were not playing in the hotel hallways, they would spill out into the streets and the square around the hotel to play.

Even my own family that had for centuries lived just outside Zagreb in the town of Petrinja was forced to suffer through four years of humbling and undignified life as refugees in the nearby city of Sisak. Their Serbian neighbors, who had for decades lived in the upstairs flat of the house built by my great-uncle and great-grandfather, had, according to my family, forced them at gunpoint to abandon all of their belongings and leave their ancestral home.

Sitting in the hotel's restaurant waiting for Vinko, my thoughts drifted back to memories of those war years and the many times I watched civilians in Zagreb fleeing for the safety of nearby buildings during the constant air raid sirens as the JNA fighter jets flew overhead on the prowl for new civilian targets. It was on that now peaceful Jelačić square that just a few years before my friends and I strolled across as air raid sirens blared in the background and police approached to reprimand us for being so careless and nonchalant and ignoring the sirens. My own wife, Sandra, who lived in a nearby apartment, was one of those civilians forced to spend many nights in the dark and damp basement of her apartment building while she waited for the "all clear" siren to sound. It was the signal that she could return to her elderly grandmother upstairs who stubbornly refused to leave her apartment for the safety of the cellar.

I was beginning to understand how it was for older people who, although living in the present, were also constantly living amongst the shadows of the past that only they and their generation could see. It becomes increasingly clear to me that if one is fortunate enough to survive the past, it becomes difficult to avoid the pervasive flood of memories experienced with the turning of every street corner.

As I anxiously waited for Vinko to arrive, the melancholy memories began to fade. They were replaced with a sense of pride as I watched young Croatian soldiers pass the windows of the restaurant. Gone were the mismatched military uniforms and tennis shoes worn by Croatia's Homeland War volunteers. Gone were the headbands of the past popularized by the movie Rambo. What I saw that day were soldiers who were part of a modern and organized military with a mission to defend the Croatian people against any enemy aggressors. These young, well-trained, professional soldiers were part of a Croatian government that was now recognized by the world. Their government, Croatia, now had a seat in the United Nations and later became a full member of NATO. I was proud that I had the honor of playing some small role in the country's development. Croatia had made the dangerous transition from a fledgling revolutionary movement to realizing full nation-state status. It was both a privilege and a blessing to have witnessed and participated in the birth of a state.

Vinko, who was always running late, apologized for keeping us waiting when he arrived. After the usual catching up regarding friends we had in common, he began to explain in some detail how I came to be free and sitting in Zagreb with him on that day.

Vinko was one of the individuals that I had contacted even before the Americans indicted me. It was Vinko who promised me that he would do everything he could to get the German federal agencies to destroy the weapons I was arrested with in October of 1991. Although he was not the only person I entrusted with this request, I thanked him for his assistance over the years. I explained what I was able to glean from the communications between the German and American Customs Departments. Those documents, as is required by law, had been released to me when my case was dismissed by the American government.

According to U.S. Federal law, a defendant who is exonerated, or whose case is dismissed, has the right to demand that all documents and evidence pertinent to the case and used by the prosecution be released to him. I was amazed when I discovered the communications between the Americans and the Germans regarding the weapons confiscated from me. The incomplete communications that I received begin with a response from the German Customs Department. The Germans state that they "have no idea where the seized weapons went." In the second German response they write to inform the Americans: "Their [sic] is a slight chance that they aren't destroyed by now, because the weapon experts within our house asked the prosecutor to turn over some of the exhibits to them for their gun exhibition. As soon as I know what really happend [sic] I'm contacting you again." The final communication from the German Customs Department was unbelievable – even for me. As I read it, I laughed out loud and knew that Croatia had succeeded in their attempt to get the evidence destroyed. In the communication sent by a German Agent named Kamala to the Americans, on September 10, 1993, the Germans reported: "Helmut called today (10th September at 12.15) and said that these evidence [sic] were destroyed on March 10, 1993!".

If the documents that I received shocked me, what Vinko told me next would astonish me even more. He went on to tell me the whole incredible story that had played out behind the scenes.

Vinko apologized that he was not able to communicate with me for the last several years during my ordeal. He went on to say: "Even if I were to see you in Jelačić Square in those years and you waved hello to me, I would have been forced to pass you by without even acknowledging that I knew you." Vinko continued: "During those years, I was myself being followed by the American CIA. This led me to ask one of the guys I knew working for HIS why the Americans were following me? My HIS contact told me, 'It's not about you. They want to know what connection you have with Palaich.' I was subsequently told to stop all contact with you." I assumed he was ordered to stop contact with me so that he could establish some sort of "plausible denial" regarding my case. What he told me next, however, revealed the full and unbelievable story of just how and why my indictment was dismissed. But, more importantly, it revealed just what lengths the Croatian government had gone to in order to save me from a life of misery in prison – not to mention saving my wife, Sandra, from a life without her husband and my two children, Monica and Nicholas, from a life without their father.

246

Vinko explained how one day he was directed to go to the Ministry of Defense headquarters and report directly to Gojko Šušak. Mr. Šušak asked Vinko for all the information he had regarding my indictment and what had been done to help me up to that point. There was an unidentified man in the office with Šušak. Mr. Šušak explained to Vinko that he was going to ask his American counterpart, Secretary of Defense William Perry, to do everything in his power to get my case quashed by the U.S. Prosecutor in Detroit. It is a well-known fact that Mr. Šušak and Mr. Perry had developed a very close and friendly relationship over several years. William Perry would demonstrate this publicly by attending Gojko Šušak's funeral in Zagreb in May 1998. When Šušak lost his battle with cancer, Perry attended the funeral as a private citizen. The Croatian government honored Perry that same year with the Grand Order of King Dmitar Zvonimir Medal.

I was both astonished and deeply humbled that Gojko Šušak, as well as others in the government at the time, would go to such lengths to save someone of my meager stature from prosecution in America. What could I say, but thank Vinko and the others for all that was done on my behalf?

It finally became clear to me why all those Croatian officials, whom I had considered friends, had discontinued all contact with me. Admittedly, it was discouraging at the time and I felt abandoned by them when their friendship was needed most. I now understood that they had no choice but to terminate their contact with me, if they were to be successful in helping me from behind-the-scenes.

Just weeks prior to my case being dismissed I also received a call at my home from an attorney named Pavelić with offices in New York. Pavelić, I would later discover, was also a Registered Agent for the Croatian government in America. I now believe that Pavelić was the nameless individual that Vinko saw sitting in Šušak's office when he was directed to the Ministry's headquarters. During his phone conversation with me, Pavelić explained that he was calling on behalf of some mutual friends in

Croatia and that he would like me to fill him in regarding the facts surrounding my case. I had absolutely no way of knowing who it was that was really calling, or whether he was being forthright with me. Being suspicious of every chance encounter not initiated by me had served me well over the years. Too many people that I knew had ended up with long jail terms for simply not having self-control and discipline over their own speech. This phone call out of the blue was no exception, so I was naturally suspicious and teased the man on the other end of the phone about the last name he shared with the assassinated NDH leader from WWII named Ante Pavelić. Since what I was about to tell him was part of my defense in court, I began to give him the details of my case. I was careful, however, to only give him the publicly known details or insert the word "alleged" when talking about the charges. At the end of the conversation he explained that he would be travelling to Croatia soon where he would meet with high officials in the Croatian government. I still remember what he said to me just before we concluded our conversation: "You have a lot of powerful friends in Croatia." I simply said, "Thank you for the call and for any help you can offer."

Of course, I never could have known how critical the intervention of Minister Šušak was in keeping me out of prison. I deeply regret that Gojko Šušak did not live long enough for me to personally thank him for all that he had done for me and my family. He died on May 3, 1998 and is buried at Mirogoj Cemetery in Zagreb.

06-SEP-1993 15:57 HU.R Abt.3/4 -42 8.4448 S.01

TELEFAX

HESSISCHES LANDESKRIMINALAMT

65187 Wiesbaden, den 06.09.1993

TELEFON: 0611 / 83-0
VERMITTLUNG FÜR ALLE ABTEILUNGEN

TELEFAX: 0611 / 83-4448
NUR FÜR ABTEILUNG 3 UND 4

AN:

U.S. CUSTOMS

Attn.: Jack M'QUADE

53179 BONN

FAX-NR.:

0228 / 334663

ABSENDER:

KHM BEER
HSG 33

Telefon-Durchwahl:

0611 / 83 - 4334

EILT !

SEITENZAHL: - 1 - (OHNE DIESES DECKBLATT)

Bei fehlerhafter Übermittlung rufen Sie bitte 0611 / 83 - 4309 an (Standort des Fax-Gerätes) !!!

Cover page of letter from German Criminal Police to U.S. Customs

Hallo Jack;

I was able to trace out your PALAICH-exhibits to a police department which is responsible for destroying seized weapons after being in illegal possess and after a valid sentence or fine. All exhibits went on 18th of february 1993 to that duty station over here in Mainz-Kastel. The man in charge is on vacation til end of this week. I left a note to call me back. Their is a slight chance that they aren't destroyed by now, because the weapon experts within our house asked the prosecutor to turn over some of the exhibits to them for their gun exhibition. As soon as I know what really happend, I'm contacting you again.

Please let me know if you need the exhibits or if you just want to know what happend !

This morning I brought Udo BÜHLER and Alfred JUNG to the airport. They used DELTA DL 107. Coming back to my office I informed Dennis about their arrival time at JFK (of course not before the official wake up time for a holiday).

Good luck

Helmut

Jack:

Helmut called today (10th September 93 at 12.15) and said that these evidence were destroyed on March 10, 1993!

Regards from Helmut.

Kamala

Letter from German National Criminal Police to U.S. Customs in Bonn

"I would give everything to see her proud and beautiful,
The way she is in my dreams."
Thompson

15

If You Can Keep It

LIFE IS STILL spent straddling two cultures as in the past. My wife Sandra and I are blessed to be able to live our lives between the two countries we love - America and Croatia. It is a luxury that my grandparents did not have when they emigrated to America more than a century ago. Thoughts of them wash over me as I look out over the Adriatic Sea and wonder what they would say about their grandson's return to the homeland they left so long ago, never to return.

Strangely enough, putting my memories on paper has not helped me to fully answer one of the questions that I originally set out to answer in writing this book: "What led you to get involved in Croatia's independence movement?" It's true that I became a fanatic and maybe even an extremist when it came to the subject of Croatian sovereignty. If we peel all the onion layers back, however, my Grandmother's love was the seed planted early in my life. I'm certain that my love for Croatia never would have blossomed to the point that it did if not for the incredible love I received from my Baka. The love for her had, in the end, become inseparable from my love for her homeland and the desire to see freedom finally come to Baka's homeland was the driving force all along.

Just a few years ago my wife Sandra and I were sitting on the patio of her family's home admiring the clear, blue Adriatic Sea on Croatia's Dalmatian coast. At the table with us was my friend of forty years, Pero Ivčec, and two of his five children, Franjo and Nikola.

Pero and I only get to see each other now once a year when we are both in Croatia during the summer. Invariably, we always come around to the same question: "Can you believe we are sitting in Croatia together after so many years of working for its independence?" Admittedly, it may sound like a strange question to a twenty-something person. Of course it is independent, they may exclaim. After all, they haven't known anything else. We, however, remember all too well being mocked and ridiculed for years because we really believed a Croatian state could one day be realized. We were seen as charging at windmills like don Quixote and "dreaming the impossible dream." We had been called many things over the years, from foolish and naïve to fanatics and lunatics – even extremists. "Croatia will never be free," they would say. "Yugoslavia is too strong." The father of Sandra's brother-in-law even warned her against dating me before we were married. "Stay away from those Croats living in emigration, they are extremists!" Looking back over the years, maybe we were a little crazy for believing in this dream. The odds of Croatia ever winning a war against the JNA was like the proverbial battle between David and Goliath.

On that particular evening Pero's son Franjo asked me a simple yet profound question as we sat overlooking the sea: "Would you do it again?" It was a question I had never asked myself. Not thinking it through completely, I responded after only a few seconds: "No." What immediately and selfishly came to mind were the ways my involvement negatively affected me personally: the various investigations directed against me, the stress of a federal indictment and the financial burdens that resulted. Mostly, I thought of how my time spent in the Croatian liberation movement had impacted my family. I naïvely believed that I could be away from my family - sometimes for months - and that my absence would have no impact on the lives of my young children, Monica and Nicholas. I was wrong. My family also paid a price for my involvement in the Croatian movement over the years.

I could see that my negative answer disturbed Pero even before he had a chance to reply. He was, as usual, thinking in political terms. "Think of all the people that were saved who now live in a free Croatia," Pero said. "You would give all that up?" We had been involved in too much together for my response not to be a reflection on him as well. Croatia's sovereignty is a subject Pero continues to be zealous about to this day.

There is a melancholy scene from the well-known play called *Les Misérables* based on the book by Victor Hugo. In the scene the character Marius, who was active in the failed Paris uprising of 1832, sings a song titled "Empty Chairs and Empty Tables." The scene is filled with flashbacks of his now-deceased friends from the revolution. In one particularly moving part of the song Marius sings, "My friends, my friends, don't ask me what your sacrifice was for." Anyone who has survived any war or revolution and considers the death and destruction that they experienced has probably had the same thoughts as Marius. The song's lyrics ring even truer for those who lost mothers, fathers, sons and daughters to war. By telling Franjo, therefore, that I would not "do it again," was I also implying that all the lives sacrificed during the Homeland War were for nothing? After all, if I personally wasn't willing to "do it again," wasn't I telling those whose loved ones were killed that their sacrifice was worthless? It forced me to consider another question: was it worth it?

Certainly, Croatia has its problems, but it is no longer an occupied land being run from a foreign capital as it had been throughout the centuries. The Croatian military vehicles that citizens and tourist may occasionally see while driving on the award-winning freeways belong to a strong and vital Croatian military that is now part of NATO – a far cry from the tennis-shoe-clad Croatian Guard volunteers of 1991.

Some Croatian politicians today place their own interests above the citizens' interests when they choose corruption over patriotism, but at least they are Croatian and not oppressive occupiers representing foreign regimes as in the past. Yes, taxes may be excessive, but they are taxes paid with Croatian kunas and not in Italian, German, Austrian, Hungarian, Turkish, Yugoslav or Serbian currency. A famous quote from Mohandas Gandhi comes to mind: "There is no people on earth that would not prefer their own bad government to the good government of an alien power."

Long before there was a Croatian State, we who were involved in the liberation movement, knew that it would take a few generations before the Croatian people would lose the mindset of a people who had been occupied for centuries. It was understandable that Croatians distrusted foreign occupiers. But there is a residual dose of cynical mistrust towards their own government as well. Croatian politicians who put their self-interest and party over their love of the nation have, thus far, done little to help the Croatian people overcome these cynical inclinations.

There is an additional issue to consider when reflecting on Franjo's question these several years later. There is a small minority of Croats who exhibit a tendency to express nostalgia for the "good old days" of Communism. The word that has developed in the Croatian lexicon to describe that baffling affinity for the past is "Yugo-nostalgia." After almost thirty years and a great deal of opposition, the city of Zagreb has only just recently chosen to remove the name of Tito from one of the main squares in the heart of the capital city. The city of Rovinj – and who knows how many other cities – still continues to honor Tito by naming a square after the dead tyrant. I was further stunned to see the former dictator's portraits hanging in a private home I visited just two years ago. This is incomprehensible to many of us. How can the man who was responsible for the murders of so many Croatian men, women and children continue to be honored by anyone belonging to the same nation that Tito and his followers had victimized for so long? Is it possible, I wonder, that "Yugo-nostalgia" is simply a larger manifestation of the Stockholm syndrome? According to Encyclopedia Britannica, "Stockholm syndrome is a psychological response wherein a captive begins to identify closely with his or her captors, as well as with their agenda and demands."

Lest we believe that this longing for former days of oppression is something unique to Croatia and modern times, it would be good to recall that the Jews of the Old Testament experienced a similar phenomenon around 3,400 years ago. While still wandering in the desert in hopes of finding the land promised to them by God, they began to attack Moses who brought them out of Egypt and nostalgically lament over their former lives as slaves. I can't help but think that Yugo-nostalgists suffer from the same affliction of the mind.

To further complicate the issue, that small minority of Croats displaying a political form of Stockholm syndrome are cognizant of the fact that it is no longer acceptable to call themselves Communist. They prefer using the deceptive title of "anti-fascists" as they systematically attempt to unravel elements of society that have unified Croatians throughout centuries. Like their fathers before them who prostrated themselves before images of Tito, these saboteurs label any patriotic Croat a Fascist. It was a favorite and effective tactic used in the past by their fathers and grandfathers; the new Communists have found it in their grandmothers' attics, dusted it off and repurposed it as today's new propaganda tool against all those who put their Croatian nation before internationalism.

This leads us to an additional divisive topic to consider when answering the question: "Would you do it again?" I am referring to the controversial topic of Croatia joining the European Union (EU) less than twenty years after winning a bloody war for independence that cost thousands of Croatian lives and untold misery for many who survived. According to the Croatian Constitution, a referendum to join the European Union was mandatory in the first place, because membership in the EU would necessarily limit Croatian sovereignty. Croatia became a member of the EU on July 1, 2013; and before the ink was dry on the agreement, a handful of politicians in Brussels were already beginning to enforce new regulations on various Croatian industries (i.e. shipyards, cheese, wine, meat, fishing, agriculture, sheep, etc.).

History will decide if it was wise to surrender even a small degree of sovereignty in the long term in exchange for some financial benefits offered by the EU in the short term. While Croatia may, like the British, discover at some point in the future that it has made a mistake in joining the EU, the EU may also come to the realization that it is very difficult to control a nation that has centuries of experience in handling the bureaucracies centered in foreign capitals. The Byzantine Empire, Turks, Hungarians, Austrians, German Nazis, Italian Fascists, Serbian Kings and Communist dictators have all tried to conquer, dominate, govern and subdue Croatians. Their empires and ideologies have all evaporated, but their former subjects – the Croats – remain.

At the time of this writing I still reflect on the question, "was it worth it?" I wish I could answer with a resounding "yes!". But while Croatia has accomplished an extraordinary feat, our rejoicing is marred by the many problems the country is experiencing. In truth, the jury is still out on what will become of Croatia. Down what path will the future nation-state proceed? Will the country succeed in maintaining its independence? Will it be successful in rooting out political corruption? Will it have the will to defend itself against future enemies, both foreign and domestic? Will Croatians continue to sell off industries and real estate to other countries until their children once again become serfs in a land their ancestors once owned and died for? Will the youth of Croatia continue choosing to work at low paying jobs outside of Croatia, serving the needs of other countries within the EU? And finally - and most importantly - will Croatia continue to worship God as their Catholic ancestors have for centuries, or will they take the path of secularism like many of their Western European neighbors?

One of America's founding fathers, Benjamin Franklin, anticipated similar concerns when answering a woman who stopped him as he was exiting Independence Hall following the signing of the U.S. Constitution. "What sort of government have you given us, Dr. Franklin?" she asked. He is said to have responded: "A republic madam, if you can keep it." Franklin understood that establishing an independent state was not the end of the journey, but the beginning.

Will Croatians be able to keep their republic? At the conclusion of every interview I conducted with survivors of Bleiburg and the death marches during the making of *The Bleiburg Tragedy*, I asked survivors if they had any words of advice for the future generations that would eventually be born in an independent Croatian state, a state that at the time of the interviews did not exist. Their responses were variations of the following: "To the Croatian generations growing up in an independent Croatia, you never experienced losing your homeland. Once you lose your state, it is very difficult to reclaim it again. Never give up! Never surrender like we did!".

While the youth of Croatia may never have heard the exhortation directly from the death march survivors I interviewed, the message has not been lost on much of the Croatian youth who flock to the concerts of the famously popular Croatian singer and war veteran named Marko Perković Thompson. His beautifully worded songs carry this baton and pass it onto the next generation, and they are embracing his music and his message. In a country with a population of only 4.5 million, Thompson's concerts routinely sell out to energetic fans at times approaching 60,000 people. Much to the dissatisfaction of those who ferociously attempt to discredit him, he continues to passionately promote love for Croatia, her culture, her people and her Catholic faith. It is my fervent hope that the message of love of country will continue to take root in the hearts of this generation and that the weeds of failed ideologies will never again choke the seeds of freedom that have been sown and watered with Croatian blood.

*One-thousand-year-old, St. Martin Church, in Ivinj, has stood
defiantly through centuries of conquerors*

Photo by Romeo Marov ©

Afterword

BAKA (Ljubica Palaich, née Vidović) passed away on February 10, 1970 when the author was sixteen years old.

Ante Beljo continues to live in Croatia and is the President of the Croatian Victimology Society where he works to highlight the war crimes committed by former regimes in Yugoslavia. After becoming director of the Croatian Information Center, he went on to become director of Matica Iseljenika, and an elected member of the Croatian Parliament.

Božimir Čačić moved back to Croatia after the Homeland War and lives today in the town of Senj.

Krešimir Ćosić was forced into retirement by then-President of Croatia, Stipe Mesić, in September of 2000, after joining eleven other generals in signing an open letter protesting the treatment of the veterans of the Croatian Homeland War that became known as the Twelve Generals' Letter. He went on to be elected to the Croatian Parliament in 2003.

Ante Čuvalo has returned to live permanently in Hercegovina and Croatia after retiring as professor of history at JJC. He and his wife Ivana own and operate CroLibertas Publishers. Dr. Čuvalo continues to be a prolific writer on all subjects Croatian and more.

Petar Ivčec remains a fierce supporter of Croatian sovereignty and is active in Canada's Croatian community. He splits his time between Windsor, Ontario, and Sveta Jana near Jastrebarsko in Croatia.

Mario Ostojić lives in Zagreb and continues to work for the Croatian Ministry of Foreign Affairs.

Dobroslav Paraga today lives in relative obscurity, occasionally speaking at public events. Tragically, most young people in Croatia do not even know the name of the man who played such an incredibly important role in the realization of the Republic of Croatia.

Ante Pranić never returned to America. He passed away from lung cancer in Zagreb on November 15, 1995.

Rodolfo Barrios Saavedra (Žuka) was ultimately promoted to the rank of Brigadier General. He retired from the Croatian Army after receiving several military awards and is said to be living with his family in Zagreb, Croatia.

Marko Stipaničić passed away in 2016 after a long battle with cancer. He was buried in his hometown of Senj after receiving a funeral with military honors. He is survived by his wife Krista, son Marko and daughter Miriam.

Gojko Šušak passed away in 1998 after his battle with lung cancer. His body is buried in Mirogoj Cemetery in Zagreb. His funeral was attended by thousands of civilians, veterans and members of the military. His friend and former Secretary of Defense, William Perry, spoke at his gravesite where he is quoted as saying: "To Croatians he was crucial to the establishment of freedom here. To Americans he was crucial to the establishment of peace and stability in the region."

"Vinko" still lives in Zagreb where he continues to work for the Republic of Croatia

Yugoslavia (Socialist Federal Republic of Yugoslavia) was officially pronounced dead in 1992. Several attempts were made to resurrect it in other forms by other names until Serbia's last ally, Montenegro, also jumped ship and declared independence on June 3, 2006.

Acknowledgements

Over the past twenty or more years, many people encouraged me tell the story of my participation in, and my witness to, the birth of the Republic of Croatia. I wish to express my gratitude to all of them for persistently stressing that there was an untold story regarding the Croatian state that needed to be told.

I would like to recognize the sacrifices made by my children, Monica and Nicholas, who, during their precious childhood, were forced to share their father with a dream.

A big thank you to Ante and Ivana Čuvalo who are not only my very dear friends, but owners of CroLibertas Publishing, without whose support and prodding this book would not have been written.

Finally, a heartfelt thank you to my editor and wife Sandra Palaich who graciously spent hours correcting, suggesting and improving the text of this book. The result is a better product than it would have been if not for her knowledge, diligence and keen eye to detail.

About the Author

Michael Palaich is a third-generation Croatian-American producer of the documentary film *The Bleiburg Tragedy*. He is a contributor to several documentaries on the subject of Yugoslav war crimes. His role in Croatia's liberation movement began in 1979 when he was recruited at the age of twenty-five. That recruitment led him on a long journey that began with anti-Yugoslav street demonstrations and ended with him becoming a Registered Foreign Agent for the Republic of Croatia during Croatia's Homeland War.

During Croatia's War of Independence, he created the Pan-National News Agency, served as a correspondent for the Croatian Information Center, WXYT Radio and *Soldier of Fortune* magazine. Ultimately, Palaich was indicted by the American government in 1996 and charged with smuggling weapons and night-vision equipment destined for Croatian forces during Croatia's Homeland War.

He graduated Cum Laude from Wayne State University where he earned a BA degree in Political Science and Psychology.

He is a father to two grown children and a grandfather to two grandchildren. Palaich is retired and lives in Croatia and Arizona with his wife, Sandra. He actively serves in the Prison Ministry for the Catholic Diocese of Phoenix.

INDEX

Index

Index

Index

K

Karlovac, 74, 138, 144, 183
Karlstruhe, 116, 118
Kemal Kurspahić, 194
KEW Gardens, 80, 85
Klagenfurt, 90
Kol Mihilli, 52
Kosovo, 38, 42, 51, 147
Krešimir Ćosić, 261
Križ-Hrastovica, 8, 18, 70

L

land for peace, 219
Laudato TV, 95
Lawrence Eagleburger, 38, 88
Lepoglava, 59, 101, 140, 212
Lincoln Battalion, 3
Livno, 131, 133, 165, 166, 167
Ljubica Vidović, 18
London Times, 135

M

Magnum Crimen, 95
Major General H.E.N. Bredin, 84
Marash Dushaj, 52
Marijan Buconjić, 53, 227, 234
Marin Sopta, 212
Mario Nobilo, 163
Mario Ostojić, 129, 130, 131, 166, 262
Marko Perković, 258
Marko Stipaničić, 23, 24, 25, 26, 28, 42, 50, 51, 52, 59, 60, 61, 71, 109, 116, 118, 122, 125, 129, 130, 132, 141, 147, 262
Maršal Tito Boulevard. *See* Sniper Alley
mass graves, 73, 77, 89, 94
Menachem Begin, 33, 34

Milan Basta, 76
Milan Šuflaj, 136
Military Professional Resources Incorporated, 218, 221
Miljacka River, 185
Mimara Museum, 91, 134
Ministry of Defense, 2, 85, 107, 207, 213, 214, 217, 220, 221, 222, 247
Ministry of Information, 134, 135, 140, 170
Mira Bakalović, 189
Mirko Kovač, 59
Miro Barešić, 53
Miro Komšić, 49, 59
Miro Vuković, 200
Mladina, 141
Mohammed Alí Seineldín, 131
Mohandas Gandhi, 254
Monica Huberts (née Palaich), 247, 253
MPRI. *See* Military Professional Resources Incorporated
Muhamed Sacirbey, 163, 165, 201
Mujahedin, 168, 169, 170
MUP, 105, 108, 127

N

Nada Prkačin, 95
National Security Office, 130
New York Times, 31, 53, 57, 104, 135, 136, 138, 202
Newsday, 200
Nicholas Palaich, 247, 253
Nidžara Šarenkapa, 184, 187, 189, 205
Nigel Nicholson, 75, 76, 77, 79, 80, 82, 86, 93, 94
Nikolai Tolstoy, 62, 71, 75, 85, 92, 93, 94
Nino Bakalović, 189

Index

Index

Index

Y

Z

Printed in Great Britain
by Amazon

35925589R00163